Visionary Women Writers of Chicago's Black Arts Movement

Visionary Women Writers of Chicago's Black Arts Movement

Carmen L. Phelps

University Press of Mississippi / Jackson

*Margaret Walker Alexander Series
in African American Studies*

www.upress.state.ms.us

The University Press of Mississippi is a member
of the Association of American University Presses.

Copyright © 2013 by University Press of Mississippi
All rights reserved

First printing 2013

∞

Library of Congress Cataloging-in-Publication Data

Phelps, Carmen L.
Visionary women writers of Chicago's Black Arts Movement /
Carmen L. Phelps.
p. cm. — (Margaret Walker Alexander series in
African American studies)
Includes bibliographical references and index.
ISBN 978-1-61703-680-4 (cloth : alk. paper) — ISBN 978-1-61703-681-1
(ebook) 1. American literature—African American authors—History
and criticism. 2. African American women authors. 3. Black Arts movement. 4. African American arts—20th century. I. Title.
PS153.N5P49 2013
810.9'928708996073—dc23   2012015855

British Library Cataloging-in-Publication Data available

Contents

3 **Introduction**
The Black Arts Movement: Let Me Count the Ways

23 **Chapter One**
Dysfunctional Functionality: Collaboration at Its Best in the Black Arts Era

56 **Chapter Two**
Women Writing Kinship in Chicago's Black Arts Movement

76 **Chapter Three**
Mirrors of Deception: Invisible, Untouchable, Beautiful Blackness in Johari Amini's Black Art

95 **Chapter Four**
Muddying Clear Waters: Carolyn Rodgers's Black Art

116 **Chapter Five**
Building a Home, Building a Nation: Family in the City and Beyond in Angela Jackson's Black Art

146 **Chapter Six**
Mixing Metaphors: Spirituality, Environmentalism, and Dystopia in Carolyn Rodgers's and Angela Jackson's Postrace Black Art

162 **Conclusion**
You Remind Me . . . "Post–BAM/Soul" Reflections

165 Notes
173 Works Cited
183 Index

Visionary Women Writers of Chicago's Black Arts Movement

Introduction

The Black Arts Movement: Let Me Count the Ways

The Black Arts Movement (BAM) of the late 1960s to mid-1970s remains an elusive and complex configuration of ideologies mutually and often paradoxically reinforced through the artistic, activist, and intellectual collaborations and exchanges between the movement's key participants and their critics. Indeed, the concept of collaboration came to signify an ideal within as much as a threat to the Black Arts Movement and Black Power Movement, as well as many other activist initiatives across the country at this time. Although there is much debate amongst scholars about when the Black Arts Movement actually began and ended, or whether or not it ended at all, even today, many individuals remain imprisoned because of their actual or alleged investment in and associations with the collaborative missions developed by activist groups like Black Artists in the interest of social justice and political empowerment for various oppressed communities.[1] Ultimately, the concept of collaboration both in practice and in vision motivated a culture of intense debate between Black Artists and their critics, and such conversations animated the landscape of black cultural expression. Furthermore, the BAM's legacy of collaboration as it was manifested in the form of politically inspired, nation-building initiatives remains influential to the work of those committed to the empowerment of black communities of the African Diaspora and other marginalized communities worldwide. As confirmed by Lisa Gail Collins and Margo Natalie Crawford, the editors of the groundbreaking collection *New Thoughts on the Black Arts Movement* (2006), "Collaboration and dialogue were at the heart of the Black Arts Movement."[2] However, rather than seize upon the rather romantic notion that the development of a collective, collaborative concept of politically inspired art was necessarily and always an inspiring or effective paradigm for achieving Black Arts goals for self-defined Black Artists, I want to contribute to the discussion of the concept of collaboration as a presumed "ideal" by addressing its varied dimensions and import as it relates to the realization of the BAM's aesthetic. More specifically, in this project, I discuss the ways in which collaboration was interrogated, undermined, and indeed parodied within the writings of a select list of understudied and in some cases "unsung" women writers, whose perspectives productively mitigated the essentialist and oftentimes normalizing and counterprogressive aspects of this in/famous collaborative moment.

As many scholars have recently noted, women writers of the BAM pushed the boundaries of the black aesthetic; however, as I discuss, too often the contributions of women artists, activists, and intellectuals have been evaluated as those which pushed the *gendered* boundaries of the movement's aesthetic, when in fact the artistic and activist work of many of these women reflects their consideration for a host of other cultural and political aspects of Black Art that ultimately went beyond the BAM's often cited sexist features.[3] Some of the most widely recognized women artists of the BAM era—such as Mari Evans, Nikki Giovanni, and Sonia Sanchez, for instance, as well as women who received less attention, like Chicago writers Johari Amini, Carolyn Rodgers, and later Angela Jackson—produced work that not only honored the black female perspective and expressed a commitment to an inclusive concept of Black Art, but as I argue throughout this project, their work ultimately reflects the ways in which the BAM was strengthened rather than weakened by a broad range of artistic ideals and perspectives. As such, a critique of their work provides an opportunity to measure the BAM's culture beyond its most recognized, polarizing, and indeed alluring controversies.

The poetry of Amini, Rodgers, and Jackson, for instance, reflects the extent to which women artists experimented with and in fact queered the conventions of Black Art from their presumed positions of "marginality," and how they consequently and paradoxically managed to transform the aesthetic for which their male peers have been credited with constructing. It is noteworthy that all three writers were affiliated with Chicago's Organization of Black American Culture (OBAC)—a local BAM initiative that emerged as one of the most successful and longest-running organizations of this historical moment. Ultimately, my evaluation of the work of Amini, Rodgers, and Jackson is an exploration into the ways in which one group of women advanced a pluralistic coalition-building aesthetic from their positions of sexual and artistic *power* rather than powerlessness. As Julia Foulkes argues with regard to black women performance artists of the BAM, such as dancer-anthropologists Katherine Dunham and Pearl

Primus, women artists "altered the message of the BAM from one of racial exclusivity to a more universalist ethos" (82). Similarly, Amini, Rodgers, and Jackson, for instance, produced Black Art that moved beyond the most notoriously exclusive features of the movement in ways that encouraged a more progressively elusive aesthetic and narrative of black culture that is often left uncharacterized and in fact overlooked in scholarly readings. While "[i]nfluential male narratives have helped to masculinize the political rebel in popular culture and memory," as aptly expressed by scholar Joy James, my readings of the poetry of Amini, Rodgers, and Jackson are intended to convey the extent to which the essentially masculine "political rebel" to which James refers indeed shares a platform with the spirit of the *female* as rebel, which is quite perceptible in the creative and activist voices of many women of the BAM era (138). As women, the perspectives of Amini, Rodgers, and Jackson promoted an aesthetic that allowed for the fullest expression and expansion of BAM goals despite the movement's otherwise and arguably restrictive elements. In addition, taken collectively, the work of these women prioritizes the deeply profound cultural and artistic kinships fomented amongst participating artists of the BAM in Chicago and beyond. According to Black Arts scholar Mike Sell, "The origins of the Black Arts Movement . . . reveal a contradictory but highly productive dynamic among organizational innovation, theoretical development, and cultural production. Moreover, they reveal a plan for institutional development that has proved extremely hardy, particularly in Chicago" (*Avante-Garde* 237).

Though it is true that collaboration amongst BAM participants led to their efforts to clarify a specific "black aesthetic," it is important to remember that the concept of such an aesthetic remained a complicated and contested term. Thus, as illustrated in the work of Amini, Rodgers, and Jackson, the concept of collaboration was both an ideal and a threat, and all three writers exemplify the extent to which collaborative practices simultaneously affirmed unity *and* aroused tensions amongst Black Artists in the marketing of a nation-building aesthetic. In addition, the earliest published poetry authored by each writer advanced paradigms for producing art which challenged and queered the elitist culture of the BAM. Furthermore, their work privileged the most marginalized voices within black communities, which ultimately perpetuated a broader, more inclusive, though less publicized and popular version of Black Art. As noted by the editors of *Want to Start a Revolution: Radical Women in the Black Freedom Struggle* (2009), "Although a new generation of scholars has greatly expanded our knowledge of black radicalism and black freedom struggle, they have left largely intact a 'leading man' master narrative that misses crucial dimensions of the postwar freedom struggle and minimizes the contributions of women" (Gore, Theoharis, and Woodard 2). Thus, as participants in, observers of, and respondents to black freedom struggles of the Black Arts Movement and Black Power Movement, Amini, Rodgers, and Jackson, in their early writing careers, compel further analysis of the artistic production of women writers, artists, activists, and intellectuals of this era of struggle and triumph, and their work should be read as important documentations of the BAM's multifarious import within the broader tradition of black activist cultural expression.

While many scholars have addressed the degree to which Black Artists collaborated around and integrated diverse mediums of artistic expression into the development of a cohesive aesthetic in order to elucidate the imperatives of the BAM, as previously expressed, paradoxically, those who were opposed to the movement's objectives contributed to the reinforcement of its goals as well. The dissenting perspectives of this latter group compelled Black Artists to strengthen their resolve in marketing their aesthetic as a progressive means toward achieving social and political empowerment in black communities throughout the African Diaspora. "During the Black Arts Movement, the inseparability of the ideological and the aesthetic was considered intuitive and self-evident" (Collins and Crawford 11). In a broader context, the collaboration of ideals in the construction of a Black Arts aesthetic takes on a globally progressive magnitude when considering the extent to which Black Artists were inspired to come together during a historical moment in which the world witnessed the rise of postcolonial struggles throughout Africa and other nations. For Black Artists and their detractors, "the example of black people rising up to throw off white European colonial governments in African countries like Chad, the Congo, Dahomey, Gabon, Ivory Coast, Mali, Nigeria, Senegal, Somalia, Upper Volta, Zaire, and others, was a potent stimulus" (T. V. Reed 8). Incidentally, coalition-building and liberation initiatives were fomented by other cultural movements amongst people of color, including Chicano, Indigenous American, Asian American, and Asian Pacific Islander movements. Many such initiatives were inspired by the practices and missions of the BAM and Black Power objectives, and many members of these various cultural communities participated in black civil rights, Black Arts, and Black Power programs, forming multicultural alliances and networks of political activism.[4] Still, among other things, the BAM in particular "articulated the relationship between Black nationalism and black art, and the black aesthetic celebrated the African origins of the Black community, championed black urban culture, critiqued Western aesthetics, and encouraged the production and reception of black arts by black people" (Pollard 175).

Yet despite its agenda, the Black Arts aesthetic of the 1960s and 1970s was ultimately an amorphous, evolving concept, as was the black nationalist ideal. According to scholar Wahneema Lubiano, "[B]lack nationalism is plural, flexible, and contested . . . [I]n its broadest sense, [it] is a sign, an analytic, describing a range of historically manifested ideas about black American possibilities . . . [It] is a constantly reinvented and reinventing discourse that generally opposes the Eurocentrism of the U.S. state . . ." (232–234). Although not every black writer chose to pursue black nationalist goals or produce art that conformed to the BAM's agenda, indeed, the movement was born out of a series of contentious though productive exchanges between its most committed architects *as well as* its critics, many of whom responded to, mocked, and even attacked their peers' competing ideas about how to advance the social and political interests of black communities through art. Simply put, the shaping of the contours of the Black Arts objective had as much to do with the ways in which the movement's participants promoted its principles as it had to do with critics' opposition to Black Artists' agenda. As artists of the BAM "attempted to unite communities dispersed across great geographical spaces," and "put into place a geographically broad, trans-American articulation of hybridity that was 'indeed a revolutionary mixture of the indigenous and the cosmopolitan,'" they did so in part because they were inspired to countermand the arguably bourgeoisie ideals of their detractors, who just as passionately expressed counter-viewpoints about these matters (Sell, "The Voice" 284). When considering the various trajectories of the debate about the relationship between art, politics, and social justice during the BAM era (and whether or not such relationships should be perpetuated and exploited as propaganda), Black Artists, their detractors, and everyone in between contributed their perspectives on the subjects. Sell's discussion of the "black voice" during the BAM is useful in this context. He writes:

> The Black voice theatricalizes and dramatizes the spaces in which it sounds, defining at once the scene and its seers, the Black voice disciplining the Black eye, configure[s] itself . . . Voice is at once the vehicle of the individual, of the self, diversity, and locality, *but it is also the guarantor of ideological homogeneity and community coherence . . .*" ("The Voice" 285, emphasis mine)

Thus, I argue that the often contentious range of black voices both within and "outside" of the BAM productively and paradoxically stimulated the movement's initiatives. The result of this fecund, artistic moment in black literary history and culture is a series of conversations among black writers worldwide, which confirms the BAM's culturally and ideologically pluralistic foundations.

In many ways, the legacy of the BAM is perpetuated through a persistent critique of its autonomous and exclusive culture as that which was alienated by and distinguishable from "other" cultures of black writers, artists, activists, and intellectuals who opposed its premise. And while such critiques can be productive, they can also reinforce particular artistic, social, and political mythologies about the BAM that audiences have come to take for granted at the expense of a more nuanced impression of the movement. According to Kimberly Benston, whose perspective regarding the BAM productively complicates what are often and otherwise perceived amongst scholars to be the polarizing aspects of the movement's culture,

> . . . the tactics we employ in decoding and recoding modern black art still turn in some measure to our interpretation of the artistic revolution whose origins stand now at a generation's remove, [and] on our attitude toward the programmatic declarations and practical performances which carry the Black Arts Movement's freight of aesthetic, ontological, and political visions. (6)

My own effort to "situate black poetics within a larger, more continuous, and more textured field of expressive desire," as further encouraged by Benston, is a response to what I perceive to be some of the limited ways in which the BAM continues to be explored by scholars.[5] As I discuss in chapter one of this project, although many researchers continue to productively remark upon the most apparent artistic and political disparities between the ideas expressed by BAM participants and those who argued against its legitimacy, such remarks discourage a more in-depth critique of the BAM that might otherwise call attention to the fluid exchange of ideas and ideological connections between the movement's participants and their critics. Thus, it is indeed fruitful to consider how the many layers of the culture of the BAM were paradoxically motivated by and reinforced through an orchestra of competing perspectives—all of which helped to elucidate the concepts of black identity, black culture, and black community and/or nation-building ideals, as well as the role of the black writer in shaping such concepts. Contemporary writers, artists, lyricists, intellectuals, theorists, and activists have drawn from the political and aesthetic legacies initiated by participants and architects of the BAM, who aspired to accomplish what they believed no other generation of black writers had before in producing a body of work that would respond to the specific cultural needs, interests, and sensibilities of people of African descent in America and beyond.[6] Indeed, as Sell further argues, "[T]he Nixon administration slashed government funding of experimental arts and the economic crisis of 1973 laid low hundreds of community theaters across the United States, many of the practical links forged between art and politics were sundered—but the theory survived in those educated by the Black Arts Movement" (*Avante-Garde* 244).

During the nascent years of the BAM, Amiri Baraka, one of the most in/famously vocal designers of the movement and perhaps the most popular figure to be associated with it, expressed that the Black Artist "is desperately needed to change the images his people identify with by asserting Black feeling, Black mind, [and] Black judgment. The Black intellectual, in this same context, is needed to change the interpretation of facts toward the Black Man's best interests . . ."[7] Baraka's equally influential contemporary, Larry Neal, suggested that black literature become part of a "ritual that affirms our highest possibilities, but is yet honest with us."[8] Both Baraka's and Neal's statements are echoed by essayist James T. Stewart, another architect of the BAM, who expressed that "the black artist must construct models which correspond to his own reality . . . Our models must be consistent with a black style, our natural aesthetic styles, and our moral and spiritual styles."[9] Whether or not self-defined Black Artists of this moment were successful in meeting such expectations continues to be a subject of debate, but as I further discuss in chapter one, what is clear is that the BAM was conceived out of a unique and perhaps paradoxical matrix of perspectives voiced between the movement's participants and their critics, which ultimately and unpredictably contributes to the continuing appeal of the BAM. Although the movement is often considered to be a contentious, antagonizing, and exclusive period of artistic production, I suggest that it can also be interpreted for its malleability and accessibility to a broad range of ideals, which contributes to its long-standing relevance. While, generally speaking, the ideals of the movement were and continue to be represented within specific political and aesthetic terms, paradoxically, the conceptualization of the Black Arts aesthetic was influenced by the constant ideological and much publicized debates between BAM writers, artists, intellectuals, and activists and their critics, including such writers as Ralph Ellison and Albert Murray. The ideological "warfare" and ongoing dialogue that ensued between artists, activists, and intellectuals representing various artistic and political sensibilities in favor of *and* opposed to BAM's tenets contributed to the shaping of the movement's aesthetics. Yet paradoxically, such discord reinforced the expectations of the movement, and this characteristic is one of the BAM's most exciting features.

In keeping with the themes of "paradox" and "collaboration" within the culture of the BAM, in chapter two I discuss the aforementioned local, grassroots Black Arts group the Organization for Black American Culture (OBAC) more fully. Although it was considered to be a branch of the BAM, its aesthetic was inspired by its own unique, culturally specific objectives through the artistic and entrepreneurial collaborations amongst key Chicago figures and institutions supporting Chicago's artistic and politically progressive culture. "What marked the intensity of cultural nationalism in Chicago was the commitment of artists and intellectuals to building and maintaining black institutions that reached a comparatively large audience," writes James Smethurst in his ambitious study of the BAM.[10] OBAC's agenda was heavily influenced by the broader national movement, and as such, its participants collaborated with BAM artists in other cities, including New York, Detroit, St. Louis, Philadelphia, Oakland, Cleveland, Los Angeles, Atlanta, etc. However, paradoxically, OBAC emerged as perhaps the most productive site from which the dissemination of the ideals of the national movement can be evaluated. In addition, OBAC existed as part of a continuing historical legacy of politically and culturally inspired art in Chicago that was, in part, conceived out of the collaboration between younger Chicago Black Artists and their mentors. As OBAC writer Carolyn Rodgers suggests, there is an "extraordinarily complex reality of [the] cultural flow that has made Chicago such a central site of Black writing in America, a site flowed to and criss-crossed over and over by thousands of migrants, and by the words, images, spirits, and bodies of the greatest Black artists in the United States and the world" (foreword i). In this context, as I discuss at length in chapter two, Gwendolyn Brooks's influence upon this younger generation of Black Arts and OBAC artists, for example, is well documented, and Brooks's collaboration with many OBAC writers afforded them the benefit of her artistic expertise and insights. Brooks was equally influenced by this eager group of younger Black Artists as they ushered in a new climate of artistic, community-inspired productivity. In addition, OBAC continued to operate well after the BAM's waning years and into the decade of the eighties. Thus, I interpret its legacy as that which is exemplary of the ways in which the ideals of the organization succeeded in doing more than fulfilling the goals of the national BAM aesthetic and in fact paradoxically became the standard by which the broader movement's "successes" or "failures" can be evaluated.

The core of this project rests between chapters three, four, and five, where I spend ample time exploring the poetry of Amini, Rodgers, and Jackson, whose careers and voices were launched via their participation in OBAC. The themes of "paradox" and "collaboration" come into play in these chapters too, for I discuss not only how each writer responds to the arguably masculine overtones and sexism embedded within the rhetoric of the BAM, as has so often been cited in scholarship regarding black women artists of this era, but I also discuss how these women managed to expand the terms of the role of the Black Arts writer despite the well-documented challenges they faced as they navigated the gendered biases of the movement. Yet even in the face of such challenges, women artists, intellectuals, and activists of this period successfully and productively collaborated with their male peers—many of whom acknowledged the roles that they played in perpetuating a climate of sexism to the detriment of women. However, in various ways, women like Amini, Rodgers, and Jackson not only became the arbiters of BAM principles, but they succeeded in productively and simultaneously queering and/or reconfiguring the concept of nation-building art as it was promoted within the movement in Chicago and beyond. In many aspects, the work of each woman reflects a visionary perspective that effectively moved beyond the immediacy of BAM aesthetics and continues to be accessible to the social, political, and artistic aspirations of contemporary audiences. Chicago's OBAC was cofounded by Amini, Rodgers, and Haki Madhubuti, each of whom assisted in advancing its imperatives during the nascent years of the BAM. In addition, Angela Jackson remained committed to maintaining the organization's objectives in later years. She also assumed a leadership role in the OBAC writers workshop during the late 1970s and worked as the editor for the organization's monthly journal, *Nommo*, which, roughly translated, means "the power of the word"—a motivating idea in the conceptualization of black nationalism. As my readings of these three writers will reveal, women were perhaps in the most advantageous positions to represent the potential of the Black Arts aesthetic *beyond* not despite its gendered parameters. Furthermore, the vision of each of these women was fundamental rather than auxiliary to the perpetuation of BAM and OBAC nation-building objectives, and their work uniquely exemplifies the complexities of such objectives. As members of OBAC, writers like Amini, Rodgers, and Jackson were capable of inspiring a progressive, expansive, and culturally inclusive version of Black Art, and OBAC's agenda inspired those of other nation-building arts organizations around the country.

Taken together, the earliest poetry produced by Amini, Rodgers, and Jackson reflects the fortitude and resiliency of the OBAC and BAM traditions in general and women artists in particular. Reviewed separately, each writer's work demonstrates the strategic ways in which she perpetuated an inclusive, continually evolving aesthetic that would appeal to and maintain relevance for future generations. Ultimately, and paradoxically—perhaps more so than the work of their male peers—much of the work produced by each of these writers during this period represents a treatment of the most honored core values of the BAM, even as such writers challenged a culture that otherwise sustained the patriarchal norms that rampantly threatened to paralyze the movement's progressive potential.

For the purposes of this project, I find Tommie Shelby's definition of "Black Power nationalism" useful in considering how the poetry of Amini, Rodgers, and Jackson perpetuated cultural and political empowerment within the African Diaspora. He writes, "According to this conception, black people should form an independent and autonomous community, with significant collective control over its sociopolitical, economic, and cultural life" (10). Shelby concludes that such a concept of nationalism, perpetuated by Black Power icons such as Stokely Carmichael, "has not adequately come to terms with the changing social conditions of blacks in the post–civil rights era, relies on the ill-founded idea of homogeneous black populations, underestimates the sociopolitical significance of class and status stratification within the black population, and fails to appreciate and truly respect differences within the group" (10). Yet I argue that the poetry of Amini, Rodgers, and Jackson, as "black nationalist poetry," *does* successfully respond to each of Shelby's expressed concerns. Therefore, and within this particular context, their work offers a more progressive approach to black nationalist goals than was advanced by their more visible male contemporaries. OBAC would ultimately afford writers like Amini, Rodgers, and Jackson the opportunity to gain exposure as Black Artists, and the organization would become a comprehensive campaign that included other branches of artistic expression, including theater, dance, music, and the visual arts. Chicago Black Artists' high regard for the BAM aesthetic was apparent in various mediums of performance developed by OBAC participants, and they were encouraged to explore the potential of a nation-building aesthetic that would have progressive import in their own communities. In addition, OBAC's aesthetic can be effectively measured by the artistic output of a culturally diverse membership, whose ideals somewhat paradoxically became a model for what could be achieved by the advancement of a culturally inclusive rather than restrictive Black Arts aesthetic.

In her essay "Unspeakable Things Unspoken," Toni Morrison writes that

> "quiet as it's kept" is a "speakerly" figure of speech that speaks and bespeaks a particular world and its ambience. Further, in its "back fence" connotation, its suggestion of illicit gossip, of thrilling revelation, there is also in the "whisper," the assumption . . . that the teller is on the inside, knows something others do not, and is going to be generous with this privileged information. (269)

Thus, one of my goals in this project is to reprioritize the "whispering" work of women writers that succeeds in paradoxically calling attention to the "particular world" of the BAM as well as its "ambiences" despite their often interpreted marginalized status within the movement. As I engage the poetry of Johari Amini, Carolyn Rodgers, and Angela Jackson as less celebrated "insiders" to the BAM culture, my goal is to frame such ambiences as those which resulted from the work produced by a select group of women artists who simultaneously collaborated with as well as challenged the masculine overtures of the period. Furthermore, instead of addressing the most noted controversies so often addressed within BAM scholarship, I am motivated by scholar Ginter Lenz's suggestion that we need to challenge a "reductive understanding of the Black Arts/Black Aesthetic Movement and have a fresh look at all of its complexity" (204). As scholar Amy Abugo Ongiri recently pointed out in *Spectacular Blackness: The Cultural Politics of the Black Power Movement and the Search for a Black Aesthetic* (2010), "The Black Arts Movement continues to be one of the most influential and yet least studied moments of African American literary and cultural production" (91). Even though the BAM is commonly perceived as an exclusive moment in the history of black expression, I hope to encourage readers to consider some of the movement's subtleties, which were influenced by a range of women's voices.

Readers continued to be intrigued by the activist energy and zeitgeist of the BAM as well as the iconography that epitomized its objectives long after the Movement's most fruitful years.[11] As suggested, with the exception of projects like the aforementioned books authored by Amy Abugo Ongiri as well as the collection of essays edited by Lisa Gail Collins and Margo Natalie Crawford entitled *New Thoughts on the Black Arts*

Movement (2006), much of the scholarship devoted to the study of the BAM calls attention to the ways in which the work of its women writers "revises" and/or "challenges" the gendered and/or sexist ideologies of its nation-building objectives. For instance, Karen Jackson Ford suggests that "[w]omen writers in the Black Arts Movement were faced with the impossible task of being revolutionary poets, who were aggressive, irreverent, and menacing, while being supportive black women, who were submissive, reverent to black men, and feminine" (192). In addition, William Van Deburg expresses that men of the BAM were criticized for "allowing aesthetic judgments to be dictated by political agendas," and that, furthermore, "by reducing artistic expression to 'black chauvinist' propaganda, cultural nationalists had succeeded only in 'vulgarizing' their own skills, thereby making it unlikely that they would leave anything of value to posterity" (296). Although these aspects of the BAM merit and have received much deserved attention, scholars seem resistant to turn their energies away from the BAM's in/famous "chauvinist propaganda" as it was enforced by some of its most well-known male figures, and instead engage the work of less popular though influential writers, whose work reflects other equally relevant and valuable features of the movement.

Perhaps such a trend is symptomatic of what black feminist scholar Barbara Christian refers to as "the race for theory," which has determined how scholars read (or consequently fail to acknowledge) texts that would help to expose the complexities of black cultural expression. According to Christian, the study of the BAM became fertile ground in which to nurture theory as a way of justifying BAM's goals. "The race for theory," Christian writes, ". . . has silenced many of us to the extent that some of us feel we can no longer discuss our own literature . . ." (622). She discusses her own investment in studying writing and/or literature of the Black Arts Movement that has "protested the literary hierarchy of dominance which declares when literature is literature" (623). Since, as Christian rightly points out, scholarship is a "collective" and/or "collaborative" endeavor, the tendency for scholars to "invent wholesale theories regardless of the complexity of the literature we study" is especially threatening to the legacy of the BAM, for instance, and our ability to preserve the integrity of the broad and varied body of work that it inspired (622).

As Christian suggests, as enticing as theory can be in revisiting the BAM's gendered practices, for instance, scholars' overwhelming investment in the subject of the politics of sexual "difference" that influenced BAM rhetoric, and the interpretation of "Black womanhood as a counterhegemonic subject position" within the context of its culture can ultimately and problematically limit our appreciation for the scope of the BAM's artistic output (Mance 122). My own intention is to move beyond this conversation and its reinforcement of the paradigm of gender "opposition" that most often characterizes the legacy of the BAM. As the poetry of Amini, Rodgers, and Jackson reveals, writing produced by many women of the movement was much more than oppositional "rhetoric"—an idea explicated in the poem "Power," authored by feminist writer Audre Lorde, who writes, "The difference between poetry and rhetoric / is being / ready to kill / yourself / instead of your children."[12] Thus, in this context, women poets of this period looked *beyond themselves* for the purpose of contributing their bodies, hearts, souls, and minds to a nation-building aesthetic. The popular contention that women participants of the BAM were essentially working in opposition to their male peers reductively perpetuates the movement as a monolithic, univocal endeavor, and creates little incentive for audiences to explore its dialectical nuances.

Black women's collective ability to withstand the gendered biases of the BAM in order to promote a more inclusive collaborative project represents a queering of the movement's principles as promoted by its most vocal male participants. Although gender empowerment was certainly a priority for many women of the BAM, their work addressed other issues of relevance to the movement's culture and agenda. The failure to acknowledge the multifarious aspects of their work and the movement as a whole ultimately stigmatizes the legacy of the BAM. Although it is a widely held contention that their male peers were responsible for defining some of the most resonating features of the BAM, and men continue to receive a disproportionate amount of credit for crafting the ideological blueprints for this critical artistic moment in the history of black expression, an overemphasis on and/or preoccupation with this particular aspect of Black Arts culture discourages new trajectories of insight that might illuminate other productive ways of thinking about this era.

As scholar Kim Whitehead offers, "A coalition adheres for the purpose of accomplishing a particular cultural or political goal or set of goals, and the relationship between the individual and the group always requires a recognition of difference" (38). Black feminist scholars like the aforementioned Barbara Christian, as well as Patricia Hill Collins and Deborah McDowell, among others, have ambitiously engaged the subject of black women's writing and politically inspired expression as "protest" work within their collective struggle to survive amidst race, class, and gender oppression.[13] For the purpose of my project, I am particularly compelled by Cheryl Clarke's valuable study of black women poets since the 1960s in the project *After Mecca: Women Poets and the Black Arts Movement* (2005), in which Clarke acknowledges that

> [w]omen's participation in art and politics signaled feminist potential and presented first and foremost challenges to male dominance. Longings for a militant literacy, sexual autonomy, and a poetics not circumscribed by whiteness and maleness, fomented the beginnings of black feminist and lesbian-feminist production . . . They shared longings for "women-identified women's space, culture, and politics." (94)

Despite the brevity of this commentary, Clarke does not restrict her analyses of the work of women writers of the BAM to the ways in which gender and sexual politics inform their productivity. Her suggestion that "critical engagement of the poetry of African American women in no way clutters the literary landscapes of either the black or the white west" is an appeal to scholars and audiences to expand existing literary and theoretical paradigms for considering the achievements of black women writers of this era (1). Among the many profound insights that Clarke shares with readers regarding the study of black women poets of the BAM, perhaps none is more resounding than the statement that "[t]he words of women cleaved art and activism, creating dangerous binaries and new *possibilities*" (1, emphasis mine). Furthermore, Clarke's contention that "black women exercised much artistic and writing agency" during the BAM compels my own attempt to argue for the potential capaciousness rather than the constraints of Black Art in my engagement of three understudied yet inspired female voices.

With a few exceptions, for each chapter dedicated to Amini, Rodgers, and Jackson, I have chosen to evaluate each writer's earliest collections of poetry, since they most urgently reflect the popular aesthetics of the BAM. Although Amini's first collection of poems, *Images in Black* (1967), was published before Rodgers's first published collection, *Paper Soul* (1968), Rodgers is perhaps the best known of all three writers, and her work appears more frequently in discussions of the BAM than the work of either Amini or Jackson.[14] Amini was a resident of Chicago during the Black Arts period, and the city materialized as a source of inspiration for her. Born in Philadelphia on February 13, 1935, to William and Alma McLawler, Jewel Christine, later Johari Amini, was six years old when her parents moved to Chicago. She married activist Jawanza Kunjufu in 1951 and had two children, Marcianna and Kim Allan. Later, as a student at Chicago's Wilson Junior College—now Kennedy-King City College—she met poet and later OBAC cofounder Haki Madhubuti. Amini's poetic voice emerges as one of the most prolific within the Chicago Black Arts aesthetic, and it was during the BAM that Latimore would change her name to Johari Amini, Swahili for "faithful jewel." In 1968 she met and began working with the founders of the Kuumba Performing Arts Company of Chicago—actor and director Val Gray-Ward and her husband, journalist Francis Ward. It was also during this period that Amini began meeting some of the most recognized and acclaimed writers in Chicago, including Gwendolyn Brooks, who, as mentioned, served as a mentor for many of the younger Black Artists of this era. Earning a BA in 1970 at Chicago State University and an MA at the University of Chicago in 1972, in her early years as a poet, Amini produced work that dared to challenge popular mediums of expression and the role of visual aesthetics in the perpetuation of racial and national identity. Her poetic critique of the legitimacy of such mediums expands the boundaries of Black Art in ways that perhaps undermined her peers' tendency to rely upon such mediums in their own work. Even more heretical is Amini's narrative invocation of the concept of the "erotic" as a sexual and performative ideal and a method of characterizing black identity in her earliest poetry. Since, generally speaking, Black Artists were discouraged from producing narratives of romantic love or sexuality that didn't neatly conform to nation-building principles, as I will later discuss, the explicitly liberating, woman-identified eroticism of Amini's work represents a radical disregard for such expectations. As with Rodgers, her contemporary, Amini's first two collections—*Images in Black* (1967) and *Black Essence* (1968)—were published by Haki Madhubuti's Third World Press, as were *A Folk Fable* (1969) and *Let's Go Somewhere* (1970), which includes an introduction by mentor and OBAC supporter Gwendolyn Brooks. Additional collections authored by Amini include *A Hip Tale in Earth Style* (1972) and the recorded spoken word projects *Spectrum in Black* (1971) and *Black Spirits* (1972).

After Amini's contemporary, Carolyn Rodgers, passed away of cancer on April 2, 2010, the international journal for the study of African Diasporic cultural expression, *Callaloo*, honored her work in a special edition entitled *The Blackbird Flies: Remembering Carolyn Rodgers*—a title inspired by the poet's second collection of poetry, *Songs of a Black Bird* (1969). This tributary volume, edited by Rodgers's OBAC kinswoman, Angela Jackson, included a host of scholarly and creative material celebrating the poet's contributions to the black vernacular tradition. Born in Chicago on December 14, 1940, to Clarence and Bazella Rodgers, the poet was educated in the city's public school system. Later, she attended the

University of Illinois in Chicago from 1960 to 1961; Roosevelt University, where she earned a BA in 1981; and later the University of Chicago, where she earned an MA in English. At various points in her career, Rodgers also served as a lecturer in African American literature at Columbia College and Indiana University in Bloomington, as well as being a writer-in-residence at Malcolm X College.

During the Black Arts era, Rodgers's work was published in such nationally recognized journals as the *Black World* and *Essence* magazine. In a rare public appearance in 2007, where she participated in a panel discussion about the Black Arts and OBAC traditions in Chicago, hosted by Northwestern University, Rodgers expressed that she had been inspired by writer Margaret Walker's poem "For My People" early in her writing life.[15] She began her career as a BAM/OBAC artist with the sensibilities of a writer increasingly inspired by the social and political aspirations of the black masses, and her work represents an artistic space in which to examine a woman's response to the ways in which ideals of community, nationhood, cultural identity, and the role of artists within the movement would be integrated into the production of Black Art. Yet Rodgers productively used her poetry to call attention to the limitations of this "new" aesthetic as well. Given her prior elusiveness in the years after the BAM, many of Rodgers's Black Arts peers had begun to speculate about her lifestyle since her participation in the movement. In an essay written by Amiri Baraka entitled "Afro-American Literature and Class Struggle," published in the collection *Paradigms of Black Studies* (1990), which was edited by former BAM writer and scholar Abdul Alkalimat, Baraka noted that "[w]e know that poets like Mari Evans are still producing good work, and Carolyn Rodgers, although she has gone heavy into the church . . . is still capable of stunning poetry" (139).

When Rodgers passed away, a *New York Times* writer referred to her as a "leading" BAM artist who "wove strands of feminism, black power, spirituality and writerly self-consciousness into a sometimes raging, sometimes ruminative search for identity."[16] Rodgers's OBAC contemporary, Haki Madhubuti, was reported as having said that "[w]hat made [Rodgers] important was her unique use of language and her descriptions of our community . . . When she read, people would sit up and take notice."[17] Unfortunately, I was unsuccessful in my own attempt to communicate with Rodgers while completing this project, and consequently, she is the only one of the three women I discuss at length with whom I didn't have the opportunity to conduct an interview. As one of the leading figures of OBAC, Rodgers developed her craft as a Black Artist and critic as part of a local community of writers and artists. Thus, the work she produced as part of this collective was at the creative center of its poetics.

In chapter four, I discuss Rodgers's earliest work, including many of the poems found in her first two collections of poetry, *Paper Soul* (1968) and *Songs of a Black Bird* (1969), both of which, as mentioned, were published by poet Haki Madhubuti's Third World Press. Additional works by the poet include *Two Love Raps* (1969); an anthology entitled *Roots* (1973), which Rodgers edited; a volume of poetry entitled *The Heart as Ever Green* (1978); *Eden and Other Poems* (1983); a novel entitled *A Little Lower than Angels* (1984); and the poetry volumes *Morning Glory* (1989) and *We're Only Human* (1994). At other points in her writing career, Rodgers served as a reviewer for the *Chicago Daily News* and a columnist for the *Milwaukee Courier*. Her collection *How I Got Ovah: New and Selected Poems* (1975) was a finalist for the National Book Award and includes an introduction written by OBAC writer Angela Jackson.

In both of her first two collections, much of Rodgers's poetry reflects the idea that the very concept of Black Art was not a "fixed" one, as so many have come to describe it, but rather one that varied and changed in form, function, and meaning with each piece of work produced by Black Artists. Despite the fact that Rodgers composed a manifesto defining Black Art in her piece "Black Poetry—Where It's At," the narration and character development found in several of her poetic pieces contradict the notion that there can or should exist a universal paradigm for constructing Black Art or for defining the role of the Black Artist in advancing community-building objectives.[18] In addition, Rodgers's earliest work suggests that the goal of defining the role of the Black Arts writer continued to be a fundamental preoccupation for self-acclaimed BAM participants such as herself, as Black Arts goals necessitated that they position themselves within unwavering spaces of political expression and cultural representation. During her later years, when she produced "cooler" poems that "lack[ed] the fire and brimstone" reminiscent of her earlier works, little was known about Rodgers's status until she resurfaced once more and began speaking about the influence of the BAM on her continuing development as a writer.[19]

In chapter five, I consider the aesthetic aspects of Angela Jackson's first two collections of poetry, which were published during the waning years of the BAM. The youngest of the three writers, Jackson is equally recognized for her poetry and fiction. As with her predecessors, Jackson's first collection of poetry, *VooDoo/Love Magic* (1974) was published by Third World Press, but her sophomore project, *The Greenville Club* (1977) was published by Bk Mk Press, which operated out of Kansas City. Born in Greenville, Mississippi, to George and Angeline Jackson in 1951, Jackson spent her earlier years there before moving to Illinois with her parents. She attended Northwestern University, (an experience she later fictionalized in her novel *Where I Must Go* [2009], which I discuss in chapter six), where she earned several literary awards, including the Edwin Schulman Fiction Prize and Academy of American Poets Prize. Jackson produced short stories as well, earning an Illinois State Arts Council Award in 1978 for her short story "Dreamer" (1977). The recipient of many other literary prizes and fellowships, in 1977 Jackson participated in the Poets in the Schools program to Lagos, Nigeria, as an elected representative of the United States at the second World Festival of Black and African Arts and Culture (FESTAC). In addition, an excerpt from a novel then in progress, entitled *"Witch Doctor"* (1977), *Treemont Stone* (1984), and *Solo in the Boxcar* (1985) were published while Jackson remained an active member of OBAC.

Jackson wrote dramatic works as well, including *Witness!*, which was performed at the Chicago Showcase Theater in 1978, and *Shango Diaspora: An African-American Myth of Womanhood and Love*, performed at the Chicago Parkway Community House Theatre in 1980. The collection of poetry *Dark Legs and Silk Kisses: The Beatitudes of the Spinners* won the 1994 Carl Sandburg Award for poetry, and *And All These Roads Be Luminous: Poems Selected and New* was published in 1997. Most recently, Jackson was interviewed about her first novel, *Where I Must Go* (2009), about which she stated, "I went down deep into the specific, but we arrive at the universal. It's about being true to yourself and arriving at yourself, despite your history or how other people see you."[20]

In Jackson's earliest work as an OBAC participant, she simultaneously engaged images reflective of contemporary, urban black American life while incorporating symbolic spatial and cultural references to ancient Africa as a motivating concept, which would inform the rhetoric of Pan-Africanism and Afrocentrism as they continued to be conceptualized by scholars in later years. For instance, Jackson's work reinforces what Pan-Africanist scholars Sidney J. Lemelle and Robin D. G. Kelley refer to in the introduction to *Imagining Home* (1994), a collection of essays that interpret versions of Pan-Africanism. They write, "The main characteristic of early Black nationalism was a concern with intellectually establishing the existence of a racial-cultural bond between continental Africans and diasporan Africans, and demonstrating the importance of Pan-African unity in building an emancipatory movement" (3). Black Power spokesperson Stokely Carmichael's statement that Black Arts participants and

Black Power activists "want to talk about Africa because it is important because we do not know anything about our mother continent" is relevant to my reading of the Afrocentric features of Jackson's early poetry, with its emphasis on a unified African Diaspora through the construction of a collective cultural memory (162, 206). In addition, poet Lorenzo Thomas's notion that "the aesthetic goal of Black Arts music and poetry [was] an attempt to recreate in modern modes the ancestral role of the African griots who are poets, musicians, and dancers whose songs record genealogies and the cosmologies of societies such as the Wolof and Mandinka" provides a context in which I interpret Jackson's work.[21] Finally, she invokes concepts of family, community, and nation in ways that privilege a woman-identified perspective, and as the youngest of the three OBAC writers that I evaluate in this project, Jackson making an affirmation of such ideals testifies to the sustained and perhaps increasing significance of women's voices as they inform the development of Afrocentrist philosophy, which "seeks . . . the creation of a harmonious environment in which all divergent cultures [can] coexist and learn from one another" (Marable 191). As I argue, Jackson's early poetry reflects the younger OBAC writer's contribution to the advancement of a Pan-Africanist ideology that continues to inspire nation-building objectives since the height of the BAM. According to Pan-Africanist scholar Tunde Adeleke, "Memories and knowledge of the earlier cooperation between Africans and Diaspora blacks, a cooperation that was instrumental to the dismantling of colonialism, have reinforced faith in Pan- Africanism" (95). In addition, scholar Molefi Asante, whom historian Manning Marable has referred to as a "chief representative" of Afrocentrism, suggests that "there exists an emotional, cultural, psychological connection between this people that spans the ocean and the separate existence" (Marable, *Beyond* 211; Asante qtd. in Adeleke 96). For the purpose of my project, I'm especially interested in Jackson's earlier Black Arts vision for black cultural empowerment through an integrated and/or collaborative New World African Diasporic consciousness—an aesthetic which predated theories of Pan-Africanism that would later be articulated by premiere scholars of Pan-Africanism long after the waning years of the BAM.

Although Amini's work was not published beyond the period of the BAM, in chapter six I extend my discussion of the movement and its legacies to readings of the writers' later work, including several pieces from Rodgers's final self-published collection *We're Only Human* (1994), as well as Jackson's novel, *Where I Must Go* (2009). Doing so exposes the extent to which the influences of the BAM remain perceptible in the postrace aesthetics of the women as they experiment with concepts of environmentalism and nostalgia and continue to incorporate themes of collaboration. Ultimately, my goal is to encourage readers to further consider the BAM as a contemporary and sustained construct. Thus, in the conclusion of my project, I encourage audiences to locate evidence of the continued impact of BAM in contemporary and mainstream contexts. In addition, I want to leave readers with a sense of the creative ways in which the artistic and performative contributions of women writers of the BAM helped to shape the contours of many of its most compelling features. As they did so, they looked with visionary eyes toward the artistic, political, and cultural aspirations of future generations who continue to find inspiration in the BAM. Despite the fact that the voices and contributions of women writers, artists, activists, and intellectuals of this period were pushed to the periphery, paradoxically, their work succeeded in broadening many features of the movement that threatened to restrict its objectives. As scholar Fahamisha Brown appropriately notes, "[W]riting and making poetry remains a highly idiosyncratic art . . . each poet makes the tradition new" (118).

I would like to add that my own completion of this project is the result of my collaboration with many artists, activists, and intellectuals who participated in the BAM, and who so graciously allowed me to interview them for the purpose of gaining further insight into the motivations behind their individual investments in one of the most contested, influential, and intriguing periods in the history of black expression beyond what I could ever hope to read about in books. For me, such a collaboration was vital, although, admittedly, the experience proved to be a paradoxical one as well. For better and sometimes for worse, I invariably found myself confused as well as enlightened by the living breathing perspectives of those who shared their lingering memories of the BAM with me, and I felt both overwhelmed by and privileged to hear their enthusiastic and sometimes frustrated recollections about the movement. Essentially, of course, those who were interviewed proved to be invaluable resources for me, and the results of our collaboration yielded fortuitously unexpected and valuable results.

Chapter One

Dysfunctional Functionality: Collaboration at Its Best in the Black Arts Era

It is important to consider how the agenda of the Black Arts Movement was shaped by and paradoxically instituted through a collaboration of competing and discordant voices. Whether artists, activists, and intellectuals defined themselves as "Black Artists" during this era or not, many of them favored a socially progressive agenda for pursuing cultural empowerment for black communities. "Historically within the United States, black resistance to domination has been pacifist, militarist, or a creative combination of the two" (James 143). Consequently, this crosscurrent of perspectives proved to be integral to the fomentation of BAM ideals. As those who opposed various aspects of the movement challenged the principles of its nationalist aesthetic, they forced those who most closely and conscientiously identified with Black Arts ideals to justify and carefully articulate their motives. Thus, any attempt to engage the BAM's legacy must include an observation of the vast and varied perspectives of artists, activists, and intellectuals representing ideologically diverse and divergent communities, and who were equally committed to a vision of cultural and individual empowerment for members of the African Diaspora.

Given the myriad of voices that informed the BAM aesthetic, it is useful to consider the extent to which it was mitigated by competing but mutually informative perspectives within and outside of the movement. It is also important to note that the BAM inspired cross-cultural conversations about predominant issues of relevance to the fate of black communities of the African Diaspora. While Black Artists and their critics may have been polarized by discourses of socio/economic development relative to the social and political status of black communities, they were equally bound together by their mutual investments in such issues. As such, the curious, inspired, and oftentimes contentious tone that defined this controversial though inspired moment in the history of black expression and freedom struggle emerges as an ostensible collaboration between BAM participants and their detractors, which contributes to the breadth of the BAM's complicated legacy.

Among the most simultaneously polarizing yet motivating issues that ultimately advanced rather than paralyzed Black Arts principles was the infamous "integrationist vs. nationalist" debate between BAM participants and their critics. This issue consequently aroused productive cross-cultural and cross-pollinating dialogues amongst black artists, activists, and intellectuals, who espoused a range of political and artistic objectives as such. Thus, the Black Arts Movement was swayed by an unpredictable social and political climate of hope, frustration, and uncertainty with regard to the future of black people in America and the broader African Diaspora. As William Van Deburg writes:

> By the mid-sixties, many activists were at an intellectual impasse, perplexed and disillusioned. Some had begun to question whether the federal government ever could become an effective promoter and protector of civil equality. Others had lost faith in the ability of black moderates to spur renewal in the northern ghettos. Still others were becoming skeptical of the white liberals' value to the movement in the South. In black communities, both large and small, the pressure of individual and group frustration was building behind a barrier of seemingly insoluble problems. (41)

In response to these matters, in a series of conversations published in the periodical *The Atlantic* in 1970, interviewer James Alan McPherson prompted writer Ralph Ellison, one of the most vocal critics of the BAM, to share his views about the "new" black consciousness compelled by the increasingly popular rhetoric of the movement's architects, to which Ellison responded:

> I think too many of our assertions continue to be in response to whites. I think that we're polarized by the very fact that we keep talking about "black awareness" when we really should be talking about black American awareness, an awareness of where we fit into the total American scheme . . . We did not develop as a people in isolation . . . We need to get a human perspective, and if we could get this we could put things into a more fruitful, creative perspective. (Rampersad 373)

Ellison's appeal for an integrated rather than separatist American cultural ideal was aggressively countered by the flaming rhetoric fanned by a younger generation of up-and-coming Black Power and BAM advocates of the late sixties and early seventies. During this period, "On the occasions when Ralph Ellison, an avatar of elegance, was invited to college campuses, blacks invariably denounced him for his failure to involve himself in the civil rights struggle, for his evident disdain of the posturing of Black Power" (Gates, "King" 18). As a counterresponse to Ellison's ideas, Amiri Baraka, one of the BAM's most vocal participants and the most frequently cited figure representing the movement, who later came to "personify for Ralph almost everything he deplored in the realm of race, art, and American culture," expressed the following:

> Nations are races. (In America, white people have become a nation, an identity, a race.) Political integration in America will not work because the Black Man is played on by special forces. His life, from his organs, i.e., the life of the body, what it needs, what it wants, to become, is different—and for this reason racial is biological, finally. We are a different species. (Rampersad 379; Baraka in "Afro-American" 166)

Although Baraka was more drawn to the poetry and ideas of the Beats and other white avant-garde movements than to the politics of black separatism earlier in his career, as scholar Christopher Beach notes, the death of Malcolm X inspired a myriad of changes in Baraka's life, including a conversion to the Muslim faith and the changing of his name from LeRoi Jones to Amiri Baraka. Beach also notes that Baraka founded the Black Arts Repertory Theatre/School in New York City and the Spirit House in Newark, which led to his becoming an integral figure of the BAM. After having been beaten by police during the 1967 Newark riots, Baraka continued to speak about the autonomy and empowerment of the black community as a separate nation from that of whites, and he became an advocate for black nationalism while developing criteria for the role of self-defined Black Artists in pursuing this agenda. "The increasing radicalization of the Black Revolt and the rise of the Black Arts Movement pulled LeRoi Jones from relative obscurity in the Beat circles of Greenwich Village, swept him into the center of the Black Power movement, christened him Imamu Amiri Baraka, and ultimately propelled the foremost black literary figure into the ranks of black national political leadership."[1] About Black Arts poetry, Baraka claimed, "We even want to use our poetry and song as yet another means to effect the destruction of this national oppression and its material base, monopoly capitalism. The bourgeoisie, and the intellectual sector that serves them, tells us we cannot. We say, Fuck you!" ("Afro-American" 119). Decades after the BAM, Baraka continued to criticize the black bourgeoisie, who "opened Negro Ensembles as defense against Black Arts [and] assorted colored cool-out canteens which would lessen the fire and divert the attack." According to Baraka, the black bourgeoisie was just as much an enemy of the black masses as were white capitalists. "They funded a Negro theater, a skin thing, so that what was hot and revolutionary would be overshadowed—a NAACP theater as opposed to a revolutionary nationalist theater" ("Afro-American" 127).

Throughout the debate about black identity and the future of black America in particular, both Ellison and Baraka suggested the extent to which writing and art produced by blacks would be capable of responding to their respective though disparate ideologies with regard to the future and fate of black people in America. As a sharp contrast to Baraka's version of cultural "awareness," Ellison fervently believed that blacks could realize a progressive and empowered cultural consciousness by acknowledging a shared and socially integrated black and white history, heritage, and future. "So many of our kids who are most militant really believe that whites are superior to them. That's why they keep asserting 'Blackness! Blackness! Blackness!'" Ellison contended with frustration, while Baraka argued that "[t]he black intellectual . . . is needed to change the interpretation of facts toward the Black Man's best interests, instead of merely tagging along reciting white judgments of the world . . . The Black man must seek a politics, an ordering of the world that is beneficial to *his* culture" (Rampersad 375; "Afro-American" 166, emphasis mine).

Clearly, this debate, clarified through the voices of two of the most influential figures in the history of black writing, represents the competing trajectories of intellectual thought with regard to ways in which to promote black social consciousness, and the debate compelled *both* writers' desires to see black communities empowered to overcome the socially, culturally, and politically oppressive forces that continue to impede their progress. "On balance, the inclusionists' strategy sought to transcend race by creating a context wherein individuals could be judged on the basis of what they accomplished rather than on the color of their skin . . . Nationalists rejected the culture and aesthetics of white Euro-America in favor of what today would be termed an Afrocentric" (Marable 219). Both Ellison's and Baraka's insights were fundamental to the construction of the BAM, for they equally encouraged a foundation upon which its principles would be fomented. In essence, the ideas of both also explicate the opposing ideologies that continued to influence the political tone of the period, which ultimately gave rise to BAM poetics. Whereas Ellison saw the limitations of BAM objectives, artists like Baraka saw this movement as an opportune initiative that would ideally discredit the integrationist politics of the black bourgeoisie personified by writers like Ellison and Richard Wright, the latter of which Baraka criticized for his lack of investment in the black community ("Afro-American" 123).

Baraka's criticisms further validated the BAM's message of race and/or culturally defined nationalism and effectively contributed to the ways in which he and his BAM peers positioned their aesthetic as *the* medium through which the interests and needs of the black masses could be heard. "If the Black Man cannot identify himself as separate, and understand what this means, he will perish along with Western Culture and the white man," Baraka proclaimed (166). The resurrection of a "new" black art stimulated by a new black racial consciousness was motivated as much by Baraka's and his BAM peers' impulse to distinguish themselves and their aesthetic from the ideologies of the likes of Ellison and Wright as it was by their desire to pursue a newly designed nationalist approach to racial and cultural empowerment for black Americans. While Ellison lamented the fact that Black Arts and Black Power rhetoric typically drove black patrons and artists "away from artistic resources almost as precious as life itself," and which did not exclusively conform to nation-building objectives as determined by Black Artists, Baraka *encouraged* black audiences and artists to consciously turn away from such venues and support art that reflected the black experience, since "Black artists must have an image of what the Black sensibility is in this land" (Rampersad 465; "Afro- American" 167).

Furthermore, regardless of their politics, both Ellison's and Baraka's artistic perspectives characterized the social and political angst of this period, and their respective views were shared by a host of other prominent black writers, artists, intellectuals, and activists, all of whom represent a collaborative mix of coalescing and oftentimes competing ideas regarding the role that politically inspired art should play in black life. Still, while recognizing the distinctions between Ellison's and Baraka's perspectives, for instance, is useful to a point—since they suggest the extent to which black writers of this period situated themselves within an already existing debate about potential methodologies for achieving social and political empowerment for black communities, as had prior generations of black writers before them—the reigning perspectives of the Black Arts era also elucidate the commonalities between the political views of writers such as Ellison and Baraka. Both artists were equally committed to advancing their objectives during this transitional historical moment, and whatever their views were on the subject of the new black consciousness, the perspectives of both were equally essential to the designing of BAM objectives. Although Black Arts writer and critic Stephen Henderson's claim that "before Negroes can become black people, they have to confront their blackness and repudiate all that makes them ashamed of it" would have invariably infuriated Ellison, the competing perspectives expressed by those in favor of as well as those who were against the rhetoric of Black Arts and black nationalism remain essential to an evaluation of what would become one of the most contentious though inspired moments in history.[2]

In addition, as writers, artists, activists, and intellectuals continued to characterize their political sensibilities and artistic priorities in response to questions of cultural identity and black empowerment during this period, they simultaneously and necessarily engaged and consumed one another's work, and in this way, they were also subject to one another's influence for the purpose of articulating their respective aesthetics. For instance, as perhaps one of the most integral figures of Chicago's Black Arts Movement, writer, editor, and mentor Hoyt Fuller critiqued the artistic and political perspective of one of his famed contemporaries, James Baldwin, who incidentally criticized many aspects of the movement. He wrote, "Even James Baldwin, one of the best writers of his generation, bought the assimilationist philosophy . . . He lived to regret it. He soon discovered as he found fame, that the same critics who had lavished praise on him for his assault on 'protest' literature lumped his own works under that label" ("The Black Aesthetic" 336).

In addition, Larry Neal's thoughts on black nationhood are particularly useful in my examination of the paradoxical collaboration between BAM participants and their detractors, for he effectively calls attention to the interlinked though oftentimes antagonizing ideologies about which black integrationists and separatists debated. As one of the BAM's most influential architects, Neal composed an overview of the categories and elements most reflective of Black Arts principles, including the privileging of a collective "race memory" among black Americans, which recalls the Transatlantic Middle Passage; the transmutation and synthesis of black folk consciousness through dance and music; the promotion of the "integral unity of culture, politics, and art"; and the perpetuation of black nationhood and community through poetry.³ Originally published in the 1968 groundbreaking *Black Fire: An Anthology of Afro-American Writing*, in his essay entitled "And Shine Swam On," Neal writes:

> [W]hat has come to be known as Black Power must be seen in terms of the ideas and persons which preceded it. Black Power is, in fact, a synthesis of all of the nationalistic ideas embedded within the double-consciousness of Black America. But it has no one *specific* meaning. It is rather a kind of feeling—a kind of emotional response to one's history ... We have attempted through these historical judgments to examine the idea of nationhood, the idea, real or fanciful, that black people comprise a separate national entity within the dominant white culture. This sense of being separate, especially within a racist society with so-called democratic ideas, has created a particular tension with the psychology of Black America ... *We must face these ideas in all of their dimensions.* (646, emphasis mine)

Although Neal was undoubtedly a proponent and architect of the BAM, as these passages suggest, he believed that the movement's agenda was susceptible to the views expressed by those who chose *not* to support its ideals, for even these individuals were committed to the realization of cultural empowerment and an improved quality of life for black communities. In addition, they, too, were compelled by a desire to empower black Americans and members of the African Diaspora with new visions and/or versions of themselves. "Slogans such as 'Black Power,' 'Black Pride,' and 'Black is Beautiful'" represented a sense of political, social, and cultural freedom for African Americans, who had gained not only a heightened sense of their own oppression but a greater feeling of solidarity with other parts of the black world" (Beach 130).

However, the debates that ensued between these divergent ideological factions had deep historical roots. Indeed, the political divides between those who favored racial integration over separatism or black nationalism—the latter of which nineteenth-century activist and writer Martin Delaney is often credited for having initiated—had begun long before the era of the BAM.⁴ "Integration vs. separation have become polarized around two main wings of racial ideology, with fateful implications for the Negro movement and the country at large," writes Harold Cruse in "Revolutionary Nationalism and the Afro-American," an essay that originally appeared in the journal *Studies on the Left* in 1962, and which was later reprinted in the first edition of the aforementioned seminal *Black Fire* anthology.

> From the Reconstruction era on, the would-be Negro bourgeoisie in the United States confronted unique difficulties quite unlike those experienced by the young bourgeoisie in colonial areas. As a class, the Negro bourgeoisie wanted liberty and equality, but also money, prestige and political power. How to achieve this within the American framework was a difficult problem, since the whites had a monopoly on these benefits... It is up to the Negro to take the organizational, political and economic steps necessary to raise and defend his status. *The present situation in racial affairs will inevitably force nationalist movements to make demands which should be supported by people who are not Negro Nationalists.* (46 and 61, emphasis mine).

Cruse ultimately forecasts that "the more the system frustrates the integration efforts of the Negro, the more he will be forced to resolve in his own consciousness the contradiction and conflict inherent in the pro- and anti-integration trends in his racial and historical background," and that "out of this process, new organizational forms will emerge in Negro life to cope with new demands and new situations" (62). As he advocates for the reconciliation of integrationist and separatist terms for black Americans, Cruse's contentions reinforce the integral relationship between these two otherwise polarizing ideals as those that are mutually informative to one another's conceptualization. Furthermore, the BAM and its political counterpart, the Black Power Movement, arose out of a collective desire amongst artists, activists, and intellectuals to combat those oppressive factors that Cruse elucidates, and which continued to encroach upon the potential for black communities to realize their post–civil rights dreams of socio/economic equality in capitalist white America. "Most textbook treatments of the Black Power movement have focused on disillusionment and despair as major goads to black activism... By the mid-sixties, the high hopes of earlier years had, for most, proven illusionary" (Van Deburg 40).

The integrated efforts of the Black Power Movement and Black Arts Movement were designed, in part, to motivate audiences and communities to see themselves not as victims but as human beings capable of determining their own fates as proud members of the African Diaspora. "The Panthers believed they directly represented the will and imagination of the people, and they utilized a model of political organization derived from Leninist vanguard theory. Black Artists, on the other hand, developed the representational and perceptual means by which the people could represent themselves" (Sell, *Avante-Garde* 233). As Stokely Carmichael suggests regarding the need for Black Power in the "integrationist vs. nationalist" debate, "Negroes are dependent on, and at the discretion of, forces and institutions within the white society which have little interest in representing us honestly ... Our concern for black power addresses itself directly to this problem ... we shall have to struggle for the right to create our own terms through which to define ourselves and our relationship to society" ("Toward Black Liberation" 119). Perhaps opportunistically, Black Artists thought of themselves as integral to the process of shaping a new black consciousness at this moment.

However, the rigorous and aggressive tone of Black Arts rhetoric was motivated as much by BAM participants as it was by those who rebelled against their agenda. According to historian Manning Marable:

> Both the nationalists and integrationists believed that they were speaking to "white power brokers" on behalf of their "constituents"—that is, black Americans ... The integrationist version of racial politics sought the deracialization of the hierarchies of power within society and the economic system. By contrast, the black nationalist approach to racial politics was profoundly skeptical of America's ability to live up to its democratic ideals. (187–188)

As Eugene Redmond notes in *Drumvoices*, an extended study of the black vernacular tradition in poetry published in 1976, "Most of the writers of the period ... have found themselves engulfed at one time or another in heated debates over questions related to the 'black aesthetic,' the relationship of writer to reader, black versus white audiences, and the part politics should play in their work" (304). For instance, Ron Karenga's nationalist message that Black Art "must be from the people and must be returned to the people"; that "the Black Artist can find no better subject than Black People themselves"; and that the black artist "who does not choose or develop this subject will find himself unproductive" echoed throughout much of the work of the BAM's most vocal and prolific artists, and was, of course, predicated upon the nationalist assumption that there exists a distinct and unique black culture and black experience from which Black Art must be drawn (33). According to Black Arts advocate and essayist Sarah Webster Fabio, who authored the essay "Tripping with Black Writing," "Black writing of the seventies [was] the Sweet Chariots of our time, swinging low/swinging high/swinging free" (181). Her contemporary, writer John Oliver Killens, further determined that "from all sides pressure is put upon the Negro artist to deny his culture, his roots, his selfhood. How many black writers have you heard engage in this abject self-denial: 'I am not a Negro writer. I am a writer who happens to be a

Negro'?" he asked, challenging the integrationist perspectives of those like Ellison, who refused to racialize himself or his work (Rampersad 486).

As the previously mentioned scholar Eugene Redmond calls our attention to the ideological and aesthetic exchanges between black poets of the BAM, whose objectives were "often precipitated or attended by critical writings, historical studies, social essays and public political statements," as I continue to suggest, it is important to consider how such debates were informed by opposing discourses on the subject of race identity as it related to their own artistic production (304). For instance, poet Robert Hayden, who received a National Book Award nomination in 1972 and was elected to the American Academy of Poets in 1975, expressed views similar to those of Ellison, rejecting any singular, all-encompassing approach to determining an agenda for artists of African descent. Like Ellison, Hayden had a perspective reflecting that of a previous generation of established black writers who recognized the potential of the younger generation of BAM participants, and who rejected their nationalistic views about black writing, referring to it as "Black Nazism" (8). In addition, writer Albert Murray produced work that seemed "wholly in the same spirit" as Ellison's (Gates, "King" 16). Murray had been a schoolmate of Ellison's at Tuskegee Institute and was perhaps Ellison's most avid champion, and the two of them developed a long-lasting, mutually supportive friendship. With the 1970 publication of his work *The Omni-Americans*—"a book in which the very language of the black nationalists was subjected to a strip search"— Murray, like Ellison, effectively tempted the rhetoric of the BAM and stirred the debate revolving around the conceptualization of a nationalist aesthetic among black writers (Gates, "King" 18). In the book, he writes:

> The bitterness of outraged black militants ... is altogether appropriate even if sometimes excessive. [Their] own insight into the pragmatic implications of the heritage of black people in America, however, is often only one-dimensional. Indeed, sometimes it seems as if they are more impressed by the white propaganda designed to deny their very existence than by the black actuality that not only motivates but also sustains them ... Identity is best defined in terms of culture, and the culture of the nation over which the white Anglo-Saxon power elite exercises such exclusive political, economic, and social control is not all-white by any measurement ever devised. American culture, even in its most rigidly segregated precincts, is patently and irrevocably composite. It is, regardless of all the hysterical protestations of those who would have it otherwise, incontestably mulatto. (38–39)

Murray's emphasis on the concept of American identity as that which eludes any particular race—black, white, Native American, or otherwise—in favor of an identity defined by the confluence of rather than the cultural disparities between race groups effectively undermined the exigencies of the BAM. "Murray poo-poohs the whole African heritage exploration fuss. A 20th Century American, he sees no point in learning Swahili, Afro haircuts and quaint costumes. He is not about to go sifting for his African ancestors . . ." (Grunwald 14). In an interview conducted twenty-six years after the publication of *The Omni-Americans*, Murray stated, "I don't see how my main purpose in being put on this earth could be to protest white people . . ." (Piazza 114). Still, for Black Artists, Murray's brand of rhetoric was especially motivating to the nation-building project, for it validated the position of Black Artists like Baraka, who had assumed the roles of architects of the nation-building aesthetic for the benefit of black communities. For instance, as Stephen Henderson acknowledges in *The Militant Black Writer*, "Black writers, black poets, black artists are trying to demolish self-hatred . . ." (100).

While Murray's comments might seem threatening to a Black Arts nation-building aesthetic, they compelled Black Artists to invest themselves in a campaign that would perpetuate his ideals as those reflective of the tragic disillusionment among members of the black bourgeoisie, who had succumbed to what they considered to be mythic, empty promises of social, political, and cultural fulfillment falsely perpetuated in the form of integrationist, white, capitalist versions of the "American Dream." "Murray has suggested that people have a choice in their disposition toward circumstances: one can be a race statistic, or one can use all the tools of art and intellect to enlarge the scope, and therefore the potential, of the larger scene" (Lamar 191). Yet, as Black Arts critic Stephen Henderson writes:

> In the first place, what the black revolution seeks is not integration into American society as it now stands . . . We have all encountered the impersonality of institutions in every aspect of our lives—in the political, the religious, the academic, the social—and as a consequence we have all experienced the demeaning sense of powerlessness and invisibility that Ellison describes so well in *Invisible Man*. (126–128)

Henderson's reference to Ellison's novel in arguing that "the real revolution which is occurring in America today is the Black Consciousness movement . . . [as] a necessary first stage in the liberation of all black people" may seem ironic; however, it confirms the idea that no matter how contrary the views of Ellison and other writers might have been to those of Black Artists, their work and perspectives were still integral to the development of the BAM's objectives. Indeed, readers of Ellison's novel *Invisible Man* will recall that his nameless main character is *himself* beguiled by the politics of nationalism as well as assimilationism in his psychological journey toward self-empowerment.[5]

While he shared similar ideas about race consciousness and artistic production with Hayden and Murray, for instance, Ellison's own opposition to BAM objectives extended beyond mere rhetoric, and perhaps subsequently influenced his decision not to endorse many of the up-and-coming writers of this new generation—many of whom would move on to become proponents of the BAM's nation-building initiatives. As one of the few black editors working at Random House in the early seventies, who stated that "all good art has always been political," Toni Morrison recalls having solicited Ellison to write a foreword to novelist Leon Forrest's work, *There Is a Tree More Ancient Than Eden (1973)*. Although Ellison eventually agreed to do so and wrote a three-paragraph foreword to Forrest's book, Morrison stated that with the exception of his support of Forrest, Ellison was not helpful when it came to expressing support for other writers, such as Toni Cade Bambara, Henry Dumas, Gayl Jones, and June Jordan, for instance (Rampersad 487). "He saw no point in pushing for change based on racial reasons. He had earned his way in. Let other blacks do the same" (488). This kind of response to new black writers by older, more established literary counterparts like Ellison was symptomatic not only of the generational divide between them, but it also implicated the extent to which Ellison, for instance, may have been wary of the talents and/or political and artistic strivings of this new crop of talent.

But while Ellison refused to offer this level of support to young black writers of the BAM, his contemporary, Gwendolyn Brooks, considered doing so her responsibility. Rightly or wrongly, Ellison may have presumed a great deal about this generation's aesthetic vision, and he clearly had no intentions of perpetuating any kind of literary "kinship" with them in the form of mentoring. Still, his views were inspired by the same prevailing artistic, political, and social concerns as those of the younger, rising BAM artists. About black writers in general, Toni Morrison offers, "The major thing that binds . . . is the clear identification of what the enemy forces are, not this person or that person and so on, but the acknowledgement of a way of life dreamed up for us by some other people who are at the moment in power, and knowing the ways in which it can be subverted. That *is* a connection" (Davis 229).

As Morrison's words suggest, whether integrationist or separatist, established or new, black writers in America are "connected" by and share concerns about the political and social forces that have historically challenged black communities in their efforts to realize collective goals of empowerment. "At least it seems to me that in any Black book, no matter what it deals with or what the story line is, you realize that the people are not free . . . So I think the lack of freedom is the omnipresent theme in any Black writer's work today," offers playwright Alice Childress (*Black Creation Annual* 9). As she calls our attention to the connective artistic tissue that underscores a binding tradition of black expression, it becomes more apparent that despite the oppositional ideas espoused by Ellison, Hayden, and Murray, for instance, such ideas are integral to and part of a shared narrative amongst black writers that continues to express a collective desire for freedom. In addition, their ideas were relevant to the expressed currency of the new Black Art, for they exemplified the presumed and quintessentially problematic brand of black consciousness that Black Artists ultimately and perhaps opportunistically exploited as that which consequently went counter to separatist nation-building goals. Thus, Black Art was, in fact, compelled by the ideal of Murray's "omni-American" figure, for instance, for such a figure represented perhaps the most urgent justification for Black Artists' competing ideals.

Indeed, the urgency of the BAM's message offered a corrective to what writer Gwendolyn Brooks later referred to as a tradition of "literary hair straightening" perpetuated by those writers who perceived a "black-identified" consciousness to be limiting and/or counterproductive.[6] Not only was Brooks intrigued by the inspired energy of these new artists, but her endorsement of their efforts and willingness to nurture their talents and introduce them to other established black writers encouraged an intergenerational dialogue about politically informed art. "A revolutionary art is being expressed today," wrote James T. Stewart. "The anguish and aimlessness that attended our great artists of the forties and fifties and which drove most of them to early graves, to dissipation and dissolution, is over" (8). As I discuss at length in the following chapter, established writers like Gwendolyn Brooks and Hoyt Fuller, who was at one point editor of Johnson Publications' popular journal, the *Negro Digest* (later named the *Black World*), as well as artist Margaret Burroughs, who was cofounder of the Du Sable Museum of African-American Art in Chicago, collaborated with this new generation of politically conscious artists and helped them to initiate new performative, community-oriented, and ideological paradigms for achieving their objectives. "The black writer," writes Fuller, "... has wasted much time and talent denying a propensity every rule of human dignity demands that he possess, seeking an identity that can only do violence to his sense of self. Black Americans are, for all practical purposes, colonized in their native land . . ." ("Black Aesthetic" 7).

But while Fuller, Baraka, Neal, and other leading voices of the BAM were far more extremist in terms of their views about the role of the Black Artist in the new artistic and cultural landscape of the post–civil rights BAM, other writers, such as novelist Chester Himes, expressed a more nuanced perspective that further provoked prevailing questions about the psychological and performative burdens of the writing practice for artists of African descent in America and beyond:

> From the start the American Negro writer is beset by conflicts. He is in conflict with himself, with his environment, with his public . . . He must decide at the outset the extent of his honesty. He will find it no easy thing to reveal the truth of his experience or even to discover it. He will derive no pleasure from the recounting of his hurts. He will encounter more agony by his explorations in to his own personality than most non-Negroes realize. For him to delineate the degrading effects of oppression will be like inflicting a wound upon himself. He will have begun an intellectual crusade that will take him through the horrors of the damned. (395)

Himes's reference to the "American Negro" writer as opposed to the "*black writer*" may signify that at the time, he had yet to adopt the more popular terminology invoked in this new transitional era of race pride and race consciousness. But more importantly, his commentary alludes to the enigmatic psychological aspects of the creative process for writers of African descent. Although he maintains that "the effects of oppression" continue to inform and indeed weigh heavily upon the productivity of the black writer, he stops short of expressing his political views in terms of the integrationist vs. nationalist debate and instead calls readers' attention to the unnamable, torturous, though courageous act of probing areas of creative exploration yet to be tamed by words. In addition, Himes furthermore discusses the dilemma of black writers who attempt to reach both white and black audiences, although, once again, he offers no conclusive insights about whether or not black writers *should* make such an effort, and rather suggests that *all* writers "have a greater motive, a nobler aim . . . [to] write not only to express our experiences, our intellectual processes, but to interpret the meaning contained in them. We search for the meaning of life in the realities of our experiences..." (394). While one might interpret Himes's words to mean that black writers need not privilege the so-called "black experience," it is noteworthy that he also expresses that it is important for artists to draw from the cultural experiences reflective or representative of their particularized cultural realities.

In addition, writer Ishmael Reed expressed that "what distinguishes the present crop of Afro-American and Black writers from their predecessors is a marked independence from Western form" (517). But like Himes, his views about the role of the black writer during the BAM draw attention to the burdens associated with black writers' artistic production.

> Sometimes I feel that the condition of the Afro-American writer in this country is so strange that one has to go to the supernatural for an analogy. Manipulation of the word has always been related in the mind to manipulation of nature. One utters a few words and stones roll aside, the dead are raised and the river beds emptied of their content. (518)

Reed adds that the black writer "is a conjuror who works JuJu upon his oppressors; a witch doctor who frees his fellow victims from the psychic attack launched by demons of the outer and inner world"—a comment that clearly implicates the black writer's role in responding to and perpetuating the "binding" narrative of oppression amongst black writers and is reminiscent of Toni Morrison's earlier expressed views that there is indeed a culturally informed aspect to artistic production amongst writers of African descent (518). Still, Baraka later criticized Reed for at one point allegedly referring to Black Artists as "fascist tribalists" ("Afro-American" 127).

While the debate about whether or not black writers should conform to specific ideologies in the interest of addressing the social and political concerns of black life was as binding and collaborative as it was polarizing, so too were discussions about sex, sexuality, and gender bias during the era of the Black Arts Movement and Black Power Movement—all of which informed the social and political priorities of black artists, activists, and intellectuals. Such issues were addressed by self-defined Black Artists as well as other figures representing diverse cultural perspectives, who took responsibility for raising the level of consciousness among black audiences about the toxic impact of sexism and homophobia, for instance, within their communities. Incidentally, Toni Morrison wrote the introductory material for Toni Cade Bambara's *The Black Woman* (1970) and Huey Newton's collection on Black Panther writing, *To Die for the People* (1972)—two texts representing competing yet mutually informative political perspectives about and between black men and women committed to the nation-building project of the late sixties and early seventies. It is noteworthy that both of these texts, ideologically disparate though mutually informative projects, were both inspired by and perceived as representative products of the Black Arts and Black Power initiatives. Morrison's having contributed to both projects further reinforces the idea that existing ideological disparities between various cultures and/or cultural perspectives of this period were nonetheless mutually inspiring, and this paradox invariably fueled the collaborative though oftentimes contentious aspects of the BAM and Black Power Movement.

In addition, both male and female artists, as participants and opponents of BAM ideals, responded to the hypermasculine rhetoric of the movement, wherein women earned less credit for the roles they played in the collaborative effort to promote its ideals. This aspect of the BAM is well documented by scholars such as Ajuan Maria Mance, who writes that "[w]hen US scholars have turned their attention to the Black Arts Movement, it has most often been to scrutinize its emphasis on the Black male experience . . ." (95–96). In addition, Madhu Dubey notes that "[t]he peculiar positioning of the black woman in the political ideology of black nationalism was exactly reproduced in the Black Aesthetic discourse of the period. In a direct reflection of black nationalism ideology, the Black Aesthetic often constructed the revolutionary black subject in explicit opposition to the black woman" (20). While the subject of gender hierarchy and gender oppression is indeed critical to an assessment of the BAM, it is important to note that both male *and* female writers of this period engaged these issues, and such conversations ultimately inspired the collaborative energy of the BAM and had a direct impact on its social and political climate.

In 1964, the women of the civil rights organization the Student Nonviolent Coordinating Committee (SNCC) published a position paper identifying the level of sexual bias that existed within their group.[7] "Perhaps in an effort to contain the supposed power of the matriarch, many black nationalist organizations prescribed clearly restricted roles for black women in the movement" (Dubey 18). Years later, women artists of the BAM, whose work reflected a similar commitment to the political and nation-building goals as those of the women of SNCC, would also express their discontent about the sexism they experienced at the hands of their male contemporaries.[8] Many women in the civil rights, ethnic power, student, and antiwar movements experienced marginalization, harassment, disrespect, and an unequal workload. "While some men within SNCC and other radical movement groups responded favorably to the claims made by women, many more did not, calling their claims trivial and a distraction from the 'real' struggles around race, class, and war ... Sensitized to issues of inequality and injustice by these other movements, they turned their analyses back upon their male colleagues ..." (T. V. Reed 86). The 1970 publication of aforementioned anthology *The Black Woman*, edited by Toni Cade Bambara, was devoted solely to the advancement of black women's voices of this era and continues to stand as a collective response to the intersecting layers of cultural oppression black women faced at the hands of black men, despite their demonstrated equal investments in community and nation-building goals. "Unwilling to keep silent about gender issues within all-black organizations, many of these women highlighted gender oppression ..." (Gore, Theoharis, and Woodard 15). In addition, "[T]he title *The Black Woman* is strategically simple as it rages against the silence and speaks 'the black woman' into existence" (Crawford, "Must Revolution..." 187). Furthermore, Eleanor Traylor shares that "[t]he speakers whose voices sound through *The Black Woman* were (and remain) active participants in an ever-evolving movement whose impact at mid-twentieth century was perhaps the most revolutionary cultural and intellectual re-imagining to have occurred in the United States since the birth of America in the Declaration of Independence" (introduction xii).

Not only were emerging black women writers of this period calling attention to their unique experiences as such within the framework of black nationalist goals, but they were also designing new black feminist perspectives articulating liberationist objectives that were highly distinguishable from those of their white female and/or feminist peers. "In the collection of poetry, stories, and essays that is the Anthology, a definition of this worldview emerges as a sensibility, not as an 'ism' ... It finds sisterly empathy with complementary selves ... It refuses the assumptions and terminology of colonial, capitalist, racist, and gendered versions of reality" (xi-xii). Traylor's review of the accomplishments of the contributors to the anthology privileges the very basis upon which I perceive the fundamental prescience of women's voices during the BAM (including those women who defined themselves as "Black Artists" and those who did *not*), for, despite all of their commitments to encouraging an aesthetic that would respond to their culturally specific experiences, many of them were determined to create strategies for advancing culturally *inclusive* and socially conscious objectives that would *not* alienate men, thereby initiating an expansive version of nation-building art. Furthermore, "the variety of ways that conventional femininity asserted itself in [women's] poetry accounts for the distinctiveness of each writer's canon" (Ford 200). Poems that addressed everything from "women in economic poverty and spiritual poverty... battering and resistance to battering... sisterly solidarity and unsisterly betrayal... factory work and maid work... men as oppressors or men as lovers or men as loving oppressors" poured forth from black women (T. V. Reed 90). In her own conceptualization of the voice of the "black woman" in the introduction to the first edition of *The Black Woman* anthology, Bambara writes:

> She is a college graduate. A drop-out. A student. A wife. A divorcee. A mother. A lover. A child of the ghetto. A product of the bourgeoisie. A professional writer. A person who never dreamed of publication. A solitary individual. A member of the Movement. A gentle humanist. A violent revolutionary. She is angry and tender, loving and hating. She is all these things—and more. (xvii-xviii)

Bambara's expressed idea that the image and desires of black women take on many forms, and that black women of this era did not conform to any one particular ideal, nor did they subscribe to an exclusive or essentialist brand of politics, not only speaks to black women's intellectual diversity, but more importantly, it reinforces the expansive scope of black women's collective interests. Taken as a body, for instance, the work of black women writers represented in *The Black Woman* anthology redefines and encourages an aesthetic that would be far more amenable to an inclusive policy of culturally conscious art than those offered by and debated about by many of their male peers, while challenging the sexist and homophobic ideals that continue to threaten liberationist agendas for black communities. "Stronger black families would lead to more empowered black communities, but many black men were reifying the 'black family' without honestly addressing the family's problems," acknowledges scholar Margo Natalie Crawford ("Must Revolution..." 191).

In addition, as further exemplary of the paradoxically though mutually informative entanglements of Black Artists and their critics on the subjects of sex and gender, in response to the conclusions drawn from the in/famous Moynihan report, many black writers—male and female, Black Artist or not—expressed their grievances and suspicions about "Moynihan and his gang," who "postulate that Black society is matriarchal, and that Black women have been the primary castrating force in the demise of Black manhood," write Jean Carey Bond and Patricia Perry in their essay "Is the Black Male Castrated?" published in *The Black Woman* anthology (117–118). Many women and men believed the report to be wholly unfounded and insidiously corrupt in its characterization of the socially mobile yet allegedly castrating black woman who presumably undermined the black man's ability to realize economic success, and whose own economic mobility led to the destabilization of the black family.[9] "We submit that in reality Black women, domineering or not, have not had the power in this male-dominated culture to effect a coup against anyone's manhood—in spite of their oft-cited economic 'advantage' over the Black man" (Bond and Perry 117–118). Still, as Toni Morrison states, "No Black woman should apologize for being educated or anything else . . ." (Wilson 135). Incidentally, Ralph Ellison also found the Moynihan report to be troubling in its "references to black culture as isolated and incapable of assimilation into American culture," and his friend and fellow writer Albert Murray questioned how anyone could "make an evaluation of a culture for official purposes" without taking into consideration that black men continued to survive and "strut" despite the adversity they faced (Rampersad 429; Grunwald 13). Yet despite the resonating implications of the report, which further perpetuated the cultural divide between black men and women, who have always struggled to overcome sex and gender bias as well as homophobia within their communities, the significance of this collective response among black artists, activists, and intellectuals, all of whom attacked the absurdity of the Moynihan report, speaks to their cross-cultural and binding interests in remaining critical of ethnocentric and racist propaganda targeted toward and to the detriment of their communities.

Writers like Sonia Sanchez, Mari Evans, and Nikki Giovanni (whose female narrator in the 1969 poem entitled "Woman Poem" asserts that *women* can be "castrated" too) forced men to confront the gendered ideologies of the BAM and courageously cited the movement for undermining the achievements and contributions of women. "Before long, it was clear that there were those within the Black Power movement who no longer would tolerate gender-based discrimination or remain silent when militant artists portrayed women as bitches, bimbos, or babymakers for the revolution" (Van Deburg 297). In her essay "Sexual Subversion, Political Inversion," Cherise Pollard finds meaning in the ways in which Sanchez and Giovanni, for instance, "critique men's power through their use of heterosexist and homophobic language" (181). However, some of the work of women writers of this period rings with bitterness and resentment as well as overtones of aggression typically appropriated by male writers. For instance, Sanchez's poem "to all brothers" addresses the sexual exploitation of a female narrator, who cautions her black sisters about black men, stating that ". . . smoother / ones will in / tegrate your / blackness," and refers to the sexual exploitation of women at the hands of their black "brothers." In addition, her poem "nigger" features a narrator who asserts herself over her male counterpart, and who ultimately undermines his authority: "I know I am / black. / beautiful. / with meaning," she expresses.[10] Yet there were many pieces like these produced by black women writers which privilege the black female voice while critiquing sexism as women simultaneously expressed their commitment to and love for black men. "I have accepted you, taken you back . . . Embraced you, empathized with your pitiful plight, because I know how they have used and abused you," writes Gail Stokes, in the essay "Black Man, My Man, Listen," also published in *The Black Woman* anthology (137). "I have tried to cease with my lamentations and taking your faults, your shortcomings in stride, made you a part of me" (137). In addition, Giovanni's poem entitled "Concerning One Responsible Negro with Too Much Power" privileges the voice of a female narrator, who insists on defining herself in her own, woman-identified terms: "i only want to reclaim myself / i even want you / to reclaim yourself."[11] While the narrator moves forward to suggest that the first step in her ability to "reclaim" herself lies in the eventual death of her male counterpart, she also expresses her intentions to one day be freed of the racist and sexist oppression of black women while she conveys a deep cultural and emotional connectivity between herself and her male counterpart and reinforces their tragic yet shared fate. A similar sentiment is expressed in Mari Evans's famed piece "I Am a Black Woman," in which the narrator communicates her implacable fortitude and resilience—"impervious" and "indestructible"—despite the challenges she faces as a black woman, and she expresses her commitment to her community with the words "Look / on me and be / renewed."[12] Furthermore, in keeping with the theme of the black heroine as a figure capable of expressing desires for freedom through self-authorized power, and who sees herself as a symbol and source of power for others, Lucille Clifton's poem "If I Stand in My Window," for instance, features a narrator who boldly invites a man to gaze upon her naked black body and "discover self . . . crying / praying in tongues."[13]

Still, as supportive as she was of all up-and-coming artists of the BAM, even Gwendolyn Brooks later admitted to her own gender biases in favor of male writers of this period. When Brooks was asked by writer Gloria T. Hull and Posey Gallagher about the subject, given that writers like Sonia Sanchez recalled that "black women [had been] told to take a back seat at the time," Brooks admitted that she had indeed celebrated male writers more often than women at the time. "You're right to want to see the other side," she conceded to Hull. "It's a legitimate complaint . . . I've never said any of the things I've said to you in a desperate attempt to understand why men came to the fore in my poetry in the late sixties. I hadn't even thought about it but it is true" (100). Although Hull herself stated that she didn't believe the BAM was inherently a "male" moment, she concluded that many black men conformed to the notion that women were subordinate figures during this period. "You're absolutely right about that," Brooks agreed once more. "I remember that when Haki [Madhubuti] was working with [Amiri] Baraka, they were both very forward about men being the leaders. The women assisted . . . Yes, you're absolutely right . . . " (101). As noted by scholar Cherise Pollard regarding black women's poetry of this period, "[T]here is a sense of doubleness reminiscent of Du Bois' 'twoness' . . . The duality that emerges is not between race and nation, but between race and gender" (179).

However, both men *and* women perceived and responded to the gendered culture of the BAM. As historian Manning Marable notes, "From the very beginning of Black political activism in the United States, Afro-American men had real difficulty in considering the 'triple oppression' (race/class/sex) of Black women with any degree of seriousness" (124). Similarly, many scholars have suggested that a disproportionately long list of male writers, including such figures as Amiri Baraka, Larry Neal, Maulana Karenga, and Haki Madhubuti, continues to be credited for having engineered the iconic and ideological foundations of black nationalism within the Black Arts Movement. To speak about the "black writer," the "black critic," or the "Black Artist" ultimately became synonymous with speaking about the "black man," as has often been observed.

However, when Haki Madhubuti credited members of the black intelligentsia, including academics, for their roles in collaborating with Black Arts participants in the advancement of the goals of the movement, as well as for assisting in the establishment of criteria of performance for Black Artists, his list of notables included an acknowledgment of such women as Catherine Hurst, Helen Johnson, and Sarah Webster Fabio. Yet Madhubuti nonetheless expressed the following in his book *Dynamite Voices* (1971): "The critic is first and foremost a blackman . . . The Black Critic, as a Black Man first and writer second—profoundly understands his responsibility to himself and to his community" (18–19). In addition, Larry Neal's reference to the role of Black Art as that which was to be perceived as the "spiritual sister" of the Black Power Movement effectively characterizes the masculinist overtures of this aesthetic, wherein the Black Arts group functioned as the feminized counterpart to its political "brother." This is a curious construct, given that, as Mike Sell acknowledges about both activist groups, "*both* groups focused their attention on bringing revolutionary cultural programs and material assistance (in the form of lobby pressure, meal programs, police monitors, educational programs, etc.) to locations that, they believed, could best support a mass cultural nationalist movement in African American society" (*Avante-Garde* 232, emphasis mine).[14]

Neal's words are perhaps the most commonly referenced by critics whose goals are to call attention to the gendered dynamics of the BAM, while counterstatements like that expressed by writer and activist Kalamu Ya Salaam, who contends that women's rights issues are relevant and indeed integral to the discussion of black liberation and/or black empowerment, have garnered much less attention. Representing a progressive male perspective that dared to challenge quotidian practices of the BAM, and which belies the reputed and much maligned male-centered priorities of the movement, Ya Salaam states, "My position is simply this: any discussion of the issue of human rights should include a discussion of women's rights." He adds:

> I am concerned about the issue of women's rights because I am striving to be a revolutionary, and without the eradication of sexism there will be no true and thoroughgoing revolution . . . There are those who argue that raising the issue of women's liberation is divisive of Black unity. They argue that, in reality, the women's movement drives a "wedge" between Black women and Black men in our social relationships . . . We are all for the unity of our women with our men, but not if that unity is to be male superior/female inferior. (113–115)

Writer Calvin Hernton's essay, "Breaking Silences," addresses the influence of gender bias and sexism in relation to the culture of the BAM as well:

> The ideology of race first and sex second fosters both white supremacy and male supremacy, and it underpins the racial oppression of black women and men . . . Men first, women second, moreover, is individually and collectively vested in the concept of Manhood . . . Race first and sex second is a misogynist ideology that mandates male appropriation of women's bodies

as object of pornography and abuse ... Nearly every black man in America, and a majority of women too, would have us believe that black women are oppressed solely because of their race and not because of their sex. (153–157)

It should be noted that, historically, black men have been inspired by feminism and have worked on behalf of women and in the interest of community empowerment as they developed their own political ideologies. Early-twentieth-century leading intellectual W. E. B. Du Bois, for instance, was inspired by nineteenth-century writer Anna Julia Cooper as he developed his own black feminist principles, and many black male writers, activists, and intellectuals wholly define themselves as black feminists and have championed the history of black women's activism. "Recovering the history of Black men's woman suffrage activism is personally inspiring for me as a man," writes Gary Lemons, himself a self-defined feminist (72). "A generation of Black men [have been] committed to the eradication of sexism [and] have had their vision of womanhood, manhood, and masculinity changed by Black women feminist/womanist scholars, teachers, mothers, sisters, friends, and lovers. Thus, as prowomanist men, the antisexist activist work we perform is historically linked to that of Du Bois" (73). Of his own black feminist identity, Lemons writes, "We are sorely in need of an emancipatory vision of liberation that honors our past struggles—struggles in which Black women and men fought together against race and *gender oppression*" (72). Furthermore, Bayard Rustin, one of the main organizers of the 1963 March on Washington, a close associate of Martin Luther King, Jr., and an advocate for women's rights also expresses that "[i]f the women's liberation movement should be criticized, it is not because its demands are unjust but because they do not go far enough" (111).

It is important to acknowledge that arguments in favor of the adoption of woman-centered and/or black feminist ideologies in the overall objective of achieving liberation for all black people were indeed expressed by men. This is true, despite the fact that the history of the sexist, misogynist cultures of the Black Arts Movement and Black Power Movement remains perhaps the most dominant and influential narrative to characterize these eras, wherein "[b]lack female icons were recognized as the lovers or partners of black male revolutionaries or prison intellectuals" (James 140). Many of the movement's most vocal and visible male figures acknowledged the overtly hostile, homophobic climate of the BAM, which, ironically, they themselves often perpetuated. For instance, Black Panther Party cofounder Huey Newton, a staunch advocate for black nationalism, wrote:

> Whatever your personal opinion and your insecurities about homosexuality and the various liberation movements among homosexuals and women (and I speak of homosexuals and women as oppressed groups) we should try to unite with them in a revolutionary fashion . . . I say "whatever your insecurities are" because, as we very well know, sometimes our first instinct is to want to hit a homosexual in the mouth and to want a woman to be quiet. We want to hit the homosexual in the mouth as soon as we see him because we're afraid we might be homosexual and want to hit the woman or shut her up because she might castrate us or take the nuts that we may not have to start with. (*Traps* 282)

Newton goes on to express that he has "hang-ups" about male homosexuality but not female homosexuality, which he perceives as "just another erotic sexual thing" (283). Although this last admission reflects Newton's desire to overcome his homophobia, he continues to cling to narcissistic, sexist notions of male power and privilege in his objectification of women's bodies and woman-identified and/or lesbian sexual expression. "[Black men] . . . have an enormous responsibility to be men. There's something very large in that word. . . ," Morrison suggests (*Black Creation Annual* 7). Newton's attempts to reconcile his own sexism with that of a desired, socially inclusive, gender-neutral revolutionary agenda are noteworthy, since, in his words, "there is nothing to say that a homosexual cannot also be a revolutionary" (283). More importantly, such comments speak to the fact that the topics of sexuality and gender remained important subjects of debate within the culture of the Black Arts Movement and Black Power Movement, and that, furthermore, many of the most influential male figures of this period did indeed acknowledge the significance of these issues as they impacted the nation-building project.

Although writer James Baldwin would become a revered figure in the eyes of key members of the BAM and the Black Power Movement, including Newton himself, his homosexuality became the target of explicit attacks by Black Panther Eldridge Cleaver.[15] Weighing in on the subject both personally and intellectually, Baldwin writes, "The American idea of masculinity . . . There are few things under heaven more difficult to understand or, when I was younger, to forgive."[16] Baldwin was an active figure of the civil rights, Black Arts, and Black Power movements, and his influence in this era of activism was paradoxically defined as much by the stigmas of homosexuality as it was by his ability to speak on behalf of the black masses in the overall struggle for human rights. "I never wanted to be a spokesman," he admitted, "but I suppose that it was something that had to happen" (Lewis 411). When asked about the new era of black pride in a 1970 interview with the editor-in-chief of *Essence* magazine, Ida Lewis, Baldwin proclaimed:

> It's not new. Black pride, baby, is what got my father through . . . Black pride is in all those cotton fields, all those spirituals, all those Uncle Tom bits . . . There's something dangerous in the notion that it is new . . . After all, I've been treated as badly by black people as I have white people . . . Most people talking about black pride and black power don't know what they're talking about . . . now they're so black they won't talk to me. (418–419)

Here, Baldwin conveys feelings of resentment about having been dispossessed as a black gay man, writer, and activist throughout his career. As scholar Kendall Thomas posits with regard to Baldwin's decision to leave America for Paris, "[W]hile Baldwin may have left America because he was black, he left Harlem, the place he called 'home,' because he was gay" (327). Similarly, the discrimination that the previously mentioned civil rights organizer Bayard Rustin faced as a gay man is addressed in his biography *Bayard Rustin: Troubles I've Seen*, published in 1997. In the book, Rustin's biographer, Jervis Anderson, writes about Rustin's having been ostracized as a gay man by his activist peers, despite his continued commitment to the social and political empowerment of black communities. "By a poignant historical irony, it was in no small part because of his homosexuality—and the fear that it would be used to discredit the mobilization—that Rustin was prevented from being named director of the 1963 march," writes Henry Louis Gates, Jr. (*The Greatest Taboo* xv). As Philip Brian Harper points out about the rhetoric of the BAM, "To the extent that such rhetoric is considered an integral element of the cultural-nationalist strategy of Black Power politics, then a violent homophobia too is necessarily implicated in this particular nationalistic position, which since the late 1960's has filtered throughout black communities in the U.S., as a major influence in African-American culture" (405).

There was also speculation amongst Black Artists about the sexuality of the aforementioned Chicago Black Arts Organization, OBAC, and BAM advocate and architect Hoyt Fuller. In response to the audience's probing questions about Fuller's life at a 2007 panel discussion on Chicago's Black Arts culture, several previous members of OBAC were protective of Fuller's legacy and readily defended his reputation, appearing hesitant to engage his personal life and in particular the subject of his sexuality.[17] As Cornel West suggests, "Black male sexuality differs from black female sexuality because black men have different self-images and strategies of acquiring power in the patriarchal structures of white America and black communities" ("Black Sexuality" 305). Thus, the impulse to preserve Fuller's legacy as a patriarch of the BAM and without acknowledging his potential homosexuality on the part of previous OBAC members, in tandem with Newton's aforementioned acknowledgment of his own internalized gender biases regarding homosexuality in the black community, and the ways in which black gay men pose immediate threats to the heterosexual black male psyche—especially in the collective preservation of the nation-building ideal—can be perceived as manifestations of the pathological impulse to protect the black masculine self-image as well as the black family ideal to which West refers in his critique.

In a reflective statement collectively composed by women writers of the black feminist group the Combahee River Collective, the foundations of black feminist expression are historically rooted in a tradition of political expression protesting sexism and homophobia that began with the early American activism of such figures as Sojourner Truth, Harriet Tubman, Frances E. W. Harper, Ida B. Wells Barnett, and Mary Church Terrell. The statement reads:

> Black feminist politics have an obvious connection to movements for Black liberation, particularly those of the 1960's and 1970's. Many of us were active in those movements (civil rights, Black nationalism, the Black Panthers), and all of our lives were greatly affected and changed by their ideology, their goals, and the tactics used to achieve their goals. It was our experience and disillusionment within these liberation movements, as well as experience on the periphery of the white male left, that led to the need to develop a politics that was antiracist, unlike those of white women, and antisexist, unlike those of Black and white men. (235)

As the Combahee group statement references the integral role of the BAM and the civil rights movement in the overall development of their black feminist agenda, it also substantiates the ways in which the aesthetics and political principles of the various cultures of the sixties and seventies were productively informed and inspired by one another. Furthermore, the intersecting ideals of the BAM, Black Power, and black feminist cultures—though often at odds with one another—were paradoxically and mutually contributory to the respective development of their agendas. "That many male activists richly deserved to be picking verbal barbs out of their sexist posteriors in no way lessened the possibility that the new black feminist critique could have deleterious effects on Black Power's image and attractive power" (Van Deburg 297). It is also important to note that the Combahee River Collective felt a "solidarity with progressive Black men and [did] not advocate the fractionalization that white women who are separatists demand," for, as they claimed, "Our situation as Black people necessitates that we have solidarity around the fact of race . . . We struggle together *with* Black men against racism, while we also struggle *with* Black men about sexism" (237, emphasis mine). Thus, as I suggest, efforts to reconcile the gender and sexual biases of these movements were initiated by some of the most vocal heterosexual male leaders of the time, as well as women and members of the gay community, who suffered most immediately under the counterproductive discriminating practices of various social justice and cultural empowerment initiatives to the detriment of the collective African Diaspora.

As mentioned, scholars continue to debate the success of the BAM as well as evaluate its import within a variety of contexts. Often such critiques consider the movement's relationship to preexisting periods of flourishing artistic expression in the black vernacular tradition, including the Harlem Renaissance and the post–World War II modernist movements. In this regard, the concept of collaboration is equally valuable, as BAM aesthetics can be interpreted as part of and/or a response to already established traditions. Thus, the conceptualization of the movement did not occur without Black Artists' careful consideration of the dialectic relationship between their emergent nationalist poetics and prior traditions of black expression. Regarding Black Arts music, for instance, Peter Labrie declared, "The attitudes, dispositions, and sounds of the new breed are with us. No one can escape their influence. The penetrating glares, the pulsating rhythms, the down-to-earth beat—those elements which have always been a part of music and culture—have been reinvigorated and given a new distinct overall quality" (76). Labrie simultaneously credits the BAM for its ability to shape a new musical aesthetic with particular resonance within the nation-building project, while commenting on the place of these "new" forms within the history of black musical expression in America dating back to plantation work songs.

Similarly, the aforementioned writer Stephen Henderson noted that while it is important to recognize the distinctions between the new Black Art and previous moments in the history of black expression, it is equally productive to see its import as an extension of and response to the accomplishments and objectives of earlier writers, artists, activists, and intellectuals, who created and produced material to accommodate the social, cultural, and political interests of post–civil rights black audiences. In his preface to *Understanding the New Black Poetry* (1973), an anthology dedicated to the discussion of the canon of black poetry, beginning with eighteenth-century writers Lucy Terry and Phillis Wheatley, Henderson claims, "The chief difference between poetry of the Harlem Renaissance and the Black poetry of the sixties comes in the full exploration and appropriation of the street experience and the formulation of an aesthetic and an ideology based in part upon it. This is no mere literary gesture, as some would have us believe . . ." (xii–xiii). As Henderson encourages readers and critics of the black poetic tradition in particular to consider the artistic continuities between various moments and movements of black expression, he reiterates that the developments of new Black Arts poetry of the sixties and seventies "were possible because of the changing world in which Black Americans of the post–World War II generation found themselves . . . The process is *continuing* . . . for in its polemical dimension it calls attention, in fact, to the problems which *still* beset Black art" (17).

In recognizing the BAM *within* as opposed to radically detached *from* the broader tradition of black expression, Henderson privileges the fruits of the new black consciousness of the sixties and seventies as those which are rooted in the past, despite what he perceives to be critics' failure to acknowledge and probe the artistic and ideological complexities tied to the history of black expression. Speaking of the Harlem Renaissance generation, for instance, Henderson notes:

> Hughes and other realistic writers of his generation were sharply censured by middle-class members of their own race, including W. E. B. Du Bois and Benjamin Brawley for portraying the "seamy side" of Black life. Seen in retrospect, the poetry of this group . . . helped to balance the pieties of the abolitionist writers on the one hand and the bucolic idylls of the dialect school on the other. (14)

As Henderson suggests, the Harlem Renaissance, like the BAM, arose out of critical, dialogic exchanges between oftentimes competing perspectives with regard to the evolution of black writing as a medium for translating the black experience. Thus, the breadth of the emerging aesthetics of the BAM must be considered as part of a preexisting conversation amongst black writers, activists, and intellectuals representing various ideological perspectives about the function of creative expression as it relates to the empowerment of black audiences, and which furthermore demonstrate the multifariousness of the black and African Diasporic experience. This idea is especially true, given that the BAM is a product of the artistic legacies of a broad range of creative and political interests espoused by writers who came before them. "Whereas the leaders of the Harlem Renaissance hoped to prove the cultural worthiness of African Americans by demonstrating their aptitude for cultivation, development, and progress in terms understood by white American society, the leaders of the Black Arts Movement hoped to celebrate a kind of proletarian and vaguely 'African' culture" (Nielsen 99–100). As readers and critics acknowledge the ways in which the multifaceted debates that ensued between BAM participants and their critics were mutually and equally informative to the movement's conceptualization, the tradition of collaboration as both a polarizing and unifying concept remains productively complicated in the fomentation of politically inspired aesthetics that were intended to be wholly distinguishable from prior movements and moments in the history of black expression.

Furthermore, artists of the BAM and their critics responded to matters of global political interest relative to Third World nations, and certainly this aspect of the movement deserves more scholarly attention than I'm able to grant it here. For instance, America's involvement in the Vietnam War, and the increasing number of African nations fighting for independence from colonial rule, encouraged conversations amongst a crosscurrent of Black Arts writers and their critics about the ideological and imperialistic relationships between the oppression of black people in the United States and the colonization of Africa and other Third World communities abroad. As Peter Labrie wrote, "[T]he determination of the U.S. government and military to win the war against the yellow people in Vietnam tends to confirm the now prevalent opinion in the black community that the white man will do almost anything to maintain his domination over the darker races" (71). Similarly, James Boggs expressed that "the American way of life is itself a way of life that has been achieved through systematic exploitation of others—chiefly the black people inside this country and the Latin Americans—and is now being maintained and defended by counterrevolutionary force against blacks everywhere . . ." (115). In a 1964 announcement of the formation of the Organization of Afro-American Unity, Malcolm X stated that one of the organization's aims would be to dedicate itself to "the unification of all people of African descent in their fight for human rights and dignity, and to the utilization of that unity to bring into being the organizational structure that will project the black people's contributions to the world" (558). In addition, as a means of expressing solidarity in global freedom struggles, SNCC issued a public statement on American foreign policy condemning the Vietnam

War and imperialism in general, and poems like writer and Vietnam veteran Clarence Major's piece "Vietnam #4," Madhubuti's "The Long Reality," and Carolyn Rodgers's "A Non-Poem About Vietnam (or Try Black)," for instance, served as creative and progressive responses to these matters.[18] "It's anybody's pessimistic guess as to what impact the Yankee mentality will have on the harmonious relationships that have developed among the Vietnamese men and women bound together, under fire, committed to common struggle to liberate their nation," wrote Toni Cade Bambara (127). Even Ralph Ellison, who joined the pro–Vietnam War group the Citizens Committee for Peace with Freedom in Vietnam in 1966, found himself openly communicating his position on America's involvement in the war (Rampersad 438).

But perhaps more than anything, for many writers, the most influential events to effectively and intimately bind together the voices of the BAM as well as their critics during the late sixties and early seventies was the loss of leading civil rights and Black Power Movement activists. As Eugene Redmond writes, "Assassinations, high-level political corruption, upheaval, violence, change, clash of ideologies, flaming rhetoric—all describe the contemporary period. Revolutions of all kinds mock and mold the world" (296). Indeed, in one way or another, the deaths of leading figures of the period was a subject that not only preoccupied the collective conscious of Black Artists and the black community in general, but it was often a subject that was "romantically pursued" (Redmond 298). Although it is beyond the scope of my project to adequately address the ways in which many writers, artists, intellectuals, and activists of this period were impacted by and subsequently responded to the emotional, cultural, and political devastation of having lost leaders like Malcolm X, Martin Luther King, Jr., and Medgar Evers, all of whom sacrificed their lives in the interest of fighting systems of social and political injustice on behalf of oppressed people, it should be noted that these losses commanded the collective attention of black writers, artists, activists, and intellectuals around the world. In the words of Gwendolyn Brooks, "[T]here was revolt all around us especially when Martin Luther King, Jr. was killed, but even before that, there was an understanding that Blacks were to think better of themselves, to have more of a respect for themselves, to care for themselves . . ." (Jabbour and Miller 127).

Ultimately, the murders of Malcolm X and Martin Luther King in particular compelled a collective response to the enduring legacies of racial hostility in America amongst key artists, activists, and intellectuals. Such responses were delivered in speeches and incorporated into essays and poetry even as the dream of social justice seemed more remote with each human loss. James Baldwin attributed his own decision to leave America for France, at least in part, to the murders of Malcolm X and Martin Luther King, Jr. "I loved Martin and Malcolm. We all worked together and kept the faith together. Now they are all dead . . . I couldn't stay in America, I had to leave . . . With those great men, the possibility of a certain kind of dialogue in America has ended. Maybe the possibility was never real, but the hope certainly was" (Lewis, "Conversation" 23–27). As Baldwin's words express discouragement about the momentum of freedom struggles in the wake of the deaths of these leading figures, they remind readers that perhaps one of the most productive aspects of these struggles was the exchange of ideas and debates about the ways in which the fate of a racially divided nation could reach its democratic potential, and in particular, how such exchanges could lead to a more empowered black community.

In a poetic homage to Malcolm X in the wake of his murder, Larry Neal wrote, "America is the world's greatest jailer, and we all in jails. Black spirits contained like magnificent birds of wonder" ("Autobiography" 315). As Malcolm X was one of the most inspirational figures of the BAM, there was a widespread consensus that his aggressive rhetoric of black separatism, nationhood, and self-reliance—over that of Martin Luther King, Jr.'s nonviolent approach to achieving civil rights goals—captured the virtues of the movement in a way that nothing else did. Countless poems memorialized the spirit of Malcolm X and his beliefs, including such poems as Johari Amini's "Saint Malcolm," Sonia Sanchez's "Malcolm," Welton Smith's "malcolm," Margaret Walker's "For Malcolm X," James A. Emanuel's "For Malcolm, U.S.A," Mari Evans's "The Insurgent," Baraka's "A Poem for Black Hearts," and Gwendolyn Brooks's "Malcolm X"—dedicated to poet and Detroit-based Broadside Press publisher Dudley Randall. He and Chicago artist Margaret Burroughs edited a four-part collection of poems dedicated to Malcolm X as well, entitled *For Malcolm*, which includes several of the poems mentioned above.[19] In addition, contemporary writers, artists, and intellectuals continue to produce material inspired by Malcolm X, whom Baraka claimed had "emerged to forcefully oppose the Black bourgeoisie's domination of the Black Liberation Movement," including Spike Lee's feature-length movie *Malcolm X* (1995); Michael Eric Dyson's book entitled *Making Malcolm: The Myth and Meaning of Malcolm X* (1995); and recently deceased and celebrated historian Manning Marable's book entitled *Malcolm X: A Life of Reinvention* (2011).[20]

Still, despite the galvanizing impact of Malcolm X's murder and the extent to which it aroused the collective consciousness of the black community and in particular those who worked within the exigencies of the black nationalist aesthetic, Ralph Ellison, for instance, "did not admire Malcolm" and resented his "mythologized" status as a leading black figure (Rampersad 413). As Ellison's biographer, Arnold Rampersad writes, "In the aftermath of Malcolm's slaying, as a generation of angry blacks attempted a revolution of spirit and psychology, [Ellison] held fast to pacifist beliefs and attitudes even as he sought to capture, in his evolving narrative, the essence of the American experience" (413). Yet, as I have suggested, Ellison's productivity as a writer was inextricably bound to the same chain of events that inspired those writers whose views he strongly criticized. "Each level of violence disturbed Ralph but also raised his stock as a public speaker, especially on college campuses" (Rampersad 396). While Ellison's sentiments about Malcolm X's political ideals were well publicized, his attempt to pursue his own aesthetics and remain committed to an integrationist position was nonetheless informed, at least in part, by his desire to distance himself from the influence of nationalist rhetoric, and such efforts ultimately and paradoxically compelled Ellison's creative pursuits.

Although it had occurred more than a decade prior to the rise of the BAM, the tragic 1955 murder in Mississippi of a fourteen-year-old youth, Emmett Till, who was brutally beaten and killed after allegedly making sexual advancements toward a white woman, continued to inspire the artists of the BAM era.[21] For instance, Sonia Sanchez's poem, "14 haiku (for Emmett Louis Till)" captures the spirit of and honors the memory of the youth's life and reads "foot prints blooming / in the night remember / your blood."[22] In addition, Langston Hughes's poem "Mississippi—1955," published in the *Chicago Defender*, and Toni Morrison's dramatic piece, *Dreaming Emmett*, which was commissioned by the New York State Writers Institute at SUNY-Albany thirty years after Till's brutal murder, each narrated Till's legacy within the history of race violence in America. Of Morrison's work, one critic writes, "This venture into theater [was] a brave act for a novelist, even for one so distinguished as Toni Morrison" (Croyden 218). Gwendolyn Brooks was equally moved to use her creativity to bring awareness to the Till incident, writing as both an activist and a mother, and calling attention to the universal issue of human suffering in the wake of this tragedy. "I was appalled like every civilized being was appalled. I was especially touched because my son was fourteen at the time, and I couldn't help but think that it could have been him down there if I'd sent him to Mississippi" (Newquist 36). Shifting her perspective as a means of alluding to the ways in which social injustice ultimately impacts us all, Brooks empathizes with the white woman toward whom the young

Till was accused of making advances. "I tried to imagine how the young woman, the one who was whistled at, felt after the murder and after the trial," Brooks offers. "What it was like to live with a man who had spilled blood. I imagined that she would have certain cringing feelings when he touched her—at least I know I would" (Newquist 35–36).

As black communities continued to suffer from racial and economic oppression and hostility in post–civil rights America, the desire amongst Black Artists *and* their critics to empower black Americans with new visions and/or versions of themselves through their work and rhetoric became increasingly urgent. Indeed the BAM and its political counterpart, the Black Power Movement, arose out of a collective desire to combat such oppression as it continued to encroach upon the potential for black communities to achieve dreams of socio/economic equality and empowerment. The integrated efforts of both movements were designed to motivate audiences and communities to see themselves not as victims but as human beings capable of determining their own fates as proud members of the African Diaspora. Although Black Artists imagined themselves to be at the center of shaping a new black consciousness that would foster this transitional moment in poetics and politics, which was meant to distinguish them from artists, activists, and intellectuals representing previous movements and moments in the black vernacular tradition, they were nonetheless inspired to conceptualize their goals through cross-cultural and oftentimes contentious debates with their critics. As I discuss in the following chapters, one of the most successful and longest running Black Arts organizations, Chicago's Organization for Black American Culture (OBAC), and in particular its female members, would consequently and paradoxically transform, expand, and productively complicate the cultural energies of this nationalist movement.

Chapter Two

Women Writing Kinship in Chicago's Black Arts Movement

For artists, activists, and intellectuals of the Black Arts Movement, the collective goal of asserting a new and clearly defined relationship between politics and art in a way that distinguished the movement from that which had been defined by artists of the Harlem Renaissance era in particular cannot be overstated. "The antibourgeois stance of the Black Arts Movement and its dismissal of the Harlem Renaissance as a failure was not merely an expression of generational revolt: it was also a carefully considered political position" (Thomas 311). However, the collaborative, group-oriented aspect of Black Arts goals oftentimes distracts scholars from determining the extent to which the body of work produced by self-defined Black Artists remains eclectic. The activist intentions expressed in the Black Arts poem "You Name It," by Carolyn Rodgers, in which the narrator declares that she "will write about Black people re-po-sses-sing this earth," was a sentiment shared by many Black Artists during a period in which the act of producing nation-building art was perceived by government authorities as criminal activity. Yet women writers like Rodgers brazenly engaged politics and art through the deployment of popular aesthetics that moved beyond the framework of some of the BAM's most recognized, celebrated, and contested features. More specifically, Rodgers and her contemporary, Johari Amini, as well as their younger OBAC successor, Angela Jackson, performed as Black Artists in simultaneously conventional and paradoxical ways, drawing from the influences of their peers in the development of an intertextually informed body of art while progressively expanding the BAM's most popular though restrictive features. As such, their work remains part of a tradition of artistic activism in which women continue to play essential roles, and which, at its best, honors the cross-cultural and pluralistic potential of community inspired initiatives and nation-building projects.

However, I hesitate to suggest that their work represents a "feminist" agenda, wherein women artists, activists, and intellectuals "found themselves questioning the gendered roles they had been playing in a repressive American culture" and began "searching for an appropriate literary avenue to express this experience," as scholar Kim Whitehead suggests. As Black Arts women, Amini, Rodgers, and Jackson, for instance, immersed themselves in the broader community and within coalition-building objectives for the benefit and empowerment of *all* black people. Although I agree with Whitehead's notion that, like many feminist poets representing other cultural traditions, Amini, Rodgers, and Jackson negotiated multiple locations of spatial, ideological, and psychological performance in the production of Black Art, I am careful not to define their work as "feminist" because I see elements of it that are much more ideologically inclusive than and in tension with the conventions of feminist poetry. As Whitehead argues, even as a multicultural concept, the feminist poetry movement "depended upon the creation and development of parallel, feminist institutions." Given my reading of the paradoxically progressive though aesthetically conventional nature of their earliest Black Arts poetry, Amini, Rodgers, and Jackson, for example, were less invested in developing "institutions" of a feminist nature than they were in advancing the cultural and political interests of the black masses and their Black Arts peers. As a result of their participation in the OBAC collaborative effort, not only can contemporary and future generations of readers see evidence of the artistic diversity and breadth of the writing culture of the BAM reproduced through women's perspectives, but they can also assess the ways in which women artists who earned less credit for having contributed to the ever-evolving poetics of the BAM succeeded in progressively challenging some of the movement's most valued features from their often cited positions of so-called marginality.

Although New York City is credited for having produced the most influential coterie of Black Arts participants, the legacies of this period have roots in cities such as Chicago, St. Louis, Detroit, Philadelphia, Houston, Cleveland, and Los Angeles as well. James Smethurst's project *The Black Arts Movement: Literary Nationalism in the 1960's and 1970's* (2005) provides an impressive historiography of the ways in which the BAM agenda was realized within the culturally specific context of various geo/political locations:

> Though the Northeast has often been the regional focus of accounts of the Black Arts movement, due largely to the national reputation of Amiri Baraka, the Midwest and the San Francisco Bay Area birthed the most important and most enduring Black Arts institutions . . . In fact, we owe much of the physical record of Black Arts literature today to Midwestern institutions, since Broadside Press, Third World Press, and Lotus Press alone produced an inordinately high proportion of the titles issued by black publishers in the 1960's and 1970's . . .[1]

Other scholars, including Margo Natalie Crawford and David Lionel Smith, for instance, have written about Chicago's Black Arts culture as an important local context in which to evaluate the execution of the ideals of the broader national Black Arts Movement during this period.[2] As Elice Rogers states with regard to the migration of black Americans to northern cities like Chicago, "People within the local community responded favorably to the goals of the Black Panther Party and warmly embraced the Panthers' social welfare efforts . . ." (48). She goes on to discuss the influence of the Civil Rights Movement upon the development of a politically conscious black culture in Chicago, which led to the aggressive attempt of the black mainstream constituency to elect the first black mayor of the city. In keeping with my own emphasis on the collaborative, intercultural aspects of this particular historical moment as it relates to the marketing of the BAM principles and the collective desire amongst Black Artists to achieve social and political empowerment for black Americans, Rogers continues, "African American leaders and activists put their philosophical differences aside and began working together in their effort to find and elect an African American mayor. Such collaboration represented the origins of a populist movement, a movement for and by the people . . . [Mayor] Washington's emphasis as mayor was on people and coalition building" (49). Rogers's claim that more women were extended opportunities in Chicago politics is noteworthy, for the increased visibility and participation of women not only in political arenas but in cultural ones as well was integral to coalition-building projects fomented throughout the city. Such visibility ultimately and paradoxically came to symbolize what could be achieved through grassroots initiatives realized through the collaborative efforts of a diverse cross section of black leaders, artists, activists, and intellectuals in local contexts. The centrality of the black woman as artist, activist, and intellectual leader is a particularly significant aspect of the cultural and political zeitgeist of the BAM in Chicago, given that both intra- and interculturally, "African American participation in social movements has historically and traditionally empowered . . ." (and has arguably been empowered *by*, as I suggest) ". . . those on the margin . . ." (Rogers 55).

The 1967 mission statement for the Organization for Black American Culture (OBAC) is particularly revealing, as it expresses the collaborative goal of its membership to invest themselves in community development and socially driven art. More specifically, they committed themselves to:

> 1. The encouragement of the highest quality of literary expression reflecting the Black experience.
> 2. The establishment and definition of the standards by which that creative writing which reflects the Black experience is to be judged and evaluated.
> 3. The encouragement of the growth and development of Black critics who are fully qualified to judge and evaluate Black literature on its own terms while at the same time cognizant of the traditional values and standards of western literature and fully able to articulate the essential differences between the two literatures. (*Dynamite Voices* 21)

Chicago writer and artist Margaret Burroughs, who cofounded the Du Sable Museum on Chicago's South Side with her husband, Charles, in 1961, attributes the long-standing success of Chicago's Black Artists to the fact that they did not solicit resources from government agencies or institutions and instead relied upon the membership of committed residents to sustain their objectives. Formerly called the Ebony Museum, the Du Sable was initially operated out of the Burroughses' home and eventually grew into one of Chicago's most important cultural institutions of the post–civil rights era. "The founding of black museums such as the Du Sable Museum in Chicago, and later the National Afro-American Museum and Cultural Center in Wilberforce, Ohio . . . serve as repositor[ies] and pedagogical instrument[s] [that] help educate patrons about the history and culture of African American people and their contributions to the larger society" (Smallwood 63). Just as for younger voices of the BAM in Chicago, for accomplished figures of the previous generation such as Margaret Burroughs and Gwendolyn Brooks, the cultural interests of black audiences in the city's urban communities continued to be important influences in their aesthetics. As Houston Baker notes about black artists of these intergenerational eras:

> In sum, black writers of the 1950's were not certain they had a country. They worked, perhaps too often, in a world of abstractions that included not only

their most esteemed values, but also their hypothetical or implied Western audience. In the 1960's and 1970's, on the other hand, black spokesmen were convinced that their real audience, like the nation to come, was black, and their values and canons were designed to accord with this conviction. (117)

Still, Burroughs's artwork, for example, had at one point been criticized by members of the Chicago Art Center for its "radicalism" as opposed to its "abstract" qualities that might otherwise appeal to (white) Western audiences, and her response to the center's conservative mission influenced her eventual founding of the Du Sable Museum. In later years, the space of the museum was often reserved by OBAC members for workshops and meetings and Burroughs recalls that there were very few places where black artists of her own generation and that of younger Black Artists could gather without arousing further suspicion or invoking hostility from government officials targeting social activist groups during this period of heightened surveillance.[3]

In addition, Chicago Black Artists purchased the Southside Arts Center, located across the street from the Du Sable Museum, for hosting meetings, exhibits, and events for patrons in their communities. Both the Du Sable Museum and the Arts Center became sacred spaces for artists and community leaders, and they provided relief from what Richard Guzman refers to as Chicago's "explosive growth and grinding materialism, which always threatened to crush the human spirit" of anticapitalists (xv). He writes, "The arts, too had to struggle harder, get scrappier, and grittier, and when artists survived here, they expressed more triumph, and sometimes more sentimentality, than elsewhere," and that

> the reality of cultural flow has made Chicago such a central *site* of Black writing in America, a site flowed to and criss-crossed over and over by thousands of migrants, and by the words, images, spirits, and bodies of the greatest Black artists in the United States and the world . . . Chicago was also the site at which so much about the "modern, urban Negro" came to be constructed . . . These social and mental constructs emanating from Chicago have been central to Black culture worldwide. (xv, xix)

For Chicago artists, activists, and intellectuals, maintaining ownership and control over their political and cultural resources was critical to the liberation of the black oppressed.[4] "African Americans in Chicago, during and after World War II, engendered unique senses of group life and imagination, restructuring ideas of racial identity and politics that remain influential today" (Green 1). In this tradition of community development in the form of entrepreneurship, Chicago artists of the BAM demonstrated more of an investment in collective objectives, and egotism took a backseat to shared goals. Generally speaking, Chicago artists and activists were persistent in their efforts to define and construct Black Art that reflected the social and political lives and aspirations of their specific communities. "Whether shown perched on the crumbling stoop of a row house, holding court in a seedy bar, or semi-permanently ensconced on a well-aged living room sofa . . . the black writer's memory and imagination joined black art and life in a fashion rarely seen in white-authored books" (Van Deburg 278). In this spirit, several of Chicago's most committed Black Artists travelled to the campus of the University of Indiana at Bloomington on a rotating basis to conduct lectures for a seminar course in which Black Arts ideals were reinforced in academic curricula.[5] This is particularly reflective of the role that the BAM played in the later development of Black Studies programs in institutions of higher learning. With regard to the establishment of a community-centered, collectively inspired initiative amongst a culturally specific group of Black Artists—all of whom were creating an aesthetic out of specific, locally inspired ideals—Madhubuti adds that "other writers in different parts of the states have adopted or are beginning to adopt similar purposes." Thus, paradoxically, the leadership of this intimate coterie of writers in the urban Midwest succeeded in expanding and making more popular the terms of the broader national movement that had originally inspired OBAC's inception.

In addition to being cofounder of OBAC, Haki Madhubuti also cofounded Third World Press along with OBAC writer Johari Amini. Modeled after Dudley Randall's Broadside Press in Detroit, at one point Third World Press relied upon Broadside's resources for the printing and distribution of some of its earliest publications. Madhubuti's press also published the *Black Books Bulletin*, which featured articles on subjects pertaining to individual and community improvement, and he hosted seminars that were open to the public on topics such as nutrition, health, and spirituality.[6] As one of the founders of the Institute of Positive Education, which began operating in 1971 and continues to provide a kindergarten through sixth-grade Afrocentric curriculum for black students on Chicago's South Side today, Madhubuti established himself as a Black Arts figure whose philosophy was deeply entrenched in activism through art, education, and business. As Smallwood notes:

> As a by-product of the social unrest related to the Civil Rights, Black liberation, and Black Power movements, African Americans expressed a demand for educational institutions to provide access traditionally denied to them and asked for revisions of the curricula needed to reflect their contributions to local, national and world civilization. Specifically, the Black Studies movement in the mid-1960's was the result of African American college students and local community residents requiring that institutions of higher education respond to the needs of people in their communities. (58)

Like other initiatives offering alternative educational programs to public schooling for black youth, Madhubuti's institute responded to the need for "Afro-American educational empowerment [and] guaranteed that all children [would] be treated as educable beings, endowed with a sense of self while at the same time instilling respect for collective responsibility and action" (Van Deburg 121). Projects such as this reflect the extent to which Chicago Black Artists and their supporters were creating a paradigm for community-inspired programming that contributed to the health and well-being of black people within their own city, after which other programs throughout the country would be modeled.

Although writers like Amini, Rodgers, and Jackson found creative strategies for expanding Black Arts principles, in general one had to be careful about taking liberties that might compromise the propagandist message of community and cultural empowerment. For writers in particular, the poetic form was considered to be the most ideal because it was amenable to individual style yet universally consumable for mainstream audiences, and it generally lacked the pretenses associated with the production and distribution of other forms of writing, including short stories and novels.[7]

> Metaphor and allusion, devices of repetition, and linguistic sound effects—the matter of oral poetry no matter what its cultural origins or specificity—are the materials through which the African American poet voices her or his art, the mother tongue. The literary traditions that the African American poet explores are both oral and written, a cultural reinvention specific to a syncretic culture. (Brown 15)

Moreover, poetry was perceived to be more accommodating to the ideals of Black Art because of its popularity and economy in mainstream contexts. The accessibility of poetry was due in part to poets' employment of popular vernacular in their work as well. "Thus, poetry, as one of the richest tools for exploring the dynamic meaning-making processes of language, was bound to become an important movement resource" (T. V. Reed 91). "The poetry of the Black Arts Movement was shaped by the context of oral presentation because the highly politicized aesthetic devised by the poets decreed that it should be," writes Lorenzo Thomas (319). "With self-anointed missionary fervor, Black Arts poets extended the venues for their performances beyond storefront theaters to neighborhood community centers, church basements, taverns, and to the streets" (309). In addition, according to scholar Johanna Drucker:

> The idea of performance in poetry is conventionally associated with a realtime event in which a live or recorded reading provides effective dimensions to a poetic work through the immediate experiences that constitute an event. But a visual performance of a poetic work on a page or canvas, as a projection or sculpture, installation or score, also has the qualities of an enactment, of a staged and realized event in which the material means are an integral feature of the work ... Written work is always at a remove from the writer, cast into an autonomous form, not dependent of the presence of the author as a performance. *In fact, there is every possibility of hiding, eclipsing, effacing, or disguising the writer through writing* ... (131, emphasis mine)

The latter critique of the performative qualities of poetry offered by Drucker must be measured carefully when considering the work of Black Arts poets, whose work was indeed a public endorsement of specific racial, cultural, and politically oriented ideals that were contingent upon an author's ability to engage them as part of the nation-building process. The demands of the aesthetic undermined the elitist perpetuation of art as separate from politics. "Black Aesthetic critics exposed the covert ideological agenda of formalism" (Dubey 9). Language functioned as an ostensible portal through which audiences could most immediately connect with Black Artists, and conversely, Black Artists could determine the impact of their words upon their listeners, invoking a kind of "call and response" method of communication. More specifically, popular street vernacular was imported and co-opted by writers and performance artists of the BAM because it represented the communities and audiences that substantiated the nation-building principles of Black Art, as referenced in Madhubuti's *Dynamite Voices 1: Black Poets of the 1960's* (1971):

> The language of the new writers seemed to move in the direction of actual music. The poets were actually defining and legitimizing their own communicative medium. Their language as a whole was not formal Anglo-Saxon English. It carried its own syntax, not conventional by Western standards, and often referred to as non-communicative, obscene, profane. In short, it was the language of the street, charged to heighten the sensitivity of the reader. (33)

Audiences could experience spoken word performances of Black Artists in coffeehouses, community centers, and other casual neighborhood venues, and performance artists and writers alike could experiment with the poetic form since it could be appropriated in various artistic ways. Thus, "live" performance was strongly encouraged by a nationwide coterie of Black Artists, and it represented an ideal, organic, and intimate form of communication that they opportunistically exploited.

Like BAM artists nationwide, OBAC Black Artists relied upon multiple collaborative mediums for producing and publicizing their ideals. "African American performance artists, whether singers, dancers, comics, actors, or jazz musicians, were a persistent influence on the movement formally and ethically" (Sell, *Avante-Garde* 229). Although, as mentioned, poetry was one of the most viable forms of communication for making BAM objectives accessible to mainstream audiences, other forms of art played essential roles in communicating the ideals of this period.[8] "The younger black poets turned away from the modernist or formal styles of [Melvin] Tolson and [Robert] Hayden and embraced a more militant poetic, one based on the language of the street" (Beach 131). Like poetry, music, for instance, was perceived to be an ideal conduit through which the BAM aesthetic was expressed. "While the poetry of Langston Hughes and others was an important model, so was the music of Charlie Parker, Miles Davis, Billie Holiday, Thelonius Monk, and John Coltrane" (Beach 135). Thus, the collaboration between artists, photographers, dancers, and musicians also contributed to the popularity, accessibility, and appeal of OBAC and other BAM organizations nationwide. In Chicago, for example, dancer Darlene Blackburn and musician Phil Cohren collaborated to produce theater in the Bronzeville area on the South Side of Chicago, and acclaimed dramatists Val Gray Ward and Ann MacNeal wrote and produced a variety of productions for OBAC, while musicians fused African drumbeats with popular music in their own efforts to inspire a Pan-Africanist and global aesthetic.[9] "The response of women dramaturges to a performance style . . . is reflective of the objective of BAM ritual theater"

(Traylor, "Black Women" 62). According to Mike Sell, BAM writer and intellectual Larry Neal "argued that the embodied qualities and necessities of theater and performance enabled a direct understanding of Black history, community, and selfhood" ("The Voice" 286).

After being recruited by Black Arts writer and educator Gerald McWhorter—later Abdul Alkalimat—Chicago artist and muralist Jeff Donaldson became the director for the visual arts workshop, and other Black Artists such as Bill Abernathy and Murray DePillars were among those who produced work under the purview of AFRI-COBRA. (Originally called COBRA for Coalition of Black Revolutionary Artists, this group was formed on the South Side of Chicago and was honored by Northwestern University in the winter of 2010—the first exhibit in decades to bring together the artwork produced by the collaborative efforts of these artists.) One of the most significant collaborative projects to come out of the initiative was the in/famous mural entitled *The Wall of Respect*, painted on Chicago's South Side, which paid visual tribute to black culture and history and drew the attention of national media.[10] By the time the mural had been destroyed (along with much of the housing in this predominantly black area of Chicago, where kitchenette buildings were eventually constructed and rented to low-income residents at exorbitant prices), hundreds of murals in other urban communities throughout the United States emulating the cultural empowerment ideals of *The Wall of Respect* had been designed. Margo Natalie Crawford, daughter of Chicago Black Arts photographer Bob Crawford, notes that participating artists responsible for this project "decided to shape the mural around the following categories: rhythm and blues, jazz, theater, statesmen, religion, literature, sports, and dance" ("Black Light" 25). There were also a number of other photographers in Chicago whose work reflected OBAC imperatives, including Bobby Sengstacke and Roy Lewis. "*The Wall of Respect*," Crawford writes, "involved the crossing of boundaries between black people who, in the 1960's, had a middle-class status due to educational opportunities and black people who were economically disenfranchised due to the lack of these educational opportunities" ("Black Light" 38). In many ways, OBAC signaled a new ideological frontier to be cultivated by local Chicago Black Arts participants that continues to exemplify what is achievable through collective, community-building efforts to empower citizens through art, and women artists Amini, Rodgers, and Jackson were integral figures in these contexts. Each of them emerged as part of a tradition of women whose commitment to community service and activism is expressed through the confluence of art and politics meant to reinforce artistic and cultural kinships, which transcended the merely practical, politically inspired collaborative initiatives that defined the culturally specific objectives of Black Artists, and had the broader impact of perpetuating an inclusive nation-building aesthetic.

Historically, the black writing tradition in America includes the role of presses, periodicals, newspapers, and popular journals as vehicles through which premier ideologies endorsed by black artists, activists, and intellectuals are publicized. In Chicago, the accessibility of Black Art of the sixties and seventies was no exception, as its ideals were dependent upon publicity and media exposure. Although mainstream papers like the *Chicago Sun-Times* and the *Tribune* reported on the activities of Black Artists, the black-owned and operated *Chicago Defender* provided news coverage of issues that appealed to the interests of black readers more than any other mainstream publication, and it became a more reliable and trusted source of information for its audiences. "Chicago became fertile ground for attempts to fuse radical and nationalist politics with commercial journalism in the 1960's," acknowledges Smethurst (204). In a valuable historiography of African American magazines and journals of the twentieth century entitled *Propaganda and Aesthetics* (1991), it is noted that

> [t]hose who identified with the black arts movement wanted their little magazines to go to the heart, or the essential reality, of blackness. Thus, they insisted the journals be black at all levels of involvement, from owner to reader ... As they sought new approaches to race and culture, the supporters of black little magazines denounced the white racist press ... (165)

In response to these ideals, Hoyt Fuller, one of the deans of Chicago's Black Arts Movement, managing editor of *Ebony* magazine at Johnson Publications in Chicago, and cofounder of the *Negro Digest* (later called the *Black World*), assisted Black Artists by providing them with a mainstream platform from which to market their work to black consumers. "Fuller defined a Black cultural mission that gave direction and assurance to an extraordinary number of artists and writers" (Guzman 138). However, in his personal narrative, *A Journey to Africa* (1971), Fuller's personal and professional disillusionment during this period is made clear. He writes:

> I had run away from America. It was an old, many times told story. In the year before I packed up and sailed to France I had spent much of the time futilely trying to find some slot in which I could fit with a reasonable degree of comfort and satisfaction. I had quit *Ebony* magazine, for the magazine did

not seem to be moving in any direction that it seemed important for me to go, and it was extremely difficult in 1957 to find meaningful work that also would not threaten my sense of racial integrity in the white publishing world ... Every single day in America had brought moments when there was need to find some refuge from the nerve-wrenching reality of the omnipresent war of race. (139)

Fuller's expressed feelings of confusion and angst regarding his career as an editor influenced his later involvement in the BAM. Under Fuller's editorial leadership, in 1969, *Ebony* magazine printed Larry Neal's "Black Art and Black Liberation," in which Neal claimed that

> [t]he Black Arts movement seeks to link, in a highly conscious manner, art and politics in order to assist in the liberation of Black people. The Black Arts movement, therefore, reasons that this linking must take place along lines that are rooted in an Afro-American and Third World historical and cultural sensibility ... We identify with all of the righteous forces in those places which are struggling for human dignity ...[11]

Ebony's publication of Neal's manifesto is characteristic of the extent to which periodicals of this era served as venues for the dissemination of Black Arts ideals for popular audiences. However, as he expressed, Fuller's editorial position at the prestigious Johnson Publications was advantageous for as well as potentially compromising to the Black Arts agenda. Many Black Artists believed that as an institution, Johnson Publications generally marketed its journals toward a black audience more interested in cultural assimilation than nationalism. However, it was under Fuller's editorial stewardship that Johnson Publications' periodical the *Negro Digest* eventually became the *Black World*, and the title change was symbolic of Black Artists' political influence upon the company's marketing objectives as it continued to produce editorial content for and advertise toward a progressive urban black readership.[12] "Fuller defined a Black cultural mission that gave direction and assurance to an extraordinary number of artists and writers" (Guzman 138). Like Gwendolyn Brooks, Fuller assisted in building Chicago's Black Arts legacy in part because of his tenacious loyalty to Black Artists' goals, even though such loyalty meant compromising his own position as editor at Johnson Publications. "A black poet must remember the horrors. / The good jobs can't last forever," writes Conrad Kent Rivers in his poem dedicated to the late Fuller, entitled "In Defense of Black Poets."[13] Following Fuller's death, OBAC members paid tribute to his contributions to their Black Arts goals in a special edition of OBAC's journal *Nommo*. As mentioned in the previous chapter, as one of the most committed mentoring figures to such writers as Carolyn Rodgers, Angela Jackson, and poet Sterling Plumpp, Fuller was remembered for his influence in Chicago's BAM at a conference and tribute to Chicago's Black Arts culture, hosted at Northwestern University in 2007.[14]

For members of OBAC, urban areas became the ideal sites for marketing community and nation-building ideals. The rigorous confluence of ideas and perspectives amongst artists, activists, and intellectuals in such areas offered a variety of resources for Black Arts participants in cities like Chicago. Most meetings, readings, and functions facilitated and sponsored by the OBAC writers workshop, for instance, were conducted in predominantly black, working-class communities, which helped to stimulate cultural consciousness amongst Black Arts audiences within these areas. The recognition of and capitalization upon the social realities of a specific, ideal "black community" was sustained through the reinforcement and reiteration of specific criteria of writing that addressed the socio/economic concerns of its readership. Thus, the OBAC writers workshop positioned itself quite literally within cultural spaces immediately accessible to the black masses, and writers narrated the realities of their participating audiences specifically for nation-building purposes. OBAC participants were eager to organize around principles that would eventually assist their communities in countering the disparaging economic and political status of black Chicagoans, many of whom had migrated to the North in search of economic opportunity years before. Despite the fact that women artists received less credit for the conceptualization of the broader national goals of Black Art, as I address in the following chapters, there is clear evidence that speaks to the integral role that Chicago women played in advancing a politically and artistically inspired nation-building agenda. For writers of OBAC, the search for ways in which to build community was realized in their shared artistic goals, the resurrection of landmark organizations, and the community-building initiatives they developed. But while Black Art existed as a strict nationalist concept for participating artists in many aspects, women such as Amini, Rodgers, and Jackson managed to create art that productively critiqued the conventions of Black Art while liberating themselves from the aesthetic expectations reinforced within the culture of the movement in the interest of community empowerment and nation-building. "Women writers of the BAM entered every literary genre and constructed a language that took poetry to the taverns, streets, bars, housing projects, libraries, prisons, parks, newly founded theaters, and time-honored churches" (Traylor, "Black Women" 51).

Perhaps Gwendolyn Brooks's support of this younger group of black poets "who focused much more heavily than their predecessors on the contemporary idiom of urban blacks, [and] referenc[ed] . . . black culture and cultural practices . . . in the inner cities," resonated with younger Chicago Black Artists more than the support of any other established writer (Beach 131–132). In an interview conducted by Ida Lewis, Brooks shared her memories of a pivotal moment in her own development as a writer in relation to the BAM:

> The real turning point for me came in 1967, when I went to the Second Black Writers' Conference at Fisk University . . . there I found what has stimulated my life these last three years: young people, full of a new spirit. They seemed stronger and taller, really ready to take on the challenges. Margaret Danner was there, another poet of my years, and she and I were both amazed to see what was happening . . . We walked around all that day, looking at these new tokens and feeling so excited. (Lewis 54)

When interviewer George Stavros acknowledged Brooks's commitment to the work of new Chicago poets, Brooks responded:

> Yes, there are some very interesting ones . . . Don Lee, whom I've mentioned. Carolyn Rodgers has put out one little book very much respected by the younger poets, those who know her, and is about to bring out another one. Jewel Latimore [Johari Amini] is about to bring out a third little book . . . These are people who are very well known in Chicago, and their poetry is almost adored. I went to a reading of a little group of poets just a couple of weeks ago in the Afro-Arts Theater in Chicago, and it was packed with young people chiefly, who had come to hear poetry. This was unheard of a few years ago. (39)

About Amiri Baraka's influence on Black Artists in particular, Brooks adds that he is the "hero" of the BAM. "He's their semi-model, the one they worship . . . his work *works*" (Stavros 39, emphasis hers). Bill V. Mullen speculates that Brooks's resurgence as a figure of black nationalism may be read as one of a number of parables of the gradual elision and revision of leftist politics in black Chicago beginning with the end of World War II.[15] Brooks frequently invited the inspired young members of OBAC to her home for mentoring, discussion, and opportunities to meet already established writers who visited her when they were in town.[16] It would be at her home that many younger "new" artists would meet and interact with internationally recognized figures such as Chinua Achebe, dramatic artists and philanthropists Ruby and Ossie Davis, James Baldwin, and Richard Wright.[17] Having been encouraged as a child to follow her dreams of becoming a writer by figures like James Weldon Johnson and Langston Hughes—who believed Brooks's poetry reflected her "engagement with and understanding of the contemporary African American experience"—Brooks endorsed the work of many new artists of the BAM in Chicago in a myriad of other ways too (Kich 40). For instance, she composed the introduction to Johari Amini's collection *Let's Go Somewhere* (1970), and saluted Don L. Lee/Haki Madhubuti in the poems "To Don at Salaam," in which she writes, "Your voice is the listened-for music. / Your act is the consolidation." In her poem "In the Mecca," Brooks continues, "Don Lee wants / . . . a new Nation."[18] In turn, OBAC Black Artists appreciated the manner in which Brooks privileged the voices of Chicago's South Side communities in her work. According to Sheila Hassell Hughes, the collection of poetry entitled *In the Mecca* (1970) was the first set of Brooks's poems to be published after the poet's immersion in BAM culture. "Situated in the cramped confines of a slum tenement on Chicago's South Side, the title poem is local—even narrow—in focus. But the work continues to speak beyond both its particular subject and its point of articulation" (Hughes 210). Although she argues that "Brooks never wrote directly or explicitly for a white audience," and "was always concerned to represent, to speak to, and to sanctify Black life as she knew it—most especially in the Bronzeville section of Chicago," Hughes also argues that Brooks's work often compels readers to see the universality of the human condition conveyed through the lens of black life. Of her own work, Brooks suggests,

> I think that my poetry is related to life in the broad sense of the word, even though the subject matter relates closest to the Negro. Although I have called my first book *A Street in Bronzeville*, I hoped that people would recognize instantly that Negroes are just like other people; they have the same hates and loves and fears, the same tragedies and triumphs and deaths, as people of any race or religion or nationality. I did not start writing to be a propagandist." (Newquist 34–35)

Brooks's support of the historic NAACP as well as the student-organized civil rights group the Student Nonviolent Coordinating Committee

(SNCC) also speaks to the intergenerational and diverse ideological political and aesthetic spaces in which she works; although she shares that her primary obligation as a poet is to herself (Newquist 34). As an accomplished poet of a prior generation who chose to embrace the arguably "propagandist" efforts of Black Artists within her own community, and who was herself inspired by the aesthetics of this new nationalist ideology, Brooks "provided direct and personal explorations of the ordinary lives of African Americans, and African American women in particular" (Whitehead 13).

Indeed, her contemporary and friend, the previously discussed artist and Du Sable Museum cofounder Margaret Burroughs, completed a tribute to Brooks in the collection *To Gwen with Love*—a collection comprised predominantly of writings and artwork of Chicago artists and published by Chicago's Johnson Publications in 1971. In the tribute entitled "She'll Speak to Generations Yet to Come," Burroughs writes:

> I have had a long association with this fine poet which began long before recognition and fame which she well deserved came to her. I am reminded that she and I have shared some mighty precious moments and passed several important milestones. Yes, back in the thirties, we marched in Anti-Lynching parades up and down the Southside as members of the NAACP Youth Council. Whether the youth of today recognize it or not, that was the most militant organization for young people going outside of the Left. (129)

Burroughs's tribute appears opposite a striking image of Brooks—a drawing by Chicago painter Murray DePillars, in which Brooks adorns an afro and a flourishing African-inspired dress and appears as the embodiment of black nationalism and Afrocentricity. Burroughs writes, "Miss Brooks and her poetry will be remembered and will speak to generations yet to come because in the first instance she is a creative human being who is concerned with all humanity . . . She does not resort to fads, tricks, or gimmicks of the moment" (130). Brooks's ability to produce timely and timeless material that would appeal to contemporary as well as future readers was especially influential to female writers of the BAM and OBAC, such as Amini and Rodgers, who were dedicated to honing their own crafts, and who looked toward Brooks's experience, aesthetic insight, and formally trained eye for direction and feedback on their work. For Jackson, whose later work progressively adapts Pan-Africanism and Afrocentric thought, Brooks's literary production, situated within an Afrocentric literary tradition, serves as a useful model in which Pan-African–inspired aesthetics are popularized and rendered accessible to mainstream black audiences, as noted by scholar Joyce Ann Joyce.[19] Ultimately, Brooks's ability to respond to "turbulent changes in the Black community's vision of itself and to the changing forms of its vibrations during decades of rapid change" laid the groundwork for each of these younger women writers to advance and elucidate the potential of the collaboration ideal and the socially conscious art forms it inspired (Kent 66).

Just as many artists, activists, and intellectuals of the BAM as well as the movement's critics were inclined to do, Brooks "responded to major events during her lifetime, including World War II, the struggle for civil rights, the murders of African American leaders, race riots, and the daily life in segregated America" (Rugoff 21). In addition, Brooks provided a voice for Chicago's African American underclass, and her investment in the black urban South Side of the city was championed by Chicago Black Artists and OBAC members in particular, who themselves sought to develop a culturally specific aesthetic reflecting the lives and aspirations of these particular communities. "The violent social explosions in the cities, the Vietnam War, which took some black lives and crippled others, the persistent emergence of Africa . . . all aided in the development of [Brooks's] new consciousness" (Redmond 8). Madhubuti's Third World Press published two of many creative and critical anthologies celebrating and responding to Brooks's work and influence, including *Say That the River Turns: The Impact of Gwendolyn Brooks* (1987), edited by Madhubuti himself, in which seventy writers discuss Brooks's impact on their work, and *Gwendolyn Brooks and Working Writers* (2007), edited by Jacqueline Imani Bryant, which includes seventeen essays that are "part reminiscent [of] and part testimonial [to]" the influence of Brooks's aesthetic in the broader tradition of black writing (Rugoff 48). Even in her later years, Brooks maintained an active role in the Chicago community, and Chicago State University would continue to honor her in the establishment of the Gwendolyn Brooks Center for Research on its campus.[20] "The idea for the creation of the Gwendolyn Brooks Center for Black Literature and Creative Writing grew out of the extraordinary influence of the poetry and life of Gwendolyn Brooks. Seldom has a poet's work and literary contribution, in her life time, inspired so many, so deeply for so long in so many places," writes Haki Madhubuti (*Warpland* Introduction 4). In posing the question "Who has known and loved black people of Chicago more than you, Gwen Baby?" writer Francis Ward prompts Brooks's fans, friends, and family to offer their perspectives about the poet in the aforementioned collection *To Gwen with Love,* in which historian Lerone Bennett expresses that Brooks's poems "celebrate the truth of blackness, which is also the truth of man. They reflect the wholeness of a person with deep roots in the soil of her people."[21] In yet another contribution to the collection, poet and instructor Sarah Webster Fabio acknowledges that Brooks will be forever "imprinted / on the OBAC / wall of respect," and Haki Madhubuti adds that "[Brooks's] voice [is] the needle for new-songs."[22] As I move forward to convey in the following chapters dedicated to Amini, Rodgers, and Jackson respectively, the "wholeness" that Bennett references with regard to Brooks's work is captured in that of her younger kinswomen—all of whom created writing that expanded the goals of the BAM so that it might too reflect the spirit of wholeness rather than the exclusivity of the BAM's nation-building potential.

Given the foundational dimensions of Black Art as the product of a collective movement meant to perpetuate and reify the relationship between art, culture, and politics, my assessment of Amini, Rodgers, and Jackson as "performative" is suggestive of the social, political, and artistic consciousness that each writer demonstrated in the production of Black Art. As Marvin Carlson notes in *Performance: A Critical Introduction*, "The term 'performance' has become extremely popular in recent years . . ." and the concept can refer to any "activity carried out with a consciousness of itself" (1, 4). For Black Artists, this heightened sense of consciousness was integral to one's ability to position oneself as a Black Artist. In fact, to perform as a Black Artist was to ostensibly privilege the group-based aesthetics of Black Art over individual impulse or artistic autonomy. In his own study of the Black Arts Movement, Mike Sell writes, "It's no accident that the Black Arts Movement grounded its political theory in performative modes of culture; theater and performance can answer very specific sociopolitical needs, particularly to a community that is both economically depressed and politically advanced" (*Avante-Garde* 243). Although Amini, Rodgers, and Jackson gained exposure through writing, as members of a multidisciplinary and multimedia organization, the cross-pollination between Black Art in the form of the written word and other modes of performance was invariable. As Sell further points out, Black Artists "knew about what we now call 'performance studies,' though much too early for them to call it such" (229). For this reason, I am hesitant to simply and/or anachronistically "apply" performance theory as a postmodern construct to my reading of Black Arts writers; instead, my primary intention is to call attention to the psychological, social, and artistic maneuverings demonstrated in the work of these three writers as they paradoxically expanded the terms of a national aesthetic and culture despite their less visible and celebrated presence, compared to that of the BAM's most iconic and recognized male figures.

As I move forward to suggest in the following chapters, the poetry of Amini, Rodgers, and Jackson promotes artistic practices that encourage a sense of responsibility and activism among and between artists and their audiences that progressively move beyond the criteria of Black Art that are so often perceived as restrictive and limiting. "During the decade of the sixties, the emphasis of [black women writers] was on the critical examination of the universal postulates of freedom and justice . . . It is significant to recognize that these voices within the veil have unveiled themselves . . . and this unveiling places them at the forefront of the struggle for identity, resistance, and rebellion" (Lynch 47). My interest in pursuing their work is also motivated in part by an attempt to revitalize the ways in which the Black Arts Movement has been assessed, and a desire to introduce readers to voices representing the initiatives of the movement within the broader black writing tradition that have yet to be given adequate attention in the scholarly community. Although Amini, Rodgers, and Jackson were all committed to the BAM's aesthetics—which called for a utilitarian approach to art as a medium for achieving nation-building goals as they were most often determined by their male peers—in no way did these women compromise their independent visions in order to meet such expectations. As I discuss more specifically in the following chapters, the earliest poetry of all three writers paradoxically exemplifies the progressive breadth and integrity of BAM's nation-building concept beyond that which was characterized or promoted by their male peers.

Even though "prescriptions for proper female behavior proliferated in the countless poems dedicated to black women during the early days of the Black Arts [M]ovement," as acknowledged by Karen Jackson Ford in her discussion of feminist poetry, to suggest that the primary goal of women of the Black Arts Movement was to undermine the ideals of their male contemporaries would be a presumptuous oversimplification of the accomplishments of Black Arts women such as Amini, Rodgers, and Jackson (192). As stated by Tim'm T. West,

> Even as the foundation of many forms of nationalisms is necessarily unstable, what remains consistent between communities and nations is the ongoing tension between those vested with the power to speak and those who not only challenge people in power but who do so by adapting the very popular discourses that communicate national consciousness. Clearly the patriarchs maintain the luxury and power not only to remain seduced by the

illusion of their hegemony, but also to affect people and policy through their illusion. However, those on the margins are by no means immobilized by the powers that be. If anything, they imagine their own communities and the potentialities for the representation of their "real." (177)

The collective goal of asserting a new and clearly defined relationship between politics and art of the sixties and seventies amongst BAM participants cannot be overstated; however, such a relationship oftentimes distracts readers from pursuing the work of individual artists to determine the complexity and eclecticism that nevertheless existed in the work of this period. Although "one of the elements of the literary thrust of the sixties was the commitment of the Black woman writer to ground with the people, to move among the masses in the community . . . ," I contend that Amini, Rodgers, and, later, Jackson produced work that offered their audiences alternative ways to imagine the ground on which they collectively stood while challenging audiences to trust in the viability of a culturally inclusive aesthetic. Within the context of the Chicago BAM, the poetry of each writer reflects her ability to navigate the male-oriented exigencies of the movement while productively complicating and critiquing some of its most popular yet otherwise exclusive, unyielding, and limiting aesthetic features.

Chapter Three

Mirrors of Deception: Invisible, Untouchable, Beautiful Blackness in Johari Amini's Black Art

In Johari Amini's "Evolution," the narrator expresses that mother Africa, as a geographical, historical, and cultural ideal, expands to "black"—a "humaneness movement breathing filling / vasculating knowledge creating soul." Such an idea is appropriated throughout Amini's earliest work, published while she served as a member of the Black Arts Organization for Black American Culture (OBAC). Dedicated to "all black people," her first published collection of poetry, *Images in Black* (1967), is a critique of images, iconography, and visual references that commonly served as aesthetic conventions defining black culture and identity for the purpose of projecting preeminent community and nation-building goals during the Black Arts Movement.[1] "Immensely important in forging the new style of the Black Arts Movement, she wrote some of its most beautiful, experimentally vernacular, and hard-edged poems" (Guzman 195). More specifically, and even predictably, the treatment of images representing BAM ideals is the focus of many poems in Amini's first collection; yet she strategically and paradoxically undermines the essentialist aspect and legitimacy of visual references and iconography that had become integral to the production of Black Art during the late sixties and early seventies. According to feminist scholar Diana Fuss, "Essentialism is classically defined as a belief in true essence—that which is most irreducible, unchanging, and therefore constitutive of a given person or thing . . ." (666). Consequently, Amini's treatment of visuality and iconography popularized during this historical and aesthetic moment exposes the ways in which such resources perhaps *failed* to authentically represent "blackness" and/or black culture, despite Black Artists' investment in their currency during this period. As Angela Davis argued after the waning years of the BAM, the reduction and packaging of political ideology into popular media representations is not emancipatory or clarifying, but counterproductive.[2] Despite her own allegiance to BAM aesthetics as they were employed by members of OBAC and Black Artists nationwide, much of Amini's poetry in the collection *Images in Black* calls attention to the limitations of visual aesthetics meant to characterize black culture and/or BAM ideals. In this way, Amini casts an ambivalent light onto some of the most conventional aspects of the movement's aesthetic culture. Furthermore, Amini's prophetic and cautionary critique of BAM aesthetics remains relevant in contemporary cultural contexts, especially when considering the ways in which current new media outlets render visual projections of identity, culture, and community more accessible. Thus, Amini's treatment of visuality dared to challenge the validity of Black Art as an aesthetic paradigm for projecting nation-building ideals during the era of the Black Arts Movement and indeed moving forward.

Amini's lifelong advocacy of healthy standards of living and physical and spiritual well-being became the impetus behind her work as a chiropractor later in her life, and such interests are reflected in her earlier poetry, where there are subtle references to practical and holistic approaches to promoting these ideals within the black community and as part of the black nation-building project.[3] This is especially apparent in the poet's consistent treatment of the image of the black body in the collection *Images in Black*. "Popular culture ... plays a role in the affirmation of black bodies and somatic features, and even in the acceptance of the label 'black' (Hay 7). Yet even as Amini's poetry calls attention to the relationship between BAM aesthetics and popular culture in reaffirming the black body, it cautions against the potential exploitation of the body and/or the immobilization of its agency under the application of BAM ideals.

In the opening piece in *Images in Black*, entitled "Coronoch," references to "burning ghettos," "bloated starvation," "burning blackness," "black blood," etc., conjure vivid and collective memories of racial violence for black Americans, and Amini's aggressive incorporation of controversial and traumatic imagery is a testament to her strategic reliance upon visual stimuli as means of recalling this traumatic past in her poetic narrative (1). The image of the "spectre" that is "unseen / by masses / sensed / by some / defined / by few" is never fully clarified in this poem, yet its illusory, ethereal qualities are meaningful. The idea that only a marginal number of individuals are capable of sensing the presence of the spectre in the poem could be a reference to the ways in which the image tragically eludes the masses and serves as a visually ambiguous yet powerful symbol, as "prophetic voices" are "shouted down, "warned of fire" and "warned of patriotism" in this spectacle of violence. The piece ends with mocking emphasis on the term "DEMOCRACY," which is itself constructed as an ideal in the poem, and which can only be perpetuated through the mass killing or oppression of black bodies. Because quotidian approaches to Black Art relied upon artists' ability to use visual references and aesthetic conventions that would appeal to black audiences, and with which such audiences would most urgently identify, artworks that would speak "directly to the needs and aspirations of Black America and consequently foment a revolution in response to the national and global oppression of people of color" were critical resources for Black Artists like Amini.[4]

Furthermore, the violent "spectre" or scene in this piece is, itself, appropriately discursive. "Revolutionary violence is that violence that seeks to overthrow an established system that serves a few people, to establish a new system that serves the masses of our people," writes Stokely Carmichael, who coined the term "Black Power" as the mantra of black revolutionary groups (157). He continues:

> In this country, America, black people have just begun to scratch the surface of armed struggle. If we're talking about true revolution in this country, we're talking about a fight of a generation . . . We are talking about a generation of young black people willing to fight and give their lives for a revolution that will benefit the generations who come after us. (158)

Carmichael moves forward to distinguish between a "black militant" and a "black revolutionary"—the former being "an angry black man" who poses as a revolutionary by adorning "afros and dashikis . . . and having a press conference on the corner"; the latter being "an angry young man who wants to tear down and destroy an entire system that is oppressing his people and replace it with a new system where his people can live like human beings" (159). This sentiment, reinforced through the rhetoric and media of the Black Arts Movement and Black Power Movement, gained momentum as writers, artists, activists, and intellectuals such as Amini relied upon and popularized images and narratives that gave visual currency to the experiences of those most marginalized. Such images and narratives needed to be constructed around narratives of collaboration, cooperation, and collectivity within the black community in order to inspire activism in response to systems of oppression in America and worldwide. Thus, the propagandistic and inspiring aspects of poems like "Coronach," which reflected principles of revolutionary nation-building as adopted by Black Arts and Black Power intelligentsia, were most solvent when they privileged and indeed exploited the collaborative social, cultural, and political lives of their audiences, transforming them into the substance of art.

Thus, in the poem "Coronach," the "spectre" of violence and subsequent uprising of the masses can only be "defined by [the] few," illustrating the moment when white power and privilege are overturned in a period of "armed struggle," as theorized in Carmichael's rhetoric of revolution (158). In this way, Amini's poem implicates both the Black Artist's role in exploiting this revolutionary image as a means of motivating audiences, and the collaborative relationship between artist and audience is idealized in a poetic narrative that arouses the consciousness of the collective into eventual activism. "Recognizing that many in their audience had to experience the revolution vicariously before they could agree to its feasibility, Black Power–era writers . . . employed culture as weapon . . . Afro-American writers showed how folk, literary, and theatrical forms could complement any militant's arsenal" (Van Deburg 284). Amini's reliance upon and reconstruction of images of violence, insurgence, and civil unrest in the poem "Coronoch"—scenes that characterize the immediate and historical epistemologies of violence against blacks—exemplifies the writer's compliance with BAM and Black Power ideals regarding black activism, which was contingent, in part, upon artists' ability to both visually and narratively homogenize and characterize the collaborative interests of their audiences. "The black power phase of the civil rights/black liberation movement dominated much of the iconography and dramaturgy of the late 1960's . . . All politics involves a theatrical element . . . The cultural front of the black power movement exerted black pride and empowerment into so many different spaces on so many levels of culture" (T. V. Reed 42). The final line of Amini's "Coronoch," which states that "atrocities preserve DEMOCRACY," implicates the "pouring of black blood," the "drying of black bones," and the "burning of black flesh" as tragic but necessary consequences of preserving the myth of American freedom and democracy. The references to the colors red, white, and blue, juxtaposed with "burning ghettos / bloated starvation / and burning bodies" simultaneously conjure theatrical visions of nationalism and freedom as well as violence and oppression. "Popular culture also plays a role in the affirmation of black bodies and somatic features," writes Michelle Hay (7). Amini's reliance upon and critique of the universally recognizable and symbolic colors red, white, and blue—images with which popular audiences could easily identify in a myriad of simultaneous and conflicting ways—as well as the incorporation of scenes of reactionary violence inspired by racial subjugation constitute the poet's methods of engaging audiences in ways that reinforce the marketability of provocative images that were capable of stirring the consciousness of her readership. As poetic "cinema," Amini's images "emanate from an essential cultural matrix deriving from a collective black socio-cultural and historical experience" (Yearwood qtd. in Regester 353). Furthermore, Amini's poetry invokes theatrics, drama, and performativity through imagistic language. "Mixed media was sometimes used to express singular visions of monolithic blackness" (Collins and Crawford 12). Thus, visual culture becomes a subject of productive critique as Amini forces readers to reckon with its impact and influence in the process of invoking the history and collective memory of trauma and dehumanizing violence that has played an invariable role in defining the black experience in America.

Although, as Reed suggests, "what counts as dramatic has often been defined in limiting ways based on male-centered visions of heroic performance," many of the pieces in Amini's collection *Images in Black* boldly and paradoxically function as "Black Art," calling into question the reliability of art and/or aesthetics as discursive references meant to reinforce nation-building objectives. Such a maneuver was indeed a daring one to be executed by a woman writer. Yet, as the cofounder of Chicago's Organization for Black American Culture (OBAC), which quickly became one of the most productive and popular BAM organizations invested in addressing the social concerns of a local constituency, Amini would have likely embraced her status and influence as a leading figure of the BAM. Despite the fact that "Black Arts poetry functioned as a weapon of the idealized black warrior's revolutionary power and as a sign of his sexual prowess," as a woman writer re/constructing imagistic narratives of revolution and historiographies of black suffering, Amini wrote poetry that disrupts the otherwise masculine conceptualization of Black Arts iconography in a meaningful way. Her ability to simultaneously centralize as well as critique the iconography of the BAM's media-driven initiatives—iconography that her audiences and peers would have readily interpreted and endorsed as fodder for revolutionary activism—allows readers to evaluate ideals of collaboration and collectivity as complex and complicated psychological concepts that ultimately served as propaganda in the marketing of BAM and indeed OBAC objectives.

In "To A Black Writer," Amini's narrator contemplates the potential influence of writing as artistic and cultural expression. The narrator calls upon her contemporaries to "record the ages / for ages of Black unborn / ... give us prose / ... write the words / of Blackness stolen / ... write of why our blood / is poured out / ... give us poetry / ... tell it like it is / Black writer," revealing the narrator's expectations as a writer and potential voice of empowerment (12). Yet the narrator intimates that the future and fate of the black community is not simply contingent upon contemporary aesthetics in community conscious, nation-building goals. Instead, she conveys the idea that the Black Artist must be inspired by an idyllic African history in the creation of her work, and Black Art must be prophetic and foreshadowing in its attempt to stimulate the collective and collaborative consciousness of its audience. As the Black Artist "pervade[s] the womb of time / record[s] the ages / ... distil[s] the wisdom of beginnings ... writ[es] the words / of Blackness stolen," ultimately, she is responsible for translating the future and fate of black people into words. Thus, even as Amini's narrator privileges the role and aspirations of the Black Artist, she recognizes that she can only write from her own perspective and ". . . tell it like it is" as she sees it—not as "truth."[5] Although the line "Blackness is Revolution" confirms the ideological and visual connectivity between the ontological and cultural concept of blackness and the enactment and execution of revolutionary and/or liberating goals, Amini's poem can also be read as a productive critique of the exploitive aspects of such images in fomenting action within the black community, despite the fact that such visual references were perceived as motivating resources in the Black Arts Movement and Black Power Movement. Scholar Mike Sell's call to examine the "efforts of cultural radicals during the sixties to open up or tear down oppressive symbolic, discursive, and institutional systems during a period of remarkable innovation" is useful to my evaluation of Amini's work, since I read her earlier poems as powerful and paradoxical confirmations and indictments of the symbolism and imagery reinforced in Black Art. However, Amini's treatment productively complicates and expands what is often read as the monotheistic tone of the BAM, and her work intimates the porous and ambiguous aspects of the movement's aesthetic culture.

In keeping with her treatment of the theme of visuality, Amini's poem "Identity" can be read as a characterization of the real-life meeting between herself and her mentor, Haki Madhubuti, a "prophet / creator of / change showing identity / to [whiteminded] Negroes" who "wears a crown / of natural" (2). Ultimately, the poem narrates the extent to which the aesthetic parameters of Black Art are enacted through dialogue and performance. Dedicated to Haki Madhubuti, the construction of his "character" in this poem is particularly significant, especially since he remained one of the most influential figures within the national and Chicago Black Arts Movements. The dialogue between the speaker/narrator (Amini) and her teacher (Madhubuti) reveals the narrator's evolving state of black consciousness. The process of "becoming black" is presented in the form of a catechism in which the narrator assumes the role of the "student" and attempts to answer the questions posed by the "teacher." The narrator's arrival at a final stage of black consciousness is achieved only after this verbal exchange takes place, and the student is "reborn" as a fully realized, black-identified woman. The conceptualization of this evolution is analogous to the birthing process, and in this regard, Amini experiments with traditional gender roles, as the male teacher (Madhubuti) administers this "birthing" process and becomes the ostensible midwife who provides the guidance, cajoling, and nurturing needed to expedite the narrator's immanent and emerging "black" identity. As the teacher poses the necessary questions used to evaluate the extent to which the narrator perceives herself to "be black," the narrator exposes the contradictions of her preconceived self-image and is conscious of the fact that she cannot answer "yes" to the question of whether or not she "THINK[S] BLACK" because of her "imitationwhite hair" and her "curlfree do." The teacher (Madhubuti) directs the questions "What are you," "Are you Black," and "Do you think Black" toward a narrator who, at the point of their encounter, only *imagines* herself to be black, and who is in fact fearful of presenting herself to her teacher as a black woman. Doubting her own self-image, the narrator is apprehensive about responding to her teacher's probing questions, "as birth is a painful process." It is not until her teacher asks her "are you B L A C K" that the narrator reveals a conscious betrayal of her race—"should i lie / say / yes . . . no I need time"—that the teacher articulates the final and most critical query "do you THINK BLACK?" and implies that simply "thinking" black justifies that one *is* black.

The teacher then proffers a list of individuals who legitimately represent "blackness" and in whom an image of this ideal is reflected. Here, racial identity is treated not as an arbitrary or elusive category of subjectivity, but is instead a concept defined by boundaries and degrees of psycho/social commitments, and any question of this is mitigated by the teacher's references to Malcolm X, James Baldwin, Amiri Baraka, Patrice Lumumba, Stokely Carmichael, and W. E. B. Du Bois—all considered politically and physically "acceptable" representatives of a standard of Black racial consciousness. Each of these male figures metaphorically assists the female narrator in reaching her phallic, climactic point of recognition and clarity, and the pain of the birthing process ends as she is able to "breathe life" and begin growth. "[T]he pain stopped i / breathed life / birth was completed / growth was begun i / was sister i had Black / Proud IDENTITY." Notably, the narrator's "sisterhood" is only confirmed by her acknowledgment of the ways in which blackness is equated with masculinity as manifested in the form of her teacher's aforementioned list of male figures. By the end of the piece, the narrator's rebirth is achieved, and her teacher considers her to be deserving of her "black sister" status after having reconciled her "identity confusion." Thus, the scene represents the narrator's veritable orgasmic release into black womanhood, which symbolizes her liberation and (black identified) self-acceptance.

The opportunity to critique this interplay of words represents not only an instructional moment between the figures of the student and her mentor, but it also serves as the sacred dialogic space wherein the narrator's racialized identity is realized. Amini's script becomes a paradigm actualizing what it means to "be black," and the narrator's ideal identity is conceived via her interaction with her male mentor. Cultural identity is conceptualized as a process that is furthermore realized through language and the reinforcement of images that characterize blackness as an ideal. It is not until the narrator accepts her instructor's version of blackness, and she believes that she emulates and embodies this ideal that "the pain stop[s]," and she becomes a "sister."

The interplay between the narrator and her teacher in this poem represents an opportunity to assess the theatricality of Black Art as well as its reliance upon collaborative and interactive contexts of logocentric expressivity. "Restive and textured, black theater manifestos comprise diverse images of dramatic intention that cohere as a dialogue on presence and mediation, authenticity and signification" (Benston 28). Black Art was frequently susceptible to the agency of images in provoking audience interaction. Read as "modern black theater considered as a collective endeavor [that] seeks ultimately not to jettison but to transmute mimesis," the dramatization of BAM ideals in community theater and public performance, for instance, and as translated into poetic dialogue is represented in the piece "Identity." Such a treatment reflects a simultaneous reverence for and exposes the tenuousness of an ideal concept of black identity as was meant to inspire the narrator's process of self-reflection and indeed that of Amini's readership.

The treatment of (black) identity as an elusive and indeed psychologically, visibly, and physically tenuous concept carries over into the piece "Faux-Semblant"—a French term, which, when translated into English, means "false truth." In this short but powerful poem, Amini's narrator cautiously attempts to confirm who she is in physical terms, yet the image with which she is confronted in the water is a false and/or illusory one (4). Furthermore, the narrator is comforted by "a slight breeze," and she becomes disillusioned as she approaches a pond in which she expects to see a reflection of her desired image. Although she is beguiled by the "slight breeze" and "soft / cool shadowed woods," the narrator's ultimate decision to approach the pond is motivated by the expectation that she will be greeted by a reflection that will confirm her preconceived self-image. Leaning into the pond "drawing [her] / to its stillness . . . to breathe / the beauty" that is certain to be seen in the reflection, the narrator is instead confronted with what becomes "the death-face." Despite the ambiguity revolving around the "actual," material image with which the narrator is ultimately confronted, her unquestioning, unwavering faith in what she will see in the pond as she leans into the water, as well as her investment in the existence of a reflection that will ideally validate her self-image "mirrors" the idea that perceptions of self-image and identity are expected to be reproduced or reaffirmed through Black Art in the form of visual representation, and that an affirmation of identity is accompanied by one's ability to actually *see* it manifested in a material form. Scholar Kimberly Benston's insights with regard to the relationship between imagery and the aesthetic principles of Black Art are useful here. As she suggests,

> performance erupts within frames of perception that are both quickly disseminated and paradoxically overlooked: because one is always *watching* new images of blackness in the public sphere, responsive acts of *witnessing* become more difficult to share and sustain over a technologically shrinking but psychically fragmenting national landscape . . . the lengthening shadows of the Black Arts performance agenda [extend] themselves with impressive reach into the province of the image, variously conceived. (311, emphasis hers)

In "Faux-Semblant," the narrator's proclivity to consciously look towards physical evidence that might validate preexisting notions of identity underscores the primary function of visual stimuli in Black Art, which were intended to elucidate the concept of identity. This is further reinforced by the narrator's preoccupation with what the reflection will yield. In this sense, the responsibility of Amini's narrator is evident—she submits to a desire to have her image confirmed by the reflection, yet the ideal image of perfect "beauty" is replaced with that of the "death-face" in the reflection. The "fault/faux" of the narrator lies not in her desire to imagine herself as physically beautiful, but is instead the consequence of her efforts to *see* or verify identity in a visible, recognizable form. As in the previously discussed piece "Identity," the possibility of realizing identity in imagistic forms is unrealistic in "Faux-Semblant," and Amini's work parodies the essentialist import of visual aesthetics as a feature of Black Art. In "Faux-Semblant," the narrator is empowered by the solitude and tranquility of the pond "drawing [her] / to its stillness." Although the singular image of the "death-face" is expressive of all that is not "beauty[ful]," and it performs in opposition to that which is favorable or ideal in reference to identity, the tragic aspect of the piece revolves around the false sense of security exhibited by the narrator in her reliance upon the reflection as a sole means of self-validation. Though one might wonder why a leading figure of Chicago's BAM would throw such ambiguous light upon visuality, given the material, textual, and physical aspects of the movement's culture, which was so contingent upon audiences' ability to envision the parameters of black performance, it is equally productive to consider how Amini's treatment of these themes affirms the complex and vulnerable aspects of Black Art.

The poem "About Communication" further complicates the legitimacy of various popular mediums that were meant to market ideal, culturally specific versions of black identity, wherein "emotions / [become] intangible etherealities / difficult to dissect." The narrator of this piece assumes the role of a critic, citing the inadequacies of "sections / specifications / blueprints / delineations / . . . words" in the struggle to conceptualize identity (11). More appropriately, she becomes a veritable voice of dissention, as her words undermine political and artistic projects that enforce the commodification and construction of aesthetic paradigms that were meant to dictate and inform black identity. Thus, the pathological tendency for Black Artists to create work that reflected a codification of cultural identity through one-dimensional representations or even *words* is critiqued here. The narrator's statement "you / know my / self," despite the absence of visual markers, verbal explanations, or prescribed resources, suggests Amini's poetic departure from the practices of her BAM contemporaries, whose work often foregrounded textual and aesthetic references as means of characterizing and/or denoting (black) authenticity. The phrase "being not other / you / understand without / sections / specifications / blueprints / delineations / . . . words" suggests that perhaps the narrator believes in her counterpart's ability to psychologically connect with her because of the similarities between their *actual* rather than idealized or projected subjectivities. As the last line of the poem reads, even "words" may not be successful in achieving this goal, which suggests that a more elusive, intuitive connection exists between the two characters. In contrast to the voices that were foregrounded in the piece "Identity," in "About Communication," words and/or "voices" become meaningless and incapable of translating emotion or identity. In this way, Amini's poem is much more aggressive in its paradoxical treatment of BAM mediums, which were intended to give voice to as well as represent the black communal experience. Mike Sell's interpretation of the "antitextual bias" of the otherwise significant "black voice" is useful here:

> The Black voice was emphasized by many BAM theorists as capable of shattering the chains of a cultural imperialism based on the imposition of textual literacy and all its correlative effects. Rejecting the text and restoring the voice would allow for the ontological grounding of philosophy, economy, culture, and identity in a post-Western moment . . . Considered a cultural strategy that unites the local and the global in a peculiarly effective manner, Black Arts vocal theory and practice can be viewed as part of a larger critical tendency, a tendency that worked to destroy whatever threatened the commodification of the Black body . . . ("The Voice" 279)

Sell's commentary on the black voice is useful to my analysis of "About Communication" in particular. Not only does the poem reflect Amini's critique of textuality, but it also potentially negates "voice" in favor of a virtual or "unscripted" methodology for perpetuating ideals of community and collectivity.

For Chicago artists like Amini, as well as Black Artists nationwide, photography, art, drama, and poetry readings promoted the ideals of the BAM in ways that encouraged a critical relationship between artists and mainstream audiences.[6] The critique of "sections / specifications / blueprints," etc., as metaphors for forced and perhaps restricted aesthetics in a Black Arts poem such as "About Communication" is quite heretical in this regard. Rather than conform to quotidian methods of communicating a black cultural identity that is palpable, visible, and measurable, Amini deconstructs and indeed challenges the underpinnings of conventional aesthetics in this piece, even though visual media and performance art were integral to the process of marketing Black Art as a socially and politically conscious, community-building aesthetic. Furthermore, the accessibility of the BAM was sustained through visual and performance media that rendered images reflective of black life central to its objectives. Thus, narratives focusing on the empowerment of black communities found artistic legitimacy in the iconography reinforced through the popularity of Black Art. Yet as several of Amini's poems convey in the collection *Images in Black*, identity and community are not necessarily translatable through aesthetics or media, and such resources may never be capable of representing black consciousness, identity, community, or nation-building ideals. Such a treatment humanizes the otherwise and often-cited caricatured propaganda of the BAM and calls attention to the vulnerability and tenuousness of its aesthetics.

While Amini produces Black Art that paradoxically critiques visual aesthetics as ideal forms of realizing individual and cultural identity in the *Images in Black* collection, then in *Black Essence* (1968), Amini's follow-up publication, the writer experiments with the concept of the "erotic" as a means of elucidating ideals of black identity, community, and nation-building. Thus, sexual performance becomes a means of expressing desires to conform and aspire to rather than escape perpetuations of black identity. In several pieces in the aptly titled *Black Essence*, erotic expressions reinforce rather than negate the "essence" of black community ideals. As one scholar notes,

> Poems of familial, romantic, and erotic love abound in the works of African American women ... Overt expressions of sexuality and desire are markers of expanding feminist consciousness ... Discussions of maleness and femaleness are complicated by considerations of sexuality. Just as a period of female assertiveness brought us to a consideration of gendered discourse, today we must also become conscious of the ways in which sexuality affects discourse. (Brown 111)

As I discuss in chapter one of this project, such themes as romantic love and erotica, as referenced in Brown's assessment of poetry authored by black women writers of previous eras, were comparatively less popular amongst later BAM writers—male *or* female. Yet as many women writers of the BAM expressed in their activist poetry, the subject of love did not *always* connote an indulgence into the "personal." "The power of love, its personal and political strength as a force for black liberation, transcended heterosexual romance. Love, redefined, could and must include both relationships among women and a healthy regard for self" (Kieta 286–287). However, as I will argue, the eroticism and sexuality characterized in several of Amini's poems in *Black Essence* expand the terms of Black Art to allow for opportunities to assess where sexual performance as identity performance and revolutionary expression coincide. In addition,

Amini's treatment of sexuality can be interpreted as that which queers the heterosexual conventions of Black Art that authenticate the black family, community, and nation, as many of her poems feature sexual- and/or gender-fluid characters and relationships. This is an especially uncharacteristic treatment, since Black Arts writers were expected to narrate conventional and/or universal experiences reflecting black life; thus, any focus on the "interior," the subconscious, or the "queer" could be considered counterproductive to preeminent consciousness-raising projects.

Ultimately, in Amini's *Black Essence* poems, "erotica" paradoxically becomes synonymous with Black Art. Amini's work is furthermore anticipatory of the concept of "black (feminist) power" as it was later expressed by poet Audre Lorde, who writes, "Our poems formulate the implications of ourselves, what we feel within and dare make real . . . If what we need to dream, to move our spirits most deeply and directly toward and through promise, is discounted as a luxury, then we give up the core—the fountain—of our power, our womanness; we give up the future of *our worlds*" ("Poetry," emphasis mine). Amini's treatment of "dreams," desires, and individual free expression *reinforces* rather than runs counter to community-building goals of the BAM. For instance, in a section titled "4 poems of blk/love" in *Black Essence*, the "body" is realized as a critical source of expression and political insurgency, maintaining a contentious yet mutually informative relationship with the political aims of its community. In all four pieces included in this section—"The Two," "Quintessence," "And When I Thought of Him," and "Orbit"—sexuality and/or sexual expression become political performances that explicate necessary and productive tensions between the community and the individual. In creating such tensions in her work, Amini exposes some of the most taboo subjects that potentially threatened the progressivism of the BAM. Although the demands of Black Art ideals were stridently expressed and enforced in much of the poetry of this period, not all BAM poetry was demanding or overtly discursive in its appeal to black audiences. For instance, Amini's "The Two"—a brief, seven-line poem—recalls the idea of "blackness" and/or black identity enacted through black love/sex (10). The first lines, "Making their love / was dessert / lush . . ." coalesce with vivid, imagistic portrayals of "lush / rich / . . . seep[ing] black pleasure," and the fluidity and continuity of black life and black culture is captured in the sexual expression characterized in this piece. Yet it is noteworthy that the narrator furthermore fails to characterize black love as "joyously consumed" in unambiguously heterosexual terms, leaving the reader to ponder both the gender and sexual orientation of both characters. While one might assume the heterosexual context of this piece, given the overarching homophobic culture of the BAM, curiously, the sexuality of the two figures is never explicitly clarified in "The Two."

This romantic portrait flows into the companion poems "Quintessence" and "And When I Thought of Him," which coincide narratively and structurally into one piece. References to "his hands / touch[ing] / mak[ing] life my flesh" in the words of the first narrator in "Quintessence" literally collide on the page with the second narrator's confession that "the ways / his love would take of mine / and drain his black / ironed blood / . . . to make me woman" in the poem "And When I Thought of Him" (10, 11). As in "The Two," in both "Quintessence" and "And When I Thought of Him," the perpetuation and consumption of black love becomes a fortifying resource for two narrators who desire that their partners "make [them] woman." Although the latter piece is a clear characterization of heterosexual love, the former piece includes characters that, once again, can be interpreted as sexually ambiguous. While "[his] darkly essence nourishment / [is] require[ed] / to make [her] woman" in "And When I Thought of Him," the narrative voice in "Quintessence" is gender-neutral, and it is not clear as to whether or not the "fevering fusion" resulting from the touch of "his hands" is experienced by a male or female narrator. However, despite the disparities in the character development between all three of the poems included in the "4 poems of blk/love" section of *Black Essence*, each poem reifies sexuality and sexual acts as those that have the potential to affirm selfhood and community belonging. Each poem privileges various versions of black love as affirmations of black nation and community-building ideals.

As sexuality, like gender, became contested areas of personal and political performance in conjunction with BAM and Black Power goals, Amini's construction of sexuality within the policed terrain of the BAM is worthy of attention, as any deviation from heterosexual representations and/or enactments of black love was tantamount to antirevolutionary practices. Yet "[m]obilization efforts during Civil Rights, Black Power, Women's, and later Queer Nation movements brought with them *a call for collaboration*" between various cultures of the black community during the era of the BAM, including lesbian, gay, bisexual, and transgender communities (Battle 2, emphasis mine). While the idea of collaboration with the Black Arts Movement and Black Power Movement, for instance, was indeed contingent upon the consensual and cross-cultural participation of various groups, consequently, the hegemonic normalization of group-based politics necessarily meant the oppression and/or exclusion of many voices. However, as a committed Black Artist and leading figure of Chicago's BAM, Amini makes no such commitment to these exclusionary paradigms, as evidenced in "The Two" and "Quintessence," wherein the nation-building concept of "black love" could legitimately and inclusively take on queer forms and/or be enacted and narrated by queer subjects and/or gender-neutral voices. In this way, Amini expands the concept of black love as that which is paradoxically and progressively perpetuated as an amorphous idea within the context of an otherwise gender-restrictive Black Arts culture.

Even more radical is Amini's treatment of the theme of black love and/or sexual desire enacted by ambiguously gendered and/or gender-neutral characters, whose expressions intimate sex acts as simultaneously pleasurable and liberating as well as oppressive and painful in the poem "Orbit"—the last piece in the "blk/love" section of *Black Essence* (11). In it, the narrator's heightened sexual consciousness and metaphysical displacement reveal a desire to transcend the immediacy of the moment in order to pursue a self-defined version of liberation through sexual empowerment. Furthermore, the characters in this piece achieve a state of nirvana in the form of violent, hypervisible, though romantic, sexual expressions that "pull spasmed substance" and "heave surge / hardenings" and "burst" in "life / rhythms." "Orbiting" is a form of psychological and physical displacement here, as the ethereality of "shimmer[ing] soft colors" combines with the "space of Dark" and contrasts with the realism of the "darkcovered nappy flesh" of hardened, moistened bodies. These two disparate yet related planes of consciousness sustain a reinforced parallelism motivated by the performance of the body as it expresses sexual desire in both earthly and spiritual contexts and aspires to community ideals of belonging in its connection to another black body. According to scholar Franny Nudelman, with regard to liberationist countercultures of the late sixties, "experiments in distorted perception provided common ground for the various subcultures . . . Advocates of the counterculture claimed that experiments in consciousness and the new forms of self-expression that resulted would pave the way for revolution" (244). In this context, I read Amini's poem "Orbit" as paradoxically experimental in its narrative expression of psychological freedom rooted in fantasy even as it validates revolutionary, nation-building ideals.

Furthermore, as references to "night" and "dark" serve as metaphors for "blackness" in the poem "Orbit," once separated from her partner, the narrator is "covered" in "alone[ness] / as night was wool," and she finds hopelessness and despair in alienation. The idea that women writers of the BAM such as Amini found creative ways to appropriate, recast, or wholly abandon the otherwise violent, hypermasculine and heterosexist tone and spirit of the movement's culture is demonstrated in the poet's treatment of imagery in this piece. "Having first attempted to imitate the model hyper masculine revolutionary poet, some female poets retreated from its vulgarity and violence into a hyper feminine mode that provided relief from certain stereotypes..." (Ford 196). In this sense, Amini's poem "Orbit" reflects a potentially transgendered version of black love in its juxtaposition of "hard" and "soft" images that are both affirming and potentially compromising. The erotic impulse characterized in this piece becomes a medium of escape or refuge from that which is "lived," "real," or even heterosexual, in favor of a virtual or hypersexual fulfillment of black love. "[T]he power of love, its personal and political strength as a force for black liberation, transcended heterosexual romance" (Kieta 287). Thus, the "moaning" figures in Amini's poem are disengaged from their communities—free to express their mutual desires as they choose. In an era when "notions of racial and gender identity [were] subjected to question, dispute, and redefinitions," Amini's love poems are particularly compelling in their paradoxical appropriation of the concept of black love typified and otherwise atrophied in social realism and the conventional heterosexual terms of Black Art (Kieta 279).

Many of the poems included in *Black Essence* portray characters as autonomous, self-defined agents of their own fates, and who enact power and desire as a way of affirming and/or rejecting "reality." In this regard, Amini's work can easily be recognized as comparatively unique to many of her BAM peers. In much of her poetry, readers find a discernible and consistent focus on the individual as a complicated figure capable of expressing agency alone or as a member of the collective in perpetuating nation-building goals. However, as she obscures the lines between the "political" or the "public" and the "private," Amini does not compromise but rather *expands* the terms of Black Art as she reflects the diverse patterns and versions of the black experience.

Other selections in this collection, such as the poem entitled "(For Nigareens)," encourage readers to consider the influence of BAM ideals as they are physically and aesthetically manifested through individual aspirations of belonging (2). In this particular piece, the narrator proudly proclaims, "my hair flows / long and straightly silken / conditioned to be so..." Competing dis/illusions of "whiteness" and/or Eurocentricity and "blackness" inform the narrator's self-image and undermine her racial identity, yet she is amused by the fact that "... even those People / black and oddly proud . . . [look] / down / in / my / direction . . ." Cloaked in and encumbered by markers of race and sex, the narrator's hair, complexion, and style are distinct markers of identity and social status, while others (blacks) criticize her physical rejection of blackness as she arrogantly celebrates her "bright lightened" complexion and "haigh British" style. Since, among other performative acts, perpetuations of black identity were popularized through displays of fashion consciousness that ultimately signified one's political sensibilities, the narrator's proclamation that "no one can . . . see . . . who I am" mocks what would otherwise be an obvious expression of her (black) identity. Amini satirizes rather than perpetuates the solvency of identity politics here, drawing attention to the import of somatic and behavioral implications of race performance. The poem addresses the consequences of social exclusion faced by the narrator, since, problematically, "no one can everguess" or determine "who" she is. In an era when defining "blackness" was an artistic and politically pathological pursuit for Black Artists, Amini's obfuscation of race performance is daring. The idea that one's conformity to the ideals of the community could be visually "perceptible" exposes the extent to which codes of behavior were enforced and decoded for the purpose of gauging individuals' allegiance to nation-building and community ideals within Black Arts and Black Power cultures. Notably, the narrator of "(For Nigareens)" articulates the social dangers of passing—not across race or color lines, but more significantly, across ideological and political ones. The narrator criticizes "those People / black and oddly proud who / smile / while looking / down / in / my / direction . . ." As "(For Nigareens)" suggests, tensions between individual performance and the expectations of the collective were mutually informative, and nation and community-building ideals were in fact mitigated by the individual's capacity to either accept or reject such expectations.

In the poem "Masque," for instance, individual performance simultaneously disrupts and informs the ideological expectations and ideals of the collective, and Amini's narrator expresses impatience for the elusive categories of race performance "as black becomes / as white / and smiles and is the same" in drawing conclusions about identity (4). As shared and collaborative enactments of Black Power during the BAM assured the unification of black people and found currency and clarification in black "soul"—"a type of primal spiritual energy and passionate joy available only to members of the exclusive racial confraternity"—for the narrator of "Masque," "a sister false is / cause / to make one bleed" (Van Deburg 195). The "fals[ity]" or fault of the "sister" is not clarified, although it is clear that in some way her actions do not comply with the expectations of her community. The clarifications of the categories "false" and/or "authentic" are complicated by the coalescing references to color, as ". . . black becomes / as white / . . . and is the same / and seems the same / . . . and yet we are betrayed." Although it is quite easy to assume that the "masque" adorned by the targeted "sister" belies the "truth" and authenticity of "blackness," the masque simultaneously perpetuates the conventions of this construct—existing as both an affirmation of racial boundaries and a reference to the performatively ambiguous nature of race. The image of the "mask" recalls W. E. B. Du Bois's "double-consciousness" or "masking" concept as it relates to the process of identity construction, deception, and self-preservation for the black subject under the white gaze and within the context of white culture—a consciousness that "yields him no true self-consciousness, but only lets him see himself through the revelation of the other [white] world" (3).[7] Yet in the poem "Masque," there is a paradoxical reconfiguration of this recurring symbol, since it clarifies the fallibility of racial authenticity *within* the black community. Amini's allusion to the ambiguous nature rather than the reliability of racial identity within the context of a black community ideal is especially ironic and haunting, as it demonstrates her willingness to critique the aesthetic references that were meant to validate concepts of black identity and image to which she herself was beholden as a self-defined Black Artist.

Amini's artistic contributions as a leading figure of the BAM in Chicago are not compromised by what can be read as an unpredictable treatment of the movement's most popular mediums of expression. Instead, her poems serve as relevant examples of the innovative ways in which some of the most committed Black Artists may have progressively and courageously cast critical lights on the terms of the aesthetic principles in which they so fervently believed. With Amini being one of the most integral figures of OBAC and the BAM, her treatment of visual media, iconography, and performance as integral but nonetheless unreliable and complicated concepts and ideals for the marketing of nation-building concepts perhaps distinguishes her as both a participant within and critic of the movement. As Amini's poetry conveys, the principles and culture of the BAM necessitated an emphasis on collaboration and group-based ideals, but the movement was also capable of accommodating elusive expressions of desire and cultural belonging. More than forty years after the publication of *Images in Black* and *Black Essence*, the impact of visual media, iconography, and politically inspired propaganda as means of perpetuating community in transnational and global contexts is even greater and more pervasive, given advanced technologies. Yet decades earlier, Amini progressively cautioned against our immersion into such trends during one of the most aggressive, resonating, and politically inspired aesthetic campaigns in American and world history.

Chapter Four

Muddying Clear Waters: Carolyn Rodgers's Black Art

Women writers of the BAM were often susceptible to gendered critiques, and writers like Chicago poet Carolyn Rodgers received their fair share of these, particularly from their male peers. The relationship between gender and artistic production and/or performance was reinforced through such critiques, which subsequently impacted the BAM's objectives and continues to influence the ways in which readers and scholars perceive the legacy of the movement today. "As they articulated black manhood through the pen, the gun, the penis, and the microphone, male poets in the Black Arts Movement defined and reified revolutionary black male identity" (Pollard 173). Chicago Black Artist Hoyt Fuller composed the introduction to Rodgers's first published collection, *Paper Soul*, published by Third World Press in 1968, which includes language reflecting the kind of critical and gendered biases to which women artists of this period were subjected by their male peers. As Fuller was then managing editor of Johnson Publications' journal the *Black World*, his review of Rodgers's work was especially influential in her emerging career as a writer.

> Her perspective, both sharp and sweeping, encompasses the broad regions of what is and also the clear image of what might be; and her language, honed with bitterness and tipped with grace, swaggers along the brutal street and prances into the parlors: it does not know its bounds . . . Her prose is spare and angular, geared to essence, but hard only when she wills it; and always it is stamped with an elegance so effortless and deep that it seems inborn: it is like her own frame, slim and straight, and as subtly feminine as a virgin's blush . . . Carolyn Rodgers will be heard. She has the artist's gift and the artist's vision . . . (1–2)

Fuller was an integral figure in the process of developing the aesthetic of the Organization of Black American Culture (OBAC), and his gendered critique of Rodgers's literary talent as a black woman poet is not without an acknowledgment of her abilities to communicate the literary and cultural ideals that defined the BAM in Chicago and nationwide. His own language in characterizing the poet's style explicates more than the craft and technique exhibited by Rodgers, but it also suggests the degree to which her work reflects an artistic perspective that is decidedly "female" within the context of the BAM's nationalist and cultural aesthetic—one for which male writers have been overwhelmingly credited for having designed. Fuller's references to Rodgers's "slim and straight" physicality are aligned with her "sharp and sweeping" perspective, and it is the employment of gendered language in his description of Rodgers's work and in referencing her femininity that is so conspicuous here. (Incidentally, Rodgers's poem "For H. W. Fuller," which appeared in OBAC's journal *Nommo*, in turn, includes references to Fuller's masculinity as a celebrated mentor and Chicago Black Arts icon.)[1] In the study entitled *The Sexual Mountain and Black Women Writers*, Calvin Hernton critiques the overtly masculine culture of the black vernacular tradition that is useful in framing Fuller's comments during the height of the BAM:

> [T]he masculine perspective itself, concerning the manhood of the black race has always occupied center stage in the drama of Afro-American literature . . . [B]eing at once Black, American, and Female, [black women] have been victimized by the mountain of sexism, not only from the white world but from the men of the black world as well . . . There is much work to be done. The mountain must not merely be scaled, it must be destroyed. (50, 56)

In keeping with the critique of the gendered dimensions of the BAM within the history of black cultural expression in Chicago and beyond, Karen Jackson Ford writes:

> Carolyn Rodgers, a Chicago poet who first learned her trade in the Organization of Black American Culture (OBAC) Writer's Workshop meetings and Gwendolyn Brooks's Writers Workshops, was distinctive as a new black woman poet in the late 1960's, when she published her first two books for her vehement adherence to the Black Arts program. Noted for her vulgarity and other excesses, Rodgers was quickly criticized by other Black Aesthetic

practitioners for her unladylike uses of the very rhetorical excesses they had promoted. (209)

Ford's critique of Rodgers includes an assessment of the ways in which the poet was received by her male contemporaries, many of whom cited Rodgers for her supposed "vulgarity" (209). While this perception of Rodgers's work speaks to the artistic double standards that existed for male and female writers of the BAM, I want to argue beyond this rather popular reading of the movement's culture and its women writers in particular to suggest the ways in which Rodgers progressively and paradoxically expanded the terms of the BAM through her unique and experimental elucidation of the BAM's most valued features, including its emphasis on coalition-building, and the collective participation between Black Artists and their audiences in the community and nation-building project. Finally, having been one of the most prolific writers among Chicago artists of this period, as well as a cofounding member of OBAC, Rodgers explores another aspect of the movement that has largely gone understudied. Indeed, some of the most powerful pieces that appear in *Paper Soul*, for instance, implicate the degree to which the ideologies of this artistic moment of cultural expression were in flux and indeed in progress, despite the popular contention that the "fixed" parameters of the BAM's aesthetic limited writers' artistic expression. More specifically, several of Rodgers's earliest published poems reflect the visionary and ambitious impulses of a generation of artists whose aspirations to define Black Art may never have been fully realized. "[Rodgers's] work grows more beautiful and compelling as it finds its uniqueness" (Ford 214). Contrary to the notion that "[t]he Black Aesthetic figuratively trapped the black woman in the past, and barred her from participating in any new emancipatory discourse of blackness or femininity," in Rodgers's work, for instance, the BAM is framed as a vulnerable and precarious concept—one that women writers such as herself were responsible for defining as much as their male peers (Dubey 20). "To be sure, [Rodgers] was clairvoyant and uncompromising. Her poetry was colored by a young woman's contempt for injustice and a young rebel's sensitivity to the cost of freedom in a corrupt world where race takes precedence over everything else."[2] According to Kim Benston, "though in decidedly different languages and domains, we witness variants of the Black Arts Movement's defining effort to become a self-interpreting entity" (18). In addition, much of Rodgers's poetry not only calls into question the exclusive, culturally specific expectations of Black Art and OBAC initiatives, but it also resists the emergent postmodernist trends of this period as well, which, like the BAM, in many ways suppressed the agency of the black female voice. In this context, cultural theorist bell hooks's thoughts on postmodernism in relation to black culture and black cultural expression are useful:

> During the sixties, the black power movement was influenced by perspectives that could easily be labeled modernist. Certainly many of the ways black folks addressed issues of identity conformed to a modernist universalizing agenda. Despite the fact that black power ideology reflected a modernist sensibility, these elements were soon rendered irrelevant as militant protest was stifled by a powerful, repressive postmodern state. (703)

Although Rodgers's work appears just prior to the rise of postmodernism, the nascent, hegemonic aspirations of a postmodernist agenda collided with those of the BAM during the movement's waning years, and Rodgers succeeded in promoting an aesthetic that effectively undermined both Black Arts and postmodernist technologies wherein the voices of women were rendered inferior and insignificant.

Early reviews of Rodgers's first two collections of poems were mixed. For instance, poet and instructor Sarah Webster Fabio's review of *Paper Soul* (1968), published in the *Negro Digest*, reads, "Carolyn Rodgers seems to know what she is about in each poem, and she does whatever it is she sets out to do with utmost precision." Yet poet and Broadside Press founder Dudley Randall's *Black World* review of Rodgers's second collection, *Songs of a Black Bird* (1969), says that Rodgers "shows herself as a sensitive and gifted poet, with variety and richness," despite "the flaws and fripperies [that] could have been eliminated by careful revision, scrupulous editing . . . or frank comment from a friend." Furthermore, Rodgers's OBAC cofounder and contemporary, Haki Madhubuti, references the "weaknesses" of Rodgers's poetry in this second collection.[3] But despite these mixed responses to her work, I want to offer a more nuanced critique of Rodgers's first two collections of poetry in order to suggest the ways in which she was able to transcend the BAM's "universalizing" agenda as well as the intercepting "repressive" aspects of postmodernism as critiqued by bell hooks during the post–civil rights era. As Rodgers's OBAC successor, Angela Jackson, points out, Rodgers is "a choir in herself."[4] Although Rodgers's reputation and affiliation with OBAC and the BAM is documented much more frequently than that of her contemporary, Johari Amini, and selections of Rodgers's work from this period occasionally appear in anthologies referencing the BAM in the history of black cultural expression, Rodgers's work deserves a great deal more attention as material authored by a cofounding member of one of the longest-running Black Arts organizations in the nation.[5] In addition, her ability to broach the aforementioned issues relative to the development of a Black Arts aesthetic in such a way that ultimately and paradoxically expands the terms of the BAM's most popular and controversial features justifies a reassessment of the movement's otherwise restrictive reputation.

The proliferation of contemporary essays and articles outlining the criteria for Black Art of the late sixties and early seventies addressed the function of an emerging poetics for self-defined Black Artists in Chicago and beyond. Madhubuti, for example, acrimoniously criticized work that did not privilege the black community over the individual, and Larry Neal writes in his essay "The Black Arts Movement" that [the movement] is "radically opposed to any concept of the artist that alienates him from his community . . . it envisions an art that speaks directly to the needs and aspirations of black America" (2039). In this context, Rodgers's piece "Breakthrough," included in the collection *How I Got Ovah* (1976), published during the waning years of the BAM, is especially revealing, as Rodgers continues to implicate the ways in which previous Black Artists were encouraged to produce work that would conform to specific nation-building criteria.[6] "How do I put my self on paper / The way I want to be or am and be?" queries Rodgers's narrator in the poem. Essayist Angelyn Jamison argues that the piece "reflects the inner turmoil of the Black woman as artist, her movement from doubt and confusion to self-knowledge . . . [and that] Carolyn Rodgers apparently recognized the need to find her own voice" (379). Furthermore, Bettye L. Parker-Smith writes, "Carolyn Rodgers was "one of the most sensitive and complex poets" of BAM (395). In "Breakthrough," the narrator expresses a complex subjectivity as she tries to reconcile her individual desires with the collaborative objectives of her peers. In this regard, the narrative voice expresses a necessary tension between acceptable forms of (black) expression, self-definition, and individual desire, all of which implicate the challenges of putting "[her] self on paper / The way [she] want[s] to be / Not like any one else in this / Black world but me." As one of the most prolific writers of Chicago's Black Arts Movement, Rodgers herself exemplifies this implied dilemma and effectively "breaks through" the essentialist potential of Black Arts rhetoric that writers such as herself were pressured to perpetuate. Thus, Rodgers challenges the expectations to which Black Artists were expected to defer and that were so often taken for granted.

As has often been discussed in scholarship addressing the BAM, many male writers of the movement have been credited (and blamed) for having developed specific criteria for the production of Black Art.[7] In his defense of a "quality-control" approach to critiquing Black Artists, for instance, Haki Madhubuti implies that art *can*, in fact, be qualitatively measured for degrees of usefulness. His references to artistic production as ostensible labor in the nation-building project implicate the cultural utility and resourcefulness of an ideal version of Black Art—a subject that Rodgers fearlessly critiques in the poem "Aunt Dolly" ("Working Classics" 208). Often considered a postindustrial, working-class poem, "Aunt Dolly" doesn't appear in Rodgers's first collection, *Paper Soul*, yet the poem appropriates Madhubuti's expressed ideas regarding Black Art alongside a narrator whose fate as a working woman is analogous to the fates of women of the BAM who were themselves committed to the goals of a collective endeavor. The lines "Sitting there on the / assembly line piecing / together frocks all alike," reinforces the performative monotony of the narrator's work, and the massive production of clothes on the assembly line—an act feminized by the emphasis on the production of "frocks" in particular—becomes symbolic of the constant exhaustive reproduction of Black Art, as "thousands by thousands for / millions to buy, the same / cheap pattern duplicated all over the world." The space of the factory can also be interpreted as a metaphoric reference to the restricted space in which the female narrator becomes invisible as she meets the expectations and standards enforced by her working peers. Although "[s]he can sew anything you / cannot even imagine" and only becomes a "queen" after completing a full day of uninspired work, the narrator's personal and artistic needs are met only when she "goes / home at night and sews / up a storm, a dream that / nobody has 'ever' seen." Her expressed frustration about the fact that the "frocks" produced on the assembly line are "all alike" parallels the idea that there is little opportunity for individualism while working in the factory alongside others. The fact that no one has "ever" seen her work and "cannot even imagine" what the narrator is capable of creating, raises the question of whether or not she will ever be acknowledged as someone capable of producing her own, self-inspired work. In this way, the narrator's circumstances in the poem become a useful metaphoric context for thinking about the limited aesthetic mobility of women forced to compromise their desires for the good of the collective. Like many women who performed as Black Artists, the narrator is indeed productive, but tragically so, for her own self-interests must be sacrificed in the interest of collaboration. As in the piece "Breakthrough," themes of authority, control, and the insular existence of the female figure within the context of her immediate community are perceptible in "Aunt Dolly," and Rodgers's subversive critique of the concept of collaborative labor as that which is potentially oppressive is in direct contention with Black Arts practices that idealize this concept.

In the piece "To White Critics," the opening poem of Rodgers's first collection, *Paper Soul*, the concepts of labor and womanhood take on resonating metaphoric meaning as well (3). The form of the "baby" of this piece legitimizes the narrator's creativity, authority, and freedom of expression. The first lines, "my baby's face is a / short story, smooth—tight and tech / ni / cally / correct," speak to the discursive nature of the baby's body as the literal and figurative embodiment of the ideals of community, nationhood, and individuality. The narrator gives birth to a child just as she gives birth to a poem, and her baby, like her work, is a medium through which her subjectivity is transcribed. Rodgers introduces the concept of motherhood in this piece and in particular the black woman as the progenitor of life and the source of creativity that ensures the continuity of black culture. The black woman is positioned as subject, narrator, heroine, interpreter, and survivor within her community in this poem, as the narrator asserts, "my baby's tears are a three-act play, a sonnet, a novel, / a volume of poems / my baby's laugh is the point and the view." She assumes the responsibilities of being a figure of re/productivity reinforcing the relationship between creativity and humanity perpetuated by and within the bodies of black women. As the word "universality" punctuates the ending of the poem, readers are reminded of the narrator's efforts to raise the collective consciousness of the black masses. More specifically, the baby becomes the text that communicates its own agency, separate from that of the narrator/mother, as expressed in the lines "my baby's laugh is a high celebration / and / a black procreation." While I acknowledge the potential objectification of the black female body as a source of production in this poem, paradoxically, the piece also reminds audiences that Black Arts women such as Rodgers "variously pursue a syntax of enactment capable of mobilizing spectatorship as a simultaneously sensate and sense-altering body, capable at once of unruly critique and revolutionary revision" in their work (Benston 21). Thus, Rodgers's treatment of woman-identified themes in the assertion of political, psychological, and creative desire as *fundamental* rather than *threatening* to the nation-building project can be interpreted here, and such a treatment encourages a concept of Black Art that is strengthened rather than weakened or undermined by a woman-identified theme and perspective.

Conversely, in the poem "Now Ain't That Love?," Rodgers's narrator is much less confident about her worth and in particular her status in her relationship with her male partner (7). She expresses, "when I'm near him / I am skinny, dumb, knock-kneed," and in posing the question, "who would, who could understand," the narrator conveys a sense of alienation and becomes susceptible to her own criticism—invoking conflicting tones of antagonism, frustration, and pride characterized by the various appellations to which she assigns herself. Moving from a "skinny dark, knock-kneed lackey" to a "bitch" and finally a "princess," the poem is an orchestration of a range of voices that in unison articulate the narrator's constant re-creation of herself within the context of the relationship with her male partner. But what is most notable about this poem is that the narrator expresses a desire for power and authority, yet she feels conflicted because she is compelled to conform to a "feminized" version of herself in order to perpetuate her romantic fantasies. "Dopey with lust," she "know[s]" that this / whole scene is not / cool" and is overcome with self-doubt. Since language "is one of the means by which individuals claim membership in the tribe," and is also one of the ways through which individuals express their personalities, it is noteworthy that Rodgers's narrator "pant[s]" for a pat from her lover's hand and expresses that "Sometimes we be so close / I can cop his pulse / and think it's my heart . . ." In posing the final ambiguously framed question, "Now ain't that Love?" the narrator simultaneously challenges audiences' perspectives about the concept of black love configured around dynamics of power and perpetuated within a heterosexual relationship. As the theme of heterosexual black love determines and is determined by the discourse of Black Art ideals of the black family, community, and nation, Rodgers's treatment of these themes daringly foregrounds and critiques some of the most egregious social tensions between men and women, which invariably threatened the progress of the BAM.

Yet in the piece entitled "A Non Poem About Vietnam, or (Try Black)," Rodgers's narrator expresses her frustrations as a writer, and her concerns about the sacrifice of black male bodies in the Vietnam War are made clear (4). Divided into four separate sections, in the first section the narrator expresses, "I have been asked to write a poem / about Vietnam. I have been asked to label my- / self, (as if I am a brandless jar) . . ." Although Rodgers's narrator is clearly hesitant to characterize her internal thoughts about the war and "deliver an opinion," by the end of the poem she offers a purposeful, emblazoned reaction to the subject, and in particular, the war's impact on the black community. As she shares her feelings of resentment about the sacrifice of black boys who are still so young "they forget to wipe the milk from / their mouths" in America's imperialist campaign against the Third World citizens of Vietnam, her tone becomes increasingly aggressive. "These are the years that [Rodgers] whipped with the lean switch, often bringing down her wrath with stinging, sharp, and sometimes excruciating pain," writes reviewer Bettye L. Parker-Smith.[8] In attempting to respond "sensibly" and deal with the subject of black boys and men "fighting for a red / white and blue democracy," Rodgers expresses that "no black man (or negro) should fight the hunkie's war, cause everytime we kill a Vietnamese, we are widening the crack in our own asses," as she embraces her revolutionary "label."

According to scholar William Van Deburg regarding the sentiment of much of the population of black America during the Vietnam War, "Black people had no quarrel with those Vietnamese or Cambodians who simply wanted to run their countries without foreign intervention" (100). The message of this poem confirms Rodgers's allegiance to BAM and Black Power nationalist goals of this time. As Black Panther activist Eldridge Cleaver states, "The black man's interest lies in seeing a free and independent Vietnam, a strong Vietnam which is not a puppet of international white supremacy. If the nations of Asia, Latin America, and Africa are strong and free, the black man in America will be safe and secure and free to live in dignity and self-respect" (515). Furthermore, the first-person narrative voice in this piece invokes a "hear me talking to you" mode of black speech common in the folk tale and sermon traditions of black culture. The idea of orality and testimony as profoundly more discursive and functional mediums over the written word is ironic, given the poet's textual achievements, and such irony is further reinforced as Rodgers's narrator conveys her inability to "record on paper anything that is waterless / or sane" on the subject of black men's involvement in the Vietnam War. As she tries to "separate the answers from [her] feelings and tears," the narrator's feelings eventually manifest in the form of a written response.

In expressing her political opinion, Rodgers's employment of a female narrator undermines the presumption that such political topics were off-limits to women, and as a poet, Rodgers disrupts the discourse that preserves concepts of black manhood as she becomes the protective figure and/or voice that takes responsibility for translating the sentiments of the black masses. According to Mance, ". . . African American women poets first entered the discourse of resistant Black manhood and . . . utilized its most revered images, initially to establish a role for Black womanhood within the patriarchal landscape of nationalism, but eventually, in order to critique and transcend it" (96). Indeed, Mance makes a valid point that is applicable to my reading of Rodgers's female narrator as the epitome of the quintessential Black Artist in this piece; yet I want to push it further by suggesting that women writers like Rodgers did more than "utilize" images and/or the language of masculinity to convey their messages. Instead, I want to suggest that such women established their presence by claiming *equal* authority to that of men in their ability to address matters of social and cultural concern to and in the interest of the entire black community. Furthermore, Rodgers transcended the restrictions of gender for the purpose of perpetuating a more inclusive, progressively gender-neutral version of Black Art as well as the role of the Black Artist, which perhaps her male contemporaries were resistant to doing. "Through her poetry, Carolyn Rodgers brings to the reader the breadth and depth of her complex vision. In her work, she captures the rage of the black community, poignantly expresses the vulnerability of the lonely, and articulates the emotional dilemma of the woman—especially the black woman . . ." (567).

Rodgers's artistic, theoretical, and political contribution to BAM principles is clearly conveyed in her essay "Black Poetry—Where It's At," first published in OBAC's journal, *Nommo*, and later in the *Negro Digest* in 1969. In the piece, she identifies a paradigm for producing Black Arts poetry, noting specific stylistic and rhetorical strategies for doing so.

> I have attempted to place all Black poetry in several broad categories, all of which have variations on the main form. Very few poems are all one type or another. It is possible and probable that a poem will be three or four different types of poetry at one time. (7)

Even as she sets forth criteria for black poetry as Black Art as follows, Rodgers's categories are much more forgiving than what readers might otherwise expect of a Black Artist, as her criteria allow space for experimentation, interpretation, and artistic freedom on the part of the Black Artist in the production of nation-building art:

1. signifying
   a. open
   b. sly
   c. with or about

2. teachin/rappin

3. coversoff
    a. rundown
    b. hipto
    c. digup
    d. coatpull

4. spaced (spiritual)
    a. mindblower (fantasy)
    b. coolout

5. bein (self/reflective)
    a. upinself
    b. uptight
    c. dealin/swingin

6. love
    a. skin
    b. space (spiritual)
    c. cosmic (ancestral)

7. shoutin (angry/cathartic)
    a. badmouth
    b. facetoface (warning/confrontation)
    c. two faced (irony)

8. jazz
    a. riffin
    b. cosmic ('Trane)
    c. grounded (Lewis)

9. du-wah
    a. dittybop
    b. bebop

10. pyramid (getting us together/building/nationhood) (7–8)

Rodgers's conceptualization of Black Art incorporates technical, thematic, and contextual references, all of which were subject to the appropriation of individual poets. For instance, she advocates independent creativity *as well as* nation-building tropes, and "teachin" as well as "signifying." She also references John Coltrane and Joe Lewis as two disparate though equally iconic figures whose images are meant to inspire black empowerment. Each category within this paradigm plays a unique role within the structural framework that characterizes the vernacular and ideological conceptualizing of Black Art. For example, the insertion of the category "bein (self/reflective)" in the center of the list implicates the centrality of the Black Artist. Thus, each category is essentially organized around and inspired by the agency of the individual, and it is this agency that ultimately substantiates the aesthetic variations rather than restrictions of Black Art. The category "love," including skin, space (spiritual), and cosmic (ancestral), suggests the fluid continuity between physical and psychological planes of existence configured around both concrete and abstract concepts of intimacy. Ultimately, the last element—the "pyramid"—is the foundation upon which the objectives of black poetry as a nation-building concept encourage a unified concept of the black community and nation.

Because the artistic praxis of the period relied upon audience response and participation, it is noteworthy that implicit within each of the categories in Rodgers's characterization of "Black Poetry" is the idea that language should in some way solicit the audience's interpretation of, reaction to, and interaction with the work itself. Although it is apparent that the categories are composed of hybrid forms of standard English and popular vernacular, I agree with Gunther Lenz's assessment that "Rodgers refrains from grounding her categories in the essentialism of the Black experience, referring, instead, to the black tradition and current black speech rituals and cultural practices in urban Black America" (208). Thus, Rodgers's criteria for poetry is politically solvent as well as self-defining, self-indulgent, and self-motivating in its appeal toward a fluid, creative approach to Black Art that would serve nation-building objectives. Ultimately, in developing this list, Rodgers constructs criteria for Black Art that rely upon artists' independent interpretation of a poetic ideology and/or poetic strategies that were in many ways more accommodating to nation-building goals and individual artistic expression than those that were most often generated by her male contemporaries. She cautions audiences that "all Black poets don't write the same KIND of poetry . . . all Black poems ain't the same kind. They differ" (7). Her interpretation of Black Art effectively mitigates the essentialist standards by which the BAM continues to be judged, and Rodgers's proclivity to resist such standards represents a dissent from popular ideals expressed by many of her (male) peers. As an inspired female voice of the BAM and a leading figure of Chicago's Black

Arts culture through her participation in OBAC, Rodgers has a perspective that is especially significant in its critique of the manner in which Black Art was fomented as well as the extent to which it encouraged an aesthetic that would be amenable to a culturally inclusive and artistically malleable nation-building paradigm.

Several poems included in Rodgers's second collection, *Songs of a Black Bird* (1969) can be more adequately categorized as vignettes or stories when considering the extent to which the poet develops characters, incorporates dialogue, and foregrounds context in constructing meaning. As expressed in the foreword to the collection, Rodgers dedicates this work to "Love," "Truth," "Organization," "Discipline," and "Liberation." As I discuss, female narrators maintain central roles in much of the material in the *Songs* collection, just as they did in *Paper Soul*, and once again, readers encounter voices that speak clearly to yet are critical of BAM principles.

In the piece "Jesus Was Crucified" for example, a verbal exchange between a mother and daughter underscores the conceptualization of black nationalism, and the comparatively unique viewpoints between the two figures reflect the contrasting idealisms of their respective generations (9). Of her mother, the narrator/daughter expresses that "she wanted tuh tell / me . . . that I shud pray or / have her (hunky) preacher / pray for me." Without the presence of a male voice, the conversation between the mother and daughter exposes their competing ideologies regarding black consciousness and black liberation, and their relationship empowers both of them to express their divergent political ideas without the influence or intervention of a male presence. About her mother, the narrator reveals, "she sd if she had evah known educashun / woulda mad me crazi, she woulda neva sent me to / school (college that is)," speaking of her mother's frustrations about her newly developed revolutionary consciousness. In turn, as the mother's character objects to the black nationalist ideals that her daughter reveres, their dissenting voices inspire mutual tones of antagonism throughout the piece. Furthermore, the mother is conscious of the fact that her daughter does not respect her own presumed allegiance to the "white man's factori," where she has "worked [her] fingers to the bone" to make her [daughter] a "de-cent somebodi"—an image reminiscent of that which appears in the previously discussed factory poem, "Aunt Dolly." The discord between the mother and daughter is further exacerbated by the mother's assertion that Communist "NegroES" are particularly threatening, and meanwhile, the daughter objects to her mother's old-fashioned, assimilationist views. Still, the poem "Jesus Was Crucified" undermines the male-dominated rhetoric that so heavily defined the culture of the BAM, and which dictated that the authoritative context in which the expression of its principles could most effectively be conveyed was that which was legitimized by male voices. Instead, Rodgers constructs an exchange in which the voices of women are privileged in a productive yet intimate political debate that retains personal meaning for both female characters.

Regarding black women writers of this era, Acklyn Lynch suggests, "In a real sense, women are talking to each other about personal matters that at first glance seem to have an apolitical tone. Yet, fundamentally their concerns challenge American society in general and male domination in particular... Self-assertion in the Black woman led to antagonisms within the family unit as well as in the larger society" (47–48). In this way, Rodgers's poem contradicts the presumption that women are less capable of initiating and/or articulating the political ideals or values of nationalism within their communities. Furthermore, not only do the voices of the mother and daughter figures in the poem elucidate their divergent, generational perspectives and characterize the controversies between those who supported and opposed BAM and Black Power objectives, but they also convey the characters' personal investments in their respective ideals as they allow one another to "agree to disagree" without severing their family ties. Thus, their dissention paradoxically informs a *loving* rather than a *polarizing* relationship. As each of the characters expresses that they hope they don't have to "straighten the truth out no mo" at the end of the poem, such a conclusion can be interpreted as a fictional treatment of the "real life" tensions that existed between Black Artists and their critics, as well as a plea for both groups to salvage their ideological tensions. As scholar Michelle Nzadi Kieta argues, female artists of Rodgers's era had to be "willing to breathe empowerment into muffled voices if they were to change the landscape of American culture and indeed politics and aesthetics" (279). Although the voices of Rodgers's characters in "Jesus Was Crucified" can hardly be interpreted as "muffled," as Kieta suggests, the poem does indeed allude to the mutually informative themes of collaboration and discord through the voices representing the perspectives of women, which often went unheard in the discourse of nationalism.

The poem "It Is Deep" reads like a continuation of the themes represented in "Jesus Was Crucified," and with a prefatory comment that reads "(don't never forget the bridge that you crossed over on)," the aforementioned tensions between the mother and daughter characters of the latter piece are reconciled in this follow-up poem (12). The narrator/daughter in "It Is Deep" struggles to connect with her mother because of her unwillingness to accept her own values and political beliefs. "She did not / recognize the poster of the / Grand le-roi (al) cat on the wall," the daughter expresses in frustration, referring to an image of Amiri Baraka that decorates her room. Although she expresses frustration about the fact that her mother resents her talking about "Black anything / other than something ugly to kill it befo it grows," by the end of the piece, the narrator/daughter acknowledges that she too has been equally judgmental of her mother's opposing perspectives. "The speaker disagrees with her mother's worldview: that there is a God, that some white people are good, that all revolutionaries are Communists, and that her daughter shouldn't curse in public" (Ford 211). Yet despite the tension between the characters, the narrator begins to appreciate and understand that her mother's struggle for liberation and self-sacrifice have all been for *her* benefit. "My mother . . . is very obviously / a sturdy Black bridge that I / crossed over, on," the narrator/daughter expresses. It is not until the daughter opens herself up to comprehend the pain of her mother's disillusionment, despair, and unfulfilled promises of the "American Dream" that she realizes that her own set of values exists within a continuum of an already-established tradition of black liberation struggles. The title of the poem, "It Is Deep," "resonates with the sixties' sense of 'deep' as something complicated and ponderous: the speaker can't fathom religious belief" (Ford 211).

In addition, it is not until the narrator/daughter comes to terms with this reality and changes her mind about what she'd once perceived as her mother's assimilationist views that she begins to understand herself. So invested in the immediacy of her own generation's rhetoric of empowerment is she that she doesn't stop to think about the seeds of liberation planted by her mother, which blossom in the form of her own existence—the "gardens" that are reminiscent of those referenced by writer Alice Walker in her discussion of her own awakening to the history of black women's struggles manifested in creative and political expression. "This ability to hold on, even in very simple ways," Walker writes, ". . . is work black women have done for a very long time" (2436). As the mother figure in Rodgers's poem "push[es]" the daughter "into [her] kitchen so / she could open [her] refrigerator to see / what [she] had to eat," she is literally pushing her way into her daughter's consciousness, reminding her that no matter what their differences, she will always hold herself accountable for her child. Both characters begin to comprehend the ways in which their histories and fates are connected even if they don't share the same political ideas. In constructing a narrative in which both women are capable of finding meaning in their differences, despite their mutually contentious ideals, it is through the voices of such women that Rodgers clarifies the urgent need for open, nonjudgmental and continued communication within black communities in the collective struggle for social, political, and economic liberation. In addition, as conjoined narratives, "Jesus Was Crucified" and "It Is Deep" represent poems of the black vernacular, sermonic tradition. "African American poets within that mode explore the historical experiences of their people, illuminating the past and giving political, social, and moral significance to everyday events" (Brown 48). Thus, both pieces allude to the process of and paradigm for achieving nation-building goals in the black community as those that are amenable to potentially discordant female voices that, in unison, promote enlightenment, respect, and empathy in the otherwise politically polarizing climate of the BAM era.

The poem entitled "The Sound of Music" reflects Rodgers's continued focus on the ways in which the construction of BAM ideals can be strengthened by and through competing political perspectives (21). Interrupted by the words of the characters in the street, the narrator as "artist" or "intellectual" is "sittin near [her] window" when she "suddenly hear[s] thunder rollin / Up from the streets, below," which forces her to acknowledge the presence of the street characters as she attempts to write. The immediacy of the words spoken between the characters in the street below undermine (and indeed mock) the narrator/writer's efforts to produce words on paper, and in this way, her productivity and authority as a writer are compromised. Reminiscent of the previously discussed narrator's challenge to produce written words of sanity in response to the Vietnam War's impact on the lives of black men, the continued perpetuation of the writing practice in this piece, as a frustrated, counterproductive, and pointless one becomes a recurring theme in Rodgers's work. This treatment ironically goes counter to the poet's own established criteria outlined in the aforementioned piece "Black Poetry—Where It's At," wherein Rodgers privileges rather than undermines the creativity and voice of the Black Artist as writer. As the narrator in "The Sound of Music" hears the words spoken between the characters on the street below, she is represented as a rather disengaged figure, who is ironically unable to produce words.

Conversely, a fluid and productive exchange takes place in the dialogue between the arguing street characters below the narrator's window. In this way, paradoxically, the authority in the poem ultimately belongs to the voices of the *latter* figures, who actively debate the meaning of the concept of a "Black Nationalist," as opposed to the narrator/writer who only sits passively at the typewriter. "Who you tryin' to fool?" demands the first speaker in the street to the second speaker. "You ain't no goddamn nationalist!" the first character continues to proclaim, accusing the second speaker of being a "sell-out" because of the fact that he's sleeping with a "wite" woman, after which the second speaker weakly tries to defend himself. The first character finalizes the discussion by expressing, "You can't explain shit to me, / you ain't no Black Nationalist, / muthafucker." The fact that the voice of the narrator/writer in the window above is never heard, and that, furthermore, the final commentary in the poem is expressed by the characters in the street is significant here, as it speaks to the way in which Rodgers yet again compromises the authoritative integrity of the narrator/writer and/or the legitimacy and import of the writing practice. The typewriter itself, as well as the blank sheets of paper, can be read as symbolic of the writer's unrealized potential—whereas she can only ponder words to type onto the blank page, the speakers in the street below are productive in their exchange, despite their disagreements. Scholar Kim Whitehead's concept of integrated intertextuality—as an "impulse toward community," characterized throughout the exchange between the speakers in the street and set against the backdrop of the writer's "silence" above—is useful here, since the poem perpetuates an interactive community that reinforces the kinship between the street characters. Furthermore, their conversation intimates that the conceptualization of "Black Nationalism" is that which should be mitigated through discussion and/or dialogue rather than be flatly documented or intellectualized on paper by a narrator/writer who sits at a typewriter and contemplates such ideas from her "high" place of privilege in the window (45).

In addition, the placement of the writer in the window in "The Sound of Music"—away from the characters below—is suggestive of the ways in which she is *removed* from the realities of the characters who productively engage in their debate in the street. "Significant numbers of BAM critics and artists, including key theorists and writers, saw the situated, communitarian, and traditionalist implications of the spoken word as the best way to articulate a critical philosophy anchored in everyday activism . . . and a commitment to folk and popular culture," writes BAM scholar Mike Sell. "The focus on vocality gave the movement as a whole a decidedly performative emphasis . . ." ("The Voice" 279). In this context, the street scene in "The Sound of Music" represents the stage on which the street characters perform and explicate the ideological demands of black nationalism. While the writer in the window remains a passive observer to the "drama" of the street speakers, her alienation is further inscribed by her "sittin near [her] window" feeling the "Cool, clear summer evening" in an unsuccessful attempt to conform to the presumed image of an activist artist at work. Rodgers's characterization of the narrator/writer as a paralyzed and/or unproductive figure compared to the street characters goes counter to the idea that writers and/or intellectuals could or should be expected to set the terms of black nationalism, despite the fact that BAM writers assumed the responsibility for doing so. In the words of Haki Madhubuti, "The poets of the Sixties and Seventies move beyond mere rage and 'black is beautiful' to bring together a new set of values, emotions, historical perspectives and futuristic direction—a transformation from the lifestyle of the *sayer* to that of the *doer*" (*Dynamite* 22, emphasis his). However, it is the voices of the speakers in the *street* rather than the writer in the window, which maintain active authority and undermine the otherwise ideal function of the black writer as an "active" revolutionary figure.

Regardless of its medium, Black Art was often evaluated on the basis of whether or not it reflected a particularized black experience that would engender a nationalist ideology. The topic of romantic love, for example, was typically not considered relevant to and was in fact trivialized within the dominant rhetoric of black nationalism. Yet as discussed in chapter one of this project, poets like Sonia Sanchez and Nikki Giovanni expressed that love was just as much a signifier of revolution as any other subject . . . that love *was* revolution.[9] Consistent with this idea, Rodgers's poem "Love—The Beginning and the End" engages the subject of romantic love between black men and women as a mutually empowering one in which both figures inform the nation-building aesthetic (38). The first lines read, "the first aspect is love / is the Black Man and the Black Woman / Intragether," leaving no question as to the heterosexual framing of the characters in this piece; nor is there any doubt that the objectification of the black woman's body that "open[s]" up to the "Black Man" to "bare [her] softest fear" and "[her] nakedest secret" perpetuates the black family/nation-building project. As the "Black Man / move[es] into a Woman . . . rush[es] into her / scatter[s] [his] seeds, plant[s] his dreams" in "Love—The Beginning and the End," the black woman once again becomes the embodiment of life, just as she does in the previously discussed poem "To White Critics." Furthermore, there is a semantic disparity between the final terms "WOMAN" and "BLACKMAN," where respectively, the words convey a rather generalized reference to the woman's racial status, where the male's subjectivity is explicitly racialized. In addition, the structural and linguistic interception of the terms on the page, represented in the following way near the end of the poem, encourages a visible, phallic, hetero/sexual, and ideological relationship between the BlackMan and Woman:

Muddying Clear Waters: Carolyn Rodgers's Black Art 113

<pre>
         W
         O
BLACKMAN
         A
         N
</pre>

Even as the narrator calls for the black woman to "open open / your self, open & bare your / softest fear, your nakedest secret," she calls for *him* to "open" *himself* as well toward the end of the piece, since, as the narrator suggests, "we have not yet learned to / hear, each other's inner voices . . ." The poem also conveys that the promise and potential of a collective, unified black community is contingent upon each character's ability to imagine this sexually equal ideal. As the narrator encourages black men and women to "open open open" up to "[their] eternity," Rodgers's poem implies that both men and women are *equally* essential to an immediate nation-building program for the benefit of future generations, and they are therefore equally responsible for its perpetuation. This idea is punctuated in the last lines of the poem, which read "the last aspect is *Love is Revolution*" (emphasis mine). As Rodgers implicates that both men and women are participatory agents in the designing of a nation-building project, the poem becomes a plea for a gender-neutral, socially inclusive paradigm for realizing the concept of black nationhood that belies the more popular notion that Black Arts goals should be determined exclusively or predominantly by men, and the reference to a shared fate for men and women takes on spiritual and social connotations that can only be assured through the collaborative and mutually informative efforts of both.

Rodgers's poem "Once" yields a quite different approach in characterizing the nation-building potential of the relationships between black men and women, as it conveys that the promise and potential of a unified black community depend upon the willingness and desire of each participant to imagine a spiritual existence *outside* of their immediate realities (17). "[T]hey'll say we was / only / sleepin round wid each otha," expresses the narrator to her male ex-lover. The dissolved relationship between the narrator and her "fast rappin revolutionist" partner subjects both of them to denigration, ostracism, and exclusion from their community, and there is a sense of foreshadowing here, as the narrator considers the consequences of a failed relationship. "[S]ome uh them'll whisphuh / . . . call me uh / simple Black woman who / ain't got her game together," she continues. The implication that these two characters will no longer be able to participate in the nation-building project as a result of their breakup reinforces the idea that black men and women were expected to conform to the social expectations of their community in a mutually cooperative way—free of hierarchy or subjugation. "[S]ome uh them'll smirk at you / and point you out," she warns her ex-lover, and although the two of them together were once "beautiful," the fate of the narrator is certain and imminent as she prepares herself for the criticism that she and her partner will invariably receive because of their separation. While her ability to maintain her relationship or "keep her man" assures her of an ideal status as a black woman capable of satisfying and supporting her mate, her male partner will *also* be subjected to skepticism by the community because of his failure to remain committed to *her*. Again, we find Rodgers's characterization of ideal "black love" as that which is distinctly heterosexual; however, what is more striking is the idea that *both* the male and female characters will be outcast by their communities and perceived as people who "ain't got [their] game together." Thus, both of their revolutionary intentions will be called into question, and they are only "beautiful" and legitimate as a couple with the potential to perpetuate the black family and nation as a means of ensuring the political and cultural empowerment of the black community. Once again, in her characterization of romantic black love in this piece, Rodgers intimates that she is looking beyond the gendered priorities of the BAM and ahead to the future, while remaining conscious of the consequences of a fractured black community and/or ruptured kinships between black men and women.

Unlike many of their male contemporaries of the BAM, women writers like Carolyn Rodgers did not pretend to have all of the answers to the questions of identity formation, nation-building, or the role of the Black Artist in pursuing liberation goals for black communities and oppressed cultures worldwide. Although "the Black Aesthetic figuratively trapped the black woman in the past, and barred her from participating in any new emancipatory discourse of blackness or femininity," as Dubey rightly observes, this did not distract writers like Rodgers from confronting the issue of gender politics in order to selflessly perpetuate the progressive potential of Black Art as a socially inclusive and aesthetically amenable concept and as a resource of empowerment for black audiences seeking social and political redemption in liberation struggles (20). This may, at least in part, explain why much of Rodgers's earliest poetry, and that of her contemporaries, Amini and Jackson, implicates the elusiveness of Black Art. Although much of the work generated by her peers perpetuated paradigmatic methods for representing black culture and/or Black Arts ideals in the nation-building project, Rodgers's work expands such terms and exposes the precarious nature of politically inspired art and the role of the Black Artist in its conceptualization. In many of her poems, the characters can only aspire to but never fully realize the social and political expectations of their communities. As one of the most committed writers of the BAM in both local and national contexts, Rodgers paradoxically challenges the notion that the ideals of Black Art could be enforced without calling into question their import or the role of the Black Artist in advancing them. More specifically, as a leading figure of Chicago's BAM and a cofounding member of OBAC, Rodgers has a perspective that productively and effectively competes with those of her male peers as she takes on the gendered norms of the period and moves forward to critique other compelling though complicated aspects of Black Art for the purpose of community empowerment. In so doing, her strategies confirm the movement's complexity and encourage readers to take note of the diverse ways in which some of the BAM's most productive though lesser-known voices promoted an aesthetic that could be expanded upon and made amenable to the needs and interests of future audiences pursuing coalition-building and liberation projects without compromising individuality and/or independence of vision in order to do so.

Chapter Five

Building a Home, Building a Nation: Family in the City and Beyond in Angela Jackson's Black Art

If much of the work of Black Artists of the late sixties and early seventies conveyed their collective aspirations to pursue methods of achieving social, political, and cultural empowerment for black communities of the African Diaspora, then Angela Jackson's "a beginning for new beginnings," published in her first collection of poetry, *VooDoo/Love Magic* (1975), suggests that black communities were still "wading. waiting" for such aspirations to be realized. As the narrator of this poem expresses, "the Fight is in the living thru." Like her OBAC predecessors Johari Amini and Carolyn Rodgers, Jackson demonstrates in her work an unyielding commitment to the nation-building goals that defined the solvency of the BAM even as she expands the aesthetic terms of the movement. In addition, many of the poems in *VooDoo/Love Magic* draw from the ideals of Pan-Africanism as means of achieving black nation-building goals. As Ajuan Mance argues:

> By the mid-1970's the era of the Black Arts Movement had passed, ushered into obsolescence by the dramatic cultural and political shifts that marked the transition of the United States away from the volatile social upheaval of the 1960's and into the increasingly tolerant social climate of the late twentieth century. The next twenty-five years saw the emergence of unprecedented numbers of African American women poets writing the Black female subject into poems whose topics and themes (such as racism, political activism, and socioeconomic equality) would have, in earlier decades, precluded the mention of any black subjects who were not male. (121–122)

In tandem with the changing social, political, and ideological climate of the mid-to-late seventies and during the waning years of the BAM, the

Chicago-based, black-owned publishing company Johnson Publications devoted an entire issue of the *Black World* to an exclusive discussion about the state and/or legitimacy of Black Art for new audiences. In it, an impressive list of acclaimed scholars, writers, and artists generously offered their predictions and perspectives about the status of the BAM then and moving forward.[1] It was during this period that Jackson's first two collections of poetry, *VooDoo/Love Magic* (1974) and *The Greenville Club* (1977) were published. Thus, her work provides an opportunity to assess the impact of the goals and imperatives of the movement's aesthetic in later years. "Jackson's strange, penetrating visions range from the apocalyptic to the everyday, from the heaviness of injustice to the lightness of being carried away by love" (Guzman 248). More specifically, Jackson's work reflects a reinvention of BAM aesthetics that continued to influence her work into the new postrace era, during which she continued to develop as a writer invested in the ideals of Pan-Africanism. She had a personal and artistic kinship with her female OBAC predecessors Amini and Rodgers, and, taken together, the work of all three women speaks to the BAM's culturally and aesthetically diverse legacy beyond that for which the movement is often credited. As a means for establishing Jackson's narrative perspective as a black woman artist who engages readers in the collective and subversively political act of reminiscing, many of the poems found in *VooDoo/Love Magic* and *The Greenville Club* engage the concept of memory as part of a culturally expressive, nation-building resource in perpetuating Black Arts goals.

Unlike many of their contemporary white female artists, activists, and intellectuals, who cultivated (white) feminist ideologies and agendas during these eras, Jackson, Amini, and Rodgers not only invested themselves in the liberation struggles of black women, but their work reflects their mutual interests in perpetuating a BAM aesthetic that was socially inclusive and amenable to various perspectives and experiences defining black life, regardless of sex and gender disparities. According to Kim Whitehead:

> In the "heyday" of the women's movement (1972–1982), when feminist organizing fairly exploded and even moved into the mainstream, feminist poetry played a central role in the radical, socialist, and lesbian feminist sectors that flourished outside the dominant culture. In this context, feminists wanted a poetry in which they could name the experiences that societal and poetic taboos had previously kept them from expressing, in which they could make the hidden known. As a result, they turned to more open poetic modes, seeking to strip language and form of excess flourish and meaning to make it accessible to ordinary women. (xix)

Whitehead's description of "feminist poetry" could very well be applied to the poetry that Jackson, Amini, and Rodgers produced during this period, since their work was intended to uplift "the people" of the African Diaspora even as it responded to the experiences and interests of black women in particular. Thus, their work reveals that they were invested in producing art that accommodated cultural diversity as a way of sustaining the integrity of a progressive nation-building ideal (37). As further noted by Johnetta Cole:

> Black feminists were especially insightful about the connections between race and gender and how differences between women made it difficult for them to bond on the basis of their common womanhood. Even more scarce are the voices of Native American, Chicana/Latina, Asian American and Arab American women in these narratives. Ignoring or devaluing the unique and often oppositional perspectives of women of color during the Movement, it is not surprising that mainstream feminists would "white-out," marginalize, or even forget these contributions in reconstructions of "their" Movement some years later. (3–4)

Although Jackson, Amini, and Rodgers never proclaimed themselves to be "feminists," certainly Cole's impression of the political agenda of black feminists and women of color as artists, activists, and intellectuals who were often excluded from white feminist projects potentially made more urgent the efforts of Black Arts women to collectively construct a gender-neutral and socially inclusive, politically inspired paradigm for black nation-building that would be distinguishable from and indeed run counter to the agendas of their white feminist contemporaries.

It is within these contexts that Jackson's *VooDoo/Love Magic* presents an opportunity to critique the potential of writing as a performative and functional tool in the perpetuation of a collaborative culture amongst Black Artists. As K. Anthony Appiah recognizes, the perpetuation of cultural solidarity relies upon popular assumptions about race, social practices, and norms that will ultimately function to preserve this ideal.[2] This argument provides a useful framework for examining Jackson's *VooDoo/Love Magic*, since the collection relies upon popular ideals of race, culture, and the theme of "blackness" or black cultural identity as epistemic concepts. Many of the poems included in Jackson's first collection foreground "memory" as a cultural medium capable of advancing the concepts of black consciousness and nationhood that continue to be relevant to Pan-Africanist and black nation-building projects today. In the words of Black Power intellectual Mercer Cook, "Our turn to Africa should, hopefully, be for the richness of its culture, an awareness of which can enable us to smooth out the rough spots of what we have stubbornly held onto." Although, as scholars Sidney J. Lemelle and Robin D. G. Kelly suggest, "even the most inchoate sense of solidarity among Black peoples in the New World, Europe and Africa is contingent, constantly shifting, and socially constructed" (Cook 188; Lemelle and Kelly 7). Furthermore, Maryse Conde's essay entitled "Pan-Africanism, Feminism and Culture" clarifies the strategies that black women artists continue to rely upon in expressing the complexities of their subjectivities as they advocated an inclusive, pluralistic, Afrocentric nation-building aesthetic.

> I believe it will be the role of future writers, male and female, to turn the minds of the people towards the other world and to make them understand that there is a need for unity, diversity and Pan-Africanism. If we are not allowed to be diverse and different, we cannot be united . . . So Pan-Africanism is not that far off; what we are witnessing now are the beginnings, the birth of a new stage of Pan-Africanism. (63, 65)

In fact, more than a decade prior to the publication of this essay, Angela Jackson had already created poetry that responded to Conde's call. In Jackson's own words, "[P]opular culture and its touchstones are where day-to-day memory is posited and reposited. As a poet, I live in popular and 'high' culture and all that lives above and between . . . I subvert popular culture and pose moral and ethical questions that arise out of my conflict with popular culture's stereotypes and communal symbols and myths" (qtd. in Traylor, "Black Women" 55). Accordingly, as Tunde Adeleke expresses:

> Affirmation of African identity derives logically from [an] Afrocentric consciousness. Africa becomes the basis of self-knowledge and identity, the quintessence of one's being. This Afrocentric consciousness, and concomitant identity formation, has increasingly gained popularity among black Americans . . . Afrocentric consciousness, and the African identity that it advances, are constituents of a very strong ideological and combative movement that has both intellectual and popular dimensions. (134–135)

Thus, today "Afrocentricity" continues to be a resourceful ideology for black artists, activists, and intellectuals. Yet in her Black Arts poem "a beginning for new beginnings," Jackson expresses and anticipates the foundations of the "birth of the new stage of Pan-Africanism" that Conde and others would promote in later years. As the title of the poem suggests, "beginnings" are about renewal and reinvention, and the potential of tomorrow lies in the ability to start again. As we see in the poem, Jackson's narrator assures audiences that "some where distantly / there is an answer" perhaps to the pending question of how to conceptualize and promote the black nation ideal in the form of a socially inclusive and culturally amenable aesthetic. Jackson's narrator insists that the "answer" to this question is not only imaginable but indeed palpable—one that s/he can "feel and be felt in." More importantly, the narrator envisions a specific future for black America and suggests that an ideal existence is not only possible but imminent and certain . . . "there is a Morning. / the rise of an Other Day." Yet even as the narrator inspires her audience to consider and believe in the plausibility of such a future, suggesting that in fact "the rise of an Other Day" is imminent, she also intimates that the likelihood that this future will be realized is ultimately dependent upon the collaborative participation of people representing various black cultural communities. This is a recurring theme conveyed in many of the poems in *VooDoo/Love Magic*, and Jackson's use of "memory"—both recent/contemporary and ancestral/historical—inspires audiences to participate in the realization of a shared fate. In this way, "memory" functions not simply as a way of recalling past experiences—both imagined and "real"—but it renders such experiences accessible and motivating in the preservation of community. For example, the narrator in "beginnings" emphasizes the need for a shared commitment among people of African descent to achieve cultural autonomy and empowerment, as expressed in the words ". . . children, together (u, me, she, and us, and him. / together. Children. / we learn How / to swim." As demonstrated in several other poems in *VooDoo/Love Magic*, a collective black cultural consciousness is realized through the medium of memory, which reflects an ancestral, mythic past that perpetuates a culturally inclusive connectivity amongst Jackson's readers. The writer's employment of history—ancestral and recent—as an aesthetic trope demonstrates the functionality of this concept as a resource in sustaining BAM and OBAC poetics. In this way, Jackson anticipates the theoretical conventions of inclusivity and collaboration that are presently relevant to Pan-Africanist thought and black nation-building objectives today.

The significance of the concept of "cultural memory" that informs postmodern movements such as the civil rights movement and Black Arts Movement was the topic of interest at a seminar facilitated by scholar Valerie Smith in 2002.[3] More specifically, concepts of race and gender were discussed as cultural constructs having necessary and profound impacts on the perpetuation of memory as a discursive ideal relevant to nation-building goals during these eras. In her reflective essay "Black Nationalism: The Sixties and the Nineties," activist Angela Davis provides further insight about the psychological and social power of memory in her own self-actualization process as she became increasingly influenced by black nationalism.

> I remember the moment when I first felt the stirrings of "nationalism" in my—as I might have articulated it then—"Negro Soul." The prise de conscience occurred during a lecture delivered by Malcolm X at Brandeis University ... But I recall that I felt extremely good—I could even say I experienced that joy Cornel West talked about—momentarily surrounded by, feeling nurtured and caressed by Black people, who, as I recall, seemed to have no particular identity other than that they were Black ... The invitation to join an empowering, but abstract community of Black people—this naïve nationalist consciousness—was extended to me in a virtually all white setting ... (317–319)

Davis's ability to reconstruct the circumstances that led to her commitment to her "community" and "nation," as well as her recognition of the symbolic relevance of this personal moment, informs my evaluation of the "black community" ideal in the development of a nationalist aesthetic during the BAM period—an ideal from which Jackson seemed to have drawn inspiration as a writer. More significantly, Davis begins to experience the psychological power and influence of her racial community as a result of a collective cathartic experience, and her ability to connect with and feel strengthened by "the community of [her] birth" can be attributed to her "memory" of a cultural, ancestral past that bounds together the histories and narratives of the collective though varied dimensions of the African Diasporic experience.

Similarly, Jackson's own invocation of the concept of "memory" in her *VooDoo/Love Magic* poems can also be understood as a strategy for restoring or reconstructing the collective "black community" ideal upon which the previously developed Black Arts and OBAC aesthetics found political potential.[4] Composed of a series of vignettes that characterize and validate the black community construct, the collection is consistent in its treatment of the collaboration ideal reinforced through cultural memory for the purpose of realizing a culturally inclusive, African Diasporic black nationalist project. The fact that Jackson's work identifies the context of an African past as essential in achieving cultural awareness amongst contemporary black audiences is noteworthy, as such a treatment implies a particular political and artistic approach that demonstrates the poet's investment in Pan-Africanism as a popular and accessible aesthetic for the purpose of engaging new audiences. But as was characteristic of writing produced by Black Artists in general and OBAC members in particular, black culture and community ideals were perpetuated as part of a contemporary and socially immediate aesthetic that encouraged audiences to mutually invest themselves in the collective goal of achieving black empowerment at that time and moving forward. Thus, Jackson's construction of a black community ideal—as an effective hybrid concept that privileges both a contemporary *and* an ancestral collective consciousness—paradoxically serves the purpose of adhering to popular Black Arts ideals while anticipating later trends in Pan-Africanism.

In her critique of the "black community" concept, scholar Patricia Hill Collins outlines the potential purpose and meaning behind a reconstruction of an African ancestral past that is applicable to my reading of Jackson's work:

> Based on the premise that Black people make up a cultural nation, Black cultural nationalism aims to reconstruct Black consciousness by replacing prevailing ideas about race with analyses that place the interests and needs of African people at the center of any discussion. For African-Americans, reclaiming Black culture involves identifying dimensions of an "authentic" Black culture that distinguish it from European-derived worldviews. Reconstructing Black history by locating the mythic past and the origins of the nation or the people is intended to build pride and commitment to the nation. These elements allegedly can be used to organize the Black consciousness of people of African descent as a "chosen people." Identifying the unique and heroic elements of the national culture, in this case, Black culture ideally enables members of the group to fight for the nation. (160)

Memory, in the context of Collins's observation and as it is employed in many of Jackson's earliest poems, performs as the medium through which black nationalism achieves political and aesthetic potential. As Collins prompts, "[T]he fundamental question raised by Black women on my block remains: how can scholars and/or activists construct critical social theories that prepare future generations for lives that we ourselves have not lived?" (191) Thus, through consistent referencing to the agency of Pan-Africanism in the evolution of an aesthetics defining Black Arts writing, such as that which I observe in Jackson's piece "a beginning for new beginnings," the poet's work intimates a clear consciousness about and responsibility for the empowerment of future generations of writers and activists beyond that of the BAM. This can also be read in the piece "if I tole you," in which the concept of memory is perpetuated as both a romantic and nostalgic African-centered principle as well as a productive resource for marketing popular Black Arts poetics that promote black identity, black community, and black nation ideals.

    (it's all so silly)
    if I tole you
    you'd laugh   if i tole you
                     my body contained spirit
                       less than twenty
                       yrs. But

                       i'm mo ancient
                       than age.

    you'd laugh
                       at
                       a longing.   distant as
                       an african sunset
                       in me.
                            this pregnant craving
                       for some unknown
                       fruit.   tired
                       thirsting an ancestral
                                 drink
                       mo ancient
                       than age.   in me.
                       the feeling of an
                       emptiness in secret
                       holes that go unfilled
                                 for a time
                       mo ancient
                       than age.   in me.

                       if I tole you the
                       warm need blowin
                       restless.   in me.   mo
                       ancient than age.

>   and you'd
>   laugh   if i tole you. Pains
>   ain't pains but ex-panding
>   spirits movin
>   in me. movin to someplace
>   whose name i
>   forgot
>   goin somewhere mo
>   ancient than age.
>   in me . . . (*VooDoo* 11)

In this poem, readers encounter a fluid mind/body consciousness on the part of a narrator whose subjectivity is informed by a contemporary as well as an African ancestral cultural perspective. As the narrator encourages her companion to "remember me with me," the functionality of memory as a shared experience is implied; yet even as the narrator invites another individual to share in this re/construction of the past, she expresses a degree of apprehension about revealing a conscious connection with an ancient, African past to her counterpart . . . "you'd laugh / at / a longing. distant as / an african sunset / in me." As mainstream aesthetics enforced by Black Artists of the BAM and OBAC encouraged audiences to evaluate and react to the realities of their contemporary social conditions in the political process of achieving cultural autonomy, the focus on and assertion of an identity "mo ancient than age" might at first be perceived as counterproductive; however, even as the narrator contemplates her current, immediate identity, she "thirsts for an ancestral drink" and maintains a connection to her ancient, cultural past.

Indeed, as Femi Ojo-Ade notes in a study of Pan-Africanism in the black literary tradition, the reference to African symbols gave the revolutionary writers of the BAM a cultural base. "Their work is geared towards validating the glorious past (Africa) and building a solid, autonomous base in the present (America). Thus, the integration of down-to-earth, popular Black English [while] refer[ing] to African deities was characteristic of the Aesthetics of this period" (17). The narrator of "if I tole you," for example, projects herself both physically and psychologically as she submits to "the feeling of an / emptiness in secret / holes that go unfilled / . . . in me. / the warm need blowin / restless. in me . . ." and acknowledges that "Pains / ain't pains but ex-panding / spirits movin / in me." The narrator's craving for a connection with the ancient "spirits" is also carnal, and in this way, Jackson implicates the mind/body connection as that which is integral to her character's political fulfillment. "Hoping to reinstate an Afrocentric vision of the world, black novelists, poets, and playwrights posited the existence of a pan-African continuum of thought and experience which bound black Americans to their forebears . . . " (Van Deburg 274). Thus, when the narrator articulates "pains / ain't pains but ex-panding / spirits movin / in me. movin to someplace / whose name i / forgot," she acknowledges a heightened social and political consciousness that is mutually compelled by the realities of a postcolonial present as well as an African past.

In the poem "Second Meeting," ideals of the contemporary and the ancient work in a mutually informative way that stimulates the consciousness of the narrator as well. Aptly titled, "Second Meeting" portrays a female narrator who encounters a former male lover, and who begins to imagine the two of them as displaced, ancient African characters.

> memba the time . . .
>   we met at home
>   that slow age ago. one day.
> me.
>   with a water jar balanced
>   on my head/
>   to fetch from the river
>   and u
>   an u wuz
> hone/n a spear for the
> hunt that night
> do u think about/—when
>   we'd met befo
>   in a /once life. one nite.
> we shared the bitter ripe/ness
>   of a
>   mango/ together
> moved a fertility dance
>   beneath the warm east sky . . .
> but I guess/ u forgot . . . til
>   we met again.
>   In this cold/ place
> chicago. The subway.
>   like:
>   hey sista wuts happen/n

>   . . . and
>   i reminded
>   u   in a smile
>   (don't I know u
>   from
>   sum/
>   where??
>   u said. and
>   i nod/ ed softly: yes.
>   afraid I'd tip/ ova
>   the water jar
>   i always think
>   is
>   balanced
>   on my head . . . (*VooDoo* 12)

As in "a beginning for new beginnings" and "if I tole you," Jackson's focus on space/place and/or environment in the fulfillment of a desired identity and/or existence is clear here. As the narrator imagines/remembers balancing the water jar and dancing the fertility dance while her partner "hone[s] a spear for the hunt," she expresses a preference for a historical time/space in which she and her lover are capable of experiencing an ideal and perhaps mythic union. This image is contrasted with a scene referencing the contemporary landscape of the urban American Midwest, and thus, the urban American "version" of the story that characterizes the present becomes a metaphor for the social restrictions and pressures of a contemporary culture that competes with and denies the narrator the presumed "freedoms" inherent within an ideal "African" context. Ironically, it is the romantic notion of an alter-reality in "Second Meeting" that intimates the psychologically limiting aspects of the present, and the narrative movement between cultural, physical, and spatial perspectives and time frames as those which inform the narrator's enlightened consciousness alludes to Jackson's experimentation with and expansion of BAM aesthetics, which typically privileged popular rather than ancient or ancestral images as means of stimulating the consciousness of black audiences.

The narrator's psychological escapism in "Second Meeting" renders her simultaneous identities in the modern world and the African cultural "past" as equally relevant, but it is within the latter that the narrator gains consciousness and empowerment, and where she is able to imagine a more ideal cultural climate in which her relationship with her lover might prosper. Thus, even as she accepts the realities of her current existence, she "always think[s] [the water jar of her ancient past] / is / balanced / on [her] head," and she continues to acknowledge and occupy an identity that lies between worlds. Jackson's invention of the ancestral is critical here, as it offers a counternarrative and/or context to that of the present or "urban," and a fluid historical context in which the projection of an ideal black consciousness can be realized. In addition, both "a beginning for new beginnings" and "if I tole you" rely upon the vision and perspective of a female narrator in the realization of the black community ideal, and as each poem intimates, such an ideal is strengthened by the cross-referencing and cross-pollinating cultural contexts of the past and present and the incorporation of multiple though unified collaborative identities.

In both of the previously discussed poems, the urban and the ancestral contexts serve as disparate though mutually informative cultural spaces. Cultural critic James Jeffries provides an interpretation of the cultural, performative, and aesthetic value of the urban landscape as a politically discursive context, which accommodates my reading of Jackson's Pan-Africanist ancestralism. In his essay "Toward a Redefinition of the Urban: The Collision of Culture," Jeffries refers to the "urban" or the "city" as "place[s] where new dimensions of black popular culture are often born."

> As a group, blacks in the diaspora have realized few, if any, of the progressive ideals associated with life in the bourgeois modern city . . . Principal among those urban bourgeois ideals was the widely held notion that if you lived in a city, you were free to be as anonymous as you desired. (159)

Jeffries's vision of the "urban" as a discursive "repertoire" for "black popular culture" acknowledges the disillusionment, despair, and false hopes associated with the "broken promise" of the American Dream for black Americans, but it also identifies the "urban" as a site for cultural expression, social immersion, and the performance of contemporary political and social ideals. Jeffries notes that ironically, however, "the parochial influences Blacks are most interested in escaping are either unambiguously racist or infected with racist overtones, and therefore, are as prevalent in urban areas as they are in rural areas" (160). This idea underscores Jackson's treatment of the urban as a symbol for spiritual and physical deterioration wherein the notion of prosperity remains an elusive concept—an idea that further substantiates the function of the African/ancestral as ideal and indeed *preferred* over the contemporary urban context. Although the narrator in Jackson's poem, for instance, is assured the freedoms that anonymity brings in the monotony of the urban context, it is within her memory of "that slow age ago" that she imagines a more ideal existence with her lover.

The re/invention of memory against the backdrop of the African ancestral context in Jackson's work expands popular aesthetics that are often perceptible in the works of BAM writers, which arouse the consciousness of audiences through the artistic treatment and portrayal of contemporary social realities with which they would presumably identify. The representation of this ideal as it is invoked by Jackson is consistent with what scholar Manthia Diawara interprets as "kitsch art" in his evaluation of the black American literary tradition, which positions the "high and rarified (ancestral) over the low and popular (contemporary)" (285). Diawara's concern is that such treatments have "become sites of temporary feel-good spaces for mass conversions that cover our wounds without healing them or redeeming the Black American community" (285). Furthermore,

> Kitsch art is often accused of cutting loose old forms from their social networks and redeploying them in utterly new contexts. And kitsch art functions to reinforce identification and to promote consumption of the object thus put forth; it requires an unmediated emotional response... Revolutionary traditions are invoked only to be co-opted in these cathartic moments. And generic pan-African symbols increasingly seem the preferred style for that mode of uplifting. (285)

In addition, as the voice of one such acclaimed "[r]evolutionary tradition," as referenced by Diawara, Jackson's writing invariably maintains a duplicitous role, appealing to the more elusive, romantic desires and consciousness of her readership while conforming to the criteria of writing that theorist Debra Pollack observes as "performative."

> Performative writing is evocative. It operates metaphorically to render absence present—to bring the reader into contact with "other-worlds," to those aspects and dimensions of our world that are other to the text as such by re-marking them. Performative writing evokes worlds that are other-wise [sic] intangible, unlocatable: worlds of memory, pleasure, sensation, imagination, affect, and in-sight [sic]. It does not describe, in a narrowly reportorial sense, an objectively verifiable event or process but uses language like paint to create what is self-evidently a *version* of what was, what is, and/or what might be.[5]

Pollack's observation is useful to my reading of Jackson's work, since the images invoked within each of the previously discussed poems are important means of rendering the "absence" of an African cultural context "present," and Jackson's method of incorporating memory as an aesthetic technique in the process of inspiring and defining identity, or "creat[ing] what is self-evidently a *version* of what was, what is, and/or what might be," as Pollack phrases it, reinforces the functional value of the work and its ideological potential in the context of Jackson's version of Black Art. Yet even as OBAC Black Artists like Jackson created work that would explicate the experiences and social consciousness of contemporary black audiences, her poetics were amenable to the broader, and indeed timeless appeal of Pan-Africanism, and the colliding framework of the "urban" and the "ancestral" reveals the political potential of this cross-culturally transcendent ideal. "Bring[ing] the reader into contact with 'other-worlds,'" as determined by Pollack, characterizes and intimates Jackson's experimentation with and treatment of varying social and historical contexts for the perpetuation of the black culture, black community, and black consciousness ideals. More importantly, Jackson's aesthetic approach is particularly compelling because it reveals the political potential inherent within the appropriation of spatial and cultural terms, as well as her ability to simultaneously conform to the poetics and traditions of her Black Arts predecessors while demonstrating the ways in which black women writers have taken on leading roles in pursuing the nation-building project in the tradition of black expression.

Pollack's aforementioned explanation of performative writing is also useful to the extent that it identifies the nature of such writing as that which necessarily relies upon the participation of the writer as well as the reader. Since BAM and OBAC writers committed themselves to satisfying prescribed criteria of art that encouraged audience reaction, the time allotted for readings and feedback during workshops was equally divided, as the interaction between artists and audiences would ideally culminate in the regeneration of the cultural and artistic ideal of collaboration as a stimulus for group empowerment. Moreover, the "production of meaning" referenced in Pollack's definition satisfies a fundamental OBAC objective that reinforced the idea that literary and textual meaning should be acquired through an interactive, dialogic exchange between artist and audience. One of the essential goals for the original group of OBAC writers, which remained consistent for later writers like Jackson, was to encourage and nurture the dialectic relationship between artist and audience, thereby undermining the perceived traditional, white, Western paradigm of communication that perpetuated the role of the artist as a privileged and/or disengaged figure. Thus, one of the desired consequences of the poetics of OBAC and the BAM was that they would promote an inclusive aesthetic and nation-building paradigm that undermined classism and social hierarchy in the artistic process.

Although one way in which memory is constructed in Jackson's work is as a means of rendering an ancient, African cultural history accessible to contemporary black audiences, the poet also relies upon this concept as an aesthetically discursive space for the re/creation and narration of universal stories characterizing the familiar and shared social realities of a cross-cultural readership. Among other things, this approach ultimately motivated the collaboration ideal in the form of catharsis. Poems like "Mak/n My Music" and "a summer story," for example, constitute a style of writing demonstrated by Jackson that seeks the community, reception, and interaction of an audience capable of identifying with the sentimental realities and memories that articulate a "common," recognizable portrait of black life. Written as intimate narratives recalling childhood memories, both pieces integrate style, music, and images of the black body into an aesthetic that effectively unifies its audience.

    Mak/n My Music

my colored child/hood wuz mostly music
    celebrate/n be/n young an Black (but we din know it)
        scream/n up the wide alleys
    an holler/n afta the walla-mellon-man.

sun-rest time
my mama she wuz yell/n
    (all ova the block
        sand/n fa us
ta git our butts in
    side.

w grew up run/n jazz rhythms
    an watch/n mr. Wiggins downstairs
        knock the blues up side his woman's
            head
we rocked. An the big boys they snuck
an rolled dice/ in the hallways at nite.

> i mean. we laughed love. an the teen
>   agers they jus slow dragged thru smokey
>   tunes.
>   life wuz a ordinary miracle an
>   have/n fun wuzn no temptation
>   we jus dun it.
> an u know
> i think we grew. thru them spirit-uals
>   the saint-tified folks wud git happy off
>   of even if we wuz jus blown/n
>   when we danced the grizzly bear an
>   felt good when the reverend
>   wid the black cadillac . . . said:
>
>   let the holy ghost come in
>   side you
> that music make you/ feel sooo/ good!
>
> any how   I wuz a little colored girl
>   then . . .
>
> so far
> my Black woman/hood ain't been noth/n but music
>
>   I found billie
>   holiday an learned
>   how
>   to cry. (*VooDoo* 8)

a summer story

> she dragged me from the backyard.
> all dirt and blacken/d further from sun.
> from chianese changeling child
> she made me a lady.
> washed me pressed me slick in bangs
> that slanted more my eyes. didn she say
> i had those o/riental eyes?
> starched me in a white dress made of stiff cloud.
> the one I first communion/d in. she

> scrubbed me and rubbed me
> vaselined me a skin of brownshine.
> she even made my knees
> knees again. turned knobs of earth and ash.
>
> she stood back
> in tired triumph and faced me
> to a mirrorgirl
> "now smile and show yo pretty big dimples!"
>
> wasn't I the most beautiful charming
> creature
> a toughhand/ed and love armed cousin
> ever made? (*VooDoo* 9)

In each of these pieces, black life isn't fixed in a specific social or cultural context, but is instead informed by psychological and physical displacement or transcendence, and space/place and/or environment are inventions of each narrator's imagination. In "Mak/n My Music," the term "colored" operates on a variety of levels to reference the narrator's racial identity, the memory of a fulfilled childhood, and the reinforcement of her cultural kinship and connection with her community. As Cornel West offers in his essay "Nihilism in Black America," "... modes of valuation and resistance are rooted in a subversive memory—the best of one's past without romantic nostalgia—and guided by a universal love ethic" (43). Thus, in this piece, the narrator's reflections demonstrate the improvisational, spontaneous nature of memory in recalling childhood experiences.

 Likewise, as the relationship between music and cultural identity is "remembered" in the piece "a summer story," the value of memory emerges as a medium through which the retrieval of childhood experiences in the process of affirming black family life becomes possible. As the narrator remembers "a toughhand/ed and love armed cousin" that cared for her and took responsibility for her as a child, she conveys a sense of pride in the ritual of being transformed from "chianese changeling child" to a "lady." The narrator's cousin is invested in and accountable for the narrator's transition, and the unifying black family ideal is perceptible as the narrator is prepared for womanhood through a collaborative family ritual. It is noteworthy that the process of her becoming an adult is a domestic one that takes place in the home, where the nation-building ideal is relative to her womanhood. The idea of the domestic space as a politically solvent, woman-centered concept appears throughout the historiography of black women's literature, as critiqued in the pioneering scholarship of such theorists as Claudia Tate and Hazel Carby, both of whom acknowledge black women as heroines of the domestic sphere and key agents in narratives of black political empowerment.[6] As such critics have noted, in many ways the accomplishments and successes of the race have been contingent upon the fate and participation of black women, and women writers like Jackson, who were dedicated to the ideologies of the BAM, can be credited for their efforts in promoting an aesthetic that privileged these ideals, despite the often-cited masculinist culture of the movement.

In "i/scattered poems," the closing poem in *VooDoo/Love Magic*, the narrator actively searches for the memories of her community and nation, and the illustrated references to the African Diaspora and/or the displacement of black people from their ancestral land emerge as consciousness-raising images.

> i
> search for seeds of remembered songs
>   scattered over seas of slaveships
> wingspread and winds
>   lover
> traveling the tracks of angels
>   traced in the sands of sorrowlands
> strutting round the souls avenues and streets
> of strange and wonderful
>   wonder.
> we are not of this
>   iced and fallen land.
> we are not of this
>   dead and barren land.
> we are not of this place of concrete
>   moneyed-haters.
>   sin-spenders.
>   disease-lenders.
> life-beaters. infant-eaters. salesmen of death.
> who
> sell us suicide. sister-rape. and mother-murder.
> bartering fathers blood

                    of pride . . .

we walk on air and on
water and make it
                            wine
    clean for fish to drink
and suns to lay horizons there:

there are songs to be sung.
wiser words to be read.
diamonds to be dug. and crowns
to be settled on the heads of dark
                            dark dreamers.

there are things to be done
        in the earths of the mine
    tangled jungles of the spirit
to be set rite. in the world.

dreams to be drummed
for ears to hear. visions to be made for eyes to see.
lands to claim for bloods
                souls and feet
to dance.
        our scattered songs (22)

The reinvention of the "past" is instrumental in the fomentation of an ideology of culture because it stimulates black cultural pride, responsibility, and achievement. As Jackson encourages her audiences to psychologically and collectively subject themselves to the act of remembering a denied past, this virtual process of transformation constitutes a ritualistic act in which her readers can be inspired through the projection of an ancestral cultural identity. "Activist writers paid homage to mere mortals. . . . While the ancestors' spirits may have watched over them, providing inspiration and guidance, it was understood that the responsibility for carrying out the Black Power revolution rested upon the shoulders of the living" (Van Deburg 275). In "i/scattered poems," the narrator's dispersion of words, thoughts, and ideas educates her community/audience, and the search for history and/or documentation or evidence of the "past" is done so with a sense of consciousness and responsibility for her community. In addition, the historical and spiritual relationship between "culture/community" and land (Africa) is underscored by the narrator's criticism of the (American) urban, "modern" world.

The relationship drawn between the urban context and the violence of "this iced and fallen land / ... dead and barren land" is clearly established in this piece, and "this place of concrete / moneyed-haters. / sin-spenders. / disease-lenders. / life-beaters. infant-eaters. salesmen of death. / who sell us suicide. sister-rape. and mother-murder. / bartering fathers blood / of pride" is identified as the source of lost innocence and spiritual imbalance and is juxtaposed with the idealization of Africa as a cultural utopia. Although America and/or the New World is referenced as "a dead and barren land [of] moneyed-haters, sin-spenders, [and] disease-lenders," the narrator's consciousness is also informed by her "strutting round the souls avenues," "walk[ing] on air," "drum[ming] of dreams," as well as the "danc[ing] of songs" of Africa. In this sense, Jackson's poem is anything but "realistic," and it borders on the speculative in its characterization of a narrator whose urban subjectivity is informed by her spiritual, African-centered consciousness. The fractured identity of the narrator, who exists between the context of the "here and now" and that of ancient Africa, is a reminder of Jackson's ability to privilege both spaces and planes of consciousness. In this poem, memory, time, and place collapse into a singular, complex consciousness for the narrator.

The cultural responsibilities of Black Artists included dispelling cultural myths and misperceptions of black culture, as well as interpreting and appropriating concepts that reflected nationalist ideologies for the empowerment of black communities. This remained consistent in the work of later OBAC writers and Black Artists such as Jackson, who continued to be motivated by a desire to produce work that was culturally and politically solvent. In this aspect, scholar Tommie Shelby's analysis of the many faces of black nationalism, including "classic," "cultural," and "racial," for instance—is useful.

> According to [classical black nationalism] . . . self-realization must be rooted in a shared African or Pan-African ethnoracial identity, which black Americans must reclaim and develop . . . [M]any nationalists vacillate between, and sometimes confuse, classical nationalism and what I call "pragmatic nationalism"—the view that black solidarity is merely a contingent strategy for creating greater freedom and social equality for blacks, a pragmatic yet principled approach to achieving racial justice. (10)

Given this explication of terms, Jackson's poems can be read as counternarratives to what we now consider to be "pragmatic nationalism," despite the poet's experimentation with abstraction and dislocation. This is so because Jackson's work relies upon a "contingent strategy for creating greater freedom" for individual expression in the process of achieving racial justice instead of dictating or projecting an essential "shared African or Pan-African . . . identity." Indeed, the subjectivity of Jackson's narrator can be construed as "African" or "Pan-Africanist," but ultimately, what is important is that she has the freedom to pattern her own identity in any way that she chooses. Furthermore, Jackson's manipulation of psychological and cultural orientations of black female consciousness as a way of "reclaiming" cultural identity responds to Shelby's concerns regarding the marketing of contemporary black nationalist concepts. Shelby writes that his own goal is to "arrive at a philosophy of black solidarity rooted in the unfinished project of achieving racial justice," noting that

> the black experience can provide philosophical insight. We can think through philosophical questions—such as the limits of state coercion . . . the distinction between reality and mere appearance, the meaning of love and happiness, and the significance of life and death—by considering them in relation to the lives and experiences of black people or, better yet, by listening attentively, critically, but open-mindedly to black people themselves as they philosophize about these questions against the background of their history, practical concerns, and long-standing aspirations. (11)

The much-needed philosophical insight that Shelby promotes in contemporary multidisciplinary black studies programs meant to advance Afrocentric ideologies resonates deeply in Jackson's Black Arts–inspired "i/scattered poems," where we see a narrator philosophizing about the collision between her abstract, spiritual self and her everyday "real" experiences. Shelby's concerns regarding the subordination or lack of philosophical perspectives in Afrocentric theory are well taken; however, such perspectives *do* indeed exist in the Black Arts work of black women such as Jackson, whose aesthetic privileges progressive, Pan-Africanist nation-building strategies.

The invocation of "memory" as a unifying concept in several of Jackson's poems assists in the development of a collective black national consciousness that Black Artists privileged, and *The Greenville Club* (1977), Jackson's second collection of poetry, employs memory as an aesthetic medium as well. In addition, several pieces in this collection reference space/place and environment in the conceptualization of black and African Diasporic identities through the collaborative process of remembering. However, within the context of a select list of poems in this volume, memory is grounded in a *recent* past rather than an ancestral one, and the perpetuation of a shared, collective cultural experience amongst and between black audiences continues to emerge as an empowering nation-building resource for the writer. Furthermore, Jackson's continued treatment of common, recognizable narratives of black life reinforcing the significance of commonplace, "everyday" scenarios is at the epicenter of black cultural identity, and memory is sustained as a means of revitalizing the past. In narrating these "stories" Jackson also substantiates contemporary historical and aesthetic exigencies of the BAM that sought to define a universal black experience. More specifically, these portrayals provide the imagistic context that foregrounds black subjectivity, and Jackson invokes a somewhat romantic, less confrontational narrative style than was often perceptible in Black Arts material. For instance, the statement that introduces *The Greenville Club* is indicative of Jackson's desire to appeal to a cross-cultural, collective black audience.

> The Greenville Club meets once a year, at least, in Chicago. The homefolk collect themselves in furs and shining cars and spirits. We style whatever we do. My family is from Greenville, but that could be anyplace, everyday Black people from an everyday city or town . . . (24)

Jackson's fictional concept of "the Greenville Club" intimates the forging of "new" black extended communities reminiscent of those that developed as a result of the massive northern migration of blacks from the South in the early-to-mid-twentieth century (Conyers 43). As a community-conscious organization in Chicago, OBAC, for instance, honored the narratives of these constantly shifting, growing, and gathering communities, as demonstrated in Jackson's collection. "The emphasis on performance, on the gathering of the people, is central to African-American cultural forms" (Whitehead 93). The idea that the black American and African Diasporic experiences transcend cultural or political boundaries, as suggested in Jackson's *Greenville Club* statement, contributes to the conceptualization of a collective, unified, black community that assists in the perpetuation of a nationalist ideology. "Greenville," then, is realized as a culturally motivating construct symbolizing a homeland, community, and nation—an "everyday" space of collaborative struggle and triumph.

But even though Jackson's conceptualization of the "Greenville Club" as a Pan-Africanist cultural metaphor is consistent with earlier BAM nation-building objectives, what I find most compelling in her description of the club's aims, as expressed in its statement of purpose, is the underlying implication of its agenda. As Jackson sets forth a mission for the Greenville Club, she leaves the impression that regardless of the fact that the group concept is a BAM and/or OBAC inspired initiative, it is inspired by "everyday Black people." In this regard, the Greenville Club/collective exists as an emancipatory objective designed by its own eclectic membership—those who come from "everyday cit[ies] or town[s]" and who maintain a cultural kinship fomented by the diverse experiences of cross-pollinating communities and experiences. Poems like "Greenville," for instance, include evocative images that arouse familiar memories of childhood and family amongst its readership, compelling contemporary audiences to find strength in the memories and narratives of their shared past.

>   mouth/greasy
> and diaper/wet
> me./in a oldmans thin arms wrinkledwarm
>   and brown
>   full of granpapas foodandfussin
>   bout them kids
>   leavin this here littlebaby
>   by herself
>
> and my brothersandsisters
> skippin down the road like
> dustorms skippin like
>
> dizzy dazzlestones across the water
>
> I couldnt catch up with. (*Greenville* 27)

Like many other poems in this collection, "Greenville" portrays a particular scene that reflects various situations and circumstances characterizing and implicating the universality of childhood experiences reflecting black life; yet readers also encounter a nostalgic narrator, who compares her "brothersandsisters" to "dustorms skippin like/dizzy dazzlestones across the water / [that she] couldnt catch up with." As in several of the poems published in Jackson's first collection, *VooDoo/Love Magic*, the narrator of this piece is psychologically and physically defined by her willingness to imagine herself and her family liberated from rather than marginalized by the monotony of their everyday experiences. The reference to "stones skippin across water" conjures a visual image of an object suddenly freed, now moving with reckless abandon in its own, random path to an indecipherable rhythm. The images are explicit, aggressive, and provocative in this piece, and the smells and sights portrayed in the poem realistically characterize the experiences of Jackson's intended audience. Incidentally, hybrid terms like "foodandfussin," "littlebaby," and "brothersandsisters" are reminiscent of the terms invented by Jackson's OBAC predecessor Carolyn Rodgers, who demonstrated similar linguistic wordplay in the essay "Black Poetry—Where It's At," published in the *Negro Digest* in 1969 (7).

Similarly, in the poem "Home Trainin," the narrator's memory of being disciplined by her father for rebellious behavior characterizes another archetypal and/or familiar family scene.

> my father never did
> heal my smart talking
> mouth. No matter
> how many pursuits
> around and unda the kitchen table
> with belt or extension cord.
>
> i had two smartin legs
>   and ass
> but my mouth
>   continued to sass (*Greenville* 27)

The narrator's memory of her exhibitionism and her father's desire to enforce disciplinary boundaries culminates in their "many pursuits / aroun and unda the kitchen table / with belt or extension cord." Even though the narrator would ultimately sustain the pain of "two smartin legs / and ass" after such performances, the fact that "[her] mouth / continued to sass" signifies the unyielding persistence and will of her character. The "home trainin" she receives functions as the ritual through which the realization of identity becomes possible, and the narrator's ability to reconstruct these moments in recalling her personal history provides opportunities to critique the development of a burgeoning gender consciousness. As "home trainin" becomes a metaphor for "life training," the implied relationship between the narrator's recollections of the past and the present supports the aesthetic value of memory. To "look back" upon these instances for the narrator in an effort to understand or reconsider her relationship with her father is critical to the establishment of the aesthetic potential of memory. In this case, a single set of perfunctory, recurring circumstances from childhood becomes a ritualistic performance revitalized through memory. The father's role as teacher, enforcer, and protector in "home trainin," and the narrator's role as a comparatively radical, deviant female figure who defies his expectations contributes to the implicit sexual tension in this piece as well. The father considers his daughter's "smart talking" to be an affliction—something that he must "heal" or at least discourage—and his efforts to physically punish and disable the narrator's willful desire to "sass" is as much about encouraging her to respect his position as a parent as it is an opportunity for him to enforce gendered expectations.

In addition, the narrator's deviancy is in direct conflict with her father's expectations in this poem, and she allows memory to become the means through which she sentimentally recalls her behavior, while inviting readers to identify, remember, and claim these stories as their own. Thus, memory serves as significantly more than an individual recollection of a personal past for the narrator, but rather it invokes and stimulates a collective historical consciousness amongst Jackson's readership. As previously mentioned, the role of the Black Artist could be reified through memory and shared catharsis, thereby encouraging community and nation-building ideals. Although the rhetoric of a nationalist Black Arts aesthetic was not as fervently marketed in the mid-to-late seventies as it had been for Jackson's OBAC predecessors, she continued to produce work that honored these ideals. Her revision of some of the most popular features of the Black Arts aesthetic make clear her interests in reinventing black community concepts for new audiences, for whom the BAM's objectives remain appealing.

Domestic or "home-centered" themes such as those found in the nostalgic poem "Home Trainin" exemplify the discursive relationships between public and private spheres of expression and performance, and furthermore speak to Jackson's strategic contribution to existing BAM and OBAC aesthetics. As Patricia Hill Collins suggests:

> Reconstructing Black culture and grounding it in a family model of community organization gave newly "Black" people a home, a family to which they were linked by ties of blood. This stance joined the bonds of consanguinity, or blood ties, characterizing the racial family with the sense of political obligation that accompanies blood ties . . . Finally, when nurtured by this unified

Black community relating as family, this newfound Black identity would stimulate a new politics for African-Americans. African-Americans in touch with their essential Blackness would be more willing to serve the Black nation, defined as a large, imagined Black community. This ethic of service to Black families, Black communities, and the Black nation, one wherein Black people would function as "brothers" and "sisters," emerged from the conversion experience of immersion in Black culture, reclaiming Black identity via racial solidarity. (161–162)

As Collins further observes, "[D]isenchantment with civil rights led many younger black Americans to Black nationalism and the search for a heroic national identity or 'Blackness'" (162). However, Jackson undermines the concept of heroism as a later Black Arts poet invested in the black nationalist project, and she portrays the beauty, simplicity, and humility of black life. In this sense, her portraits engage the consciousness of audiences eager to embrace a poetics that promised sincere reflections of their worlds—past, present, and future.

The poems "Early Evenings" and "Other Evenings" are drawn from the substance of commonplace narratives of the black experience as well, and the import of Jackson's realism inspires audiences to participate in remembering a shared past. The poems complement one another, and together they convey the intertextuality of two disparate yet mutually informative narratives of black life.

Early Evenings

early evenings and the streetlights
not yet on
we carry/d the backyard
to the front
cement
and study/d the street
while jumping double dutch
or irish in case of tie
waiting for the seven fifteen
bus
bearing our mama

bus rush by kicking dust and paper
and us all raggedy

me. a rather wild child
racing to the corner

mama would wait out a light
and rest
    her shoppingbag
we would rip it from her and
worry
it
for a surprise
empty or not
       there was a happiness:
the gift of her
brownred/yellow and laughing
       weariness
rests easy in our eyes . . . (*Greenville* 30)

Other Evenings

other evenings when we called
ourselves ladies
of leisure
too cute for doing dishes and
washing and sweeping and cooking
chores like our mama did for life
beings too much women
grown and fine we decorated
the streets
flirted and jived
til the sun blinked a warning
about work to be done
before the old girl
arrived (*Greenville* 31)

As in her words in *The Greenville Club* statement of purpose, Jackson reminds readers that cultural consciousness and community-building initiatives must be self-motivated, and that there is no pretense for or ideal place in which such expressions should take root. In "Early Evenings," the narrator's daily routine of waiting for her mother to arrive home after work becomes a ritual that perpetuates and affirms family, and in this way, Jackson's recurring sentimentalism is consistent with the popular strategies invoked by earlier Black Artists, who capitalized upon the commonality of their audiences' shared, cultural experiences. The narrator's voice transcends the singular "I" as she remembers that "we carry/d the backyard . . . waiting for the . . . bus bearing our mama . . . and us all raggedy . . .". The consistency with which the characters perform these daily greetings is implied by the narrator's ability to recall the repetitive nature and details of these occasions, as the bus "rush[es] by kicking dust and paper . . . mama would wait out a light / and rest / her shoppingbag / we would rip it from her and / worry / it / for a surprise . . .".

In "Other Evenings," however, the narrator is uninspired by the routine of her mother's life, and she is disheartened by the idea that her own future may be characterized by the same responsibilities and domestic tasks that her mother is forced to perform on her family's behalf. "[T]oo cute for doing dishes and / washing and sweeping and cooking / . . . like our mama did for life," the narrator and her sisters attempt to extricate themselves from the mundane realities of their existence, and the everyday ritual of greeting their mother as she returns home from work is a grim and inescapable reminder of their own future responsibilities as women and mothers. Feelings of resentment, devotion, and an increasing consciousness about the realities of adulthood inspire the girls to pretend that they are "ladies / of leisure . . . women / grown and fine . . .". To behave as a "woman" required "flirt[ing]" and "jiv[ing]" in "the streets." Yet at the end of the day, the girls must transform themselves back into the comparatively mundane realities of their youth. Read together, both "Early Evenings" and "Other Evenings" reflect a distinct plot and character development demonstrating the subjectivities of each narrator. In the first piece, the youth and innocence that the character recalls during her youth is juxtaposed with the second narrator's expressions of disillusionment with and anxieties about adulthood. As in several other poems in *The Greenville Club*, the invocation of memory works concomitantly as an aesthetic context in which the narrator is both compelled and discouraged by the past. In this way, Jackson's narrative treatment represents the voices of a new generation of black (women) searching for ways to address their fears about the fate of the black community and in particular the roles they may be required to play in sustaining the black family and black nation ideals, as they are torn between the "work to be done" at home and the freedom to "decorate / the streets / [with their] flirt[ing] and jiv[ing]."

The sentimentalism of Jackson's work manages quite unsuspectingly to expose the political potential of themes of domesticity and community that characterize the black experience. The poem "In the Echo I Remember," for example, is grounded within the context of particular scenes and circumstances that the narrator recalls from her past, yet the vivid scenes serve as metaphors for the elusive nature of memory as well.

> in
> the echo of the monkey
> cigartree
> a
> coming/chill
> chattering autumn
> shadow scattered around us
> leaves fell away from the tree
> i
> remember
>
> > my uncle
> > sweet&
> > me
> > negotiating a bike
> > built of junk
> > his hands
> > hard
> > crafted
> > out of refusal
> > trading
> > my two dollar dustingmoney
> > for a laidaway ride:some wheels
> > & a
> > handlebar
> > i
> > remember
> > just
> > that
> > leaves fell away from the tree
> > falling
> >
> > not too far (*Greenville* 32)

Here, Jackson constructs a parallel consciousness in which the present and past are duplicated, as the narrator watches the current falling of the leaves in the "coming / chill [of the] chattering autumn" that provokes images of the falling leaves of her past that "fell away from the tree / falling / not too far," and the "dustingmoney" becomes a symbol for the shadowy, nearly indistinguishable past. Childhood memories of the narrator's uncle are also conjured within this moment of reflection, and the narrator's memory in reconstructing the details of her experiences "negotiating a bike / built of junk . . . a laidaway ride" with her uncle's assistance is as significant as her memory of "his hands / hard / crafted / out of refusal"—hands that serve as veritable "texts" revealing the physical signs of years of intense labor and struggle. The narrator is encouraged and comforted by her uncle's demonstrated commitment to her, and the memory of the leaves of her youth that "fell away from the tree / falling / not too far" are symbolic references to the memories themselves which are never "too far" and exist as virtual "maps" of consciousness that preserve and define identity. The subjectivity of the female narrator is defined by the memories of her past as well as her ability to construct and access the details of these experiences. In this way, memory and nostalgia become resources that compel readers to pursue the legacies of their families and loved ones in developing strategies for community and self-empowerment.

Although the fact that Jackson foregrounds the female perspective in many of the poems in *The Greenville Club* may be a consequence of "the strict delineations of gender differences [that] rendered a woman writing in the voice of a man unlikely," I submit that such a strategy successfully introduces woman-identified narratives of political empowerment as well as trepidation that may not have otherwise been privileged in the Black Arts nation-building aesthetic of the time, but which nonetheless prioritizes essential perspectives that reveal the vulnerabilities and triumphs of the era's most underrepresented populations (Ford 192). In characterizing the realistic life stories of hope, survival, and possibility, as we see in her later postrace-era work, Jackson continues to find meaning in the concept of memory. The collective act of "remembering"—as both a romantic and affirming nation-building act—may indeed be one of the most effective means of stimulating the consciousness of generations of readers who remain tragically invested in the urgency of their particularized moments, and who fail to look back to the priorities, narratives, and past legacies of their predecessors or forward to the hopeful potential of their future.

Chapter Six

Mixing Metaphors: Spirituality, Environmentalism, and Dystopia in Carolyn Rodgers's and Angela Jackson's Postrace Black Art

Although the legacy of the BAM is often critiqued within the context of the activist practices and art produced by its participants at the height of the movement, it can also be evaluated in later work, since many Black Artists remained prolific beyond the BAM. In many aspects, self-defined Black Artists continue to reprise BAM ideals in more recent work, which further substantiates the idea that the Black Arts aesthetic was and remains an evolving concept. Artists, activists, and intellectuals who worked toward the realization of the BAM and who were most immediately inspired by and committed to its agenda continued to work in the interests of and within various liberationist capacities long after the energy of the movement had dissipated. For instance, on October 16, 2007, Carolyn Rodgers, Angela Jackson, and poet Sterling Plumpp gathered at Northwestern University in Evanston, Illinois, for a panel discussion focusing on the past and continuing legacies of the Black Arts Movement and OBAC traditions.[1] Although the absences of Haki Madhubuti and Johari Amini were conspicuous, given their roles as founding members of OBAC, Rodgers, Jackson, and Plumpp provided an impressive overview of the organization's goals while sharing their memories of the politically inspired, artistic zeitgeist of Chicago's BAM, recalling the ways in which their own development as writers was attributed to a collaborative vision of Black Art as activist art. Each of them commented on the life-altering impact that the BAM and Chicago artistic traditions had upon their personal lives and professional careers as well. As I mentioned in the introduction for this project, prior to this panel discussion Rodgers had been an elusive figure for several years after the BAM, having distanced herself from the culture of OBAC and many of her Black Arts peers. Thus, her participation in this celebratory event was especially meaningful.[2]

At one point during the panel discussion, Jackson reminisced about having been an aspiring writer during the early seventies, when a stranger on a train encouraged her to read a "real poet" and referred her to a copy of Rodgers's first collection, *Paper Soul* (1968). After becoming acquainted with the more established writer's work, Jackson began to take a personal interest in Rodgers's poetry, perceiving her as her "spirit sister." Rodgers's own feelings of respect and mutual support for Jackson were clear when she credited the younger writer for her ability to remember and explicate the cultural intricacies of the organization during the discussion. In addition, Rodgers expressed the ways in which she'd been socially and politically "transformed" by the BAM, remembering that everything from her poetry to her style of dress changed once she'd been introduced to the concepts of Black Power and Black Art. Prior to her participation in these nation-building movements, she recalled that she wasn't "angry about anything or anyone," and that she wasn't the kind of person to be "fired up" ("The Black Arts"). Never having thought of herself as a writer or poet in any way, Rodgers expressed that she'd been more interested in pursuing a career as a singer, and her affiliation with the BAM inspired a life and an identity that she hadn't imagined for herself. "I thought poetry was something that I'd write and toss aside," she recalled, marveling at the fact that for a while, and without knowing it, she lived in an apartment in Chicago that was directly underneath that of the famed intellectual and writer Arna Bontemps, who had been working on his Ph.D. at the University of Chicago at that time ("The Black Arts").

Rodgers also expressed her desire to devote her creative energies and emergent political awakening to the development of the new black aesthetic of this era. "I made the decision like crossing a wide stream of water I could not see the beginnings or the ends of," she recalled about her decision to become a member of OBAC. While she participated in the organization's writing activities, she was invited to join Gwendolyn Brooks's own "elite" writers' workshop, for which Brooks herself selected a group of writers. Rodgers recalled the following about feeling inspired by Chicago's Black Arts culture.

> Chicago became a Mecca where people came together. I was accepting something that was being passed down to me. We were fellowshipping. I realized that [she] was giving us something . . . like breathing, like air . . . We were aligned with people from all over the world. Her being a Pulitzer

Prize winner didn't alienate her, it brought her closer to people worldwide. It attracted people to her. ("The Black Arts")

During the early years of OBAC's existence, Brooks had encouraged Rodgers and her peers to publish their own materials, and Rodgers experienced an unprecedented sense of empowerment when she began to do so. "Amazing things happen when you take responsibility for your own life," she said ("The Black Arts"). After her second collection, *Songs of a Black Bird* (1969), had been published by Madhubuti's Third World Press, Rodgers worked with the mainstream publisher Doubleday Books, which, in her words, "wasn't a pleasant experience but a learning one." Much of her own creative and personal development in her later years culminated in the eventual establishment of her own Eden Press with the help of an Illinois Arts Council grant, through which she published her last collections of poetry.[3] Speaking during the panel discussion of her emerging career as a young writer, Rodgers referred to her growing sense of political consciousness as she began to formulate opinions about popular, urgent issues of the time—all of which members of OBAC discussed with regularity—including the concept of Black Power, reparations, oppression, and whether or not black people in America should embrace the idea of emigrating to Africa.

> We discussed artistic points of view which were of interest to our people. I was introduced to a new way of thinking. I wasn't going to write meaningless poems. Art was to be as useful as shoes or coats—indispensible to the spirit, body, and soul. Otherwise, I would be wasting my time. I had an obligation to provide these kinds of words . . . We were speaking to the world. We were trying to break down barriers between us and Africans. We wanted to be Africans and African Americans. We wanted to reclaim that heritage. We went to Africa to find roots, support, and the heart and soul of what we were. We began to embrace our heritage and write about that. ("The Black Arts")

Still, as much of her earliest poetry conveys, Black Artists and members of OBAC "never could define blackness," and such a quest was an ongoing process. "It's 2007, and I don't know if we've moved at all . . . Writers are still talking about the gospel, jazz, a love for our people and ourselves, but the problems we face are still here. You can't say that we've moved or stood still," she confided. Contrary to the notion that all artists of the BAM perpetuated essentialist notions of their aesthetic, Rodgers suggested that

OBAC members simply wanted to "control [their] own voices and critique one another's work without being negative" ("The Black Arts").

As I've argued, the Black Arts poems produced by Rodgers during the earliest years of the movement illustrate her awareness of the impossible but inspired activist and artistic responsibilities which Black Artists challenged themselves to undertake. Her most recent commentary on the subject—expressed just a few years prior to her death—reminds audiences that even some of the most inspired writers of the movement were less interested in the idealization of its goals than advancing an aesthetic that would remain rooted in and progressively amenable to rather than restricted by the cultural and social priorities of their audiences. This rather expansive vision was an especially motivating approach for members of OBAC in particular, and it exemplifies the extent to which the organization paradoxically advanced rather than merely conformed to the most popular objectives of the national movement.

There are clear signs of the vestiges of the BAM's most popularized features in Rodgers's later work, including the emphasis on collaboration in the advent of a new aesthetic meant to inspire the process of nation-building within the black community. Indeed, such a concept remained a priority for writers like Rodgers and Jackson, who continued to be productive in the years following the BAM. Yet examples of the more recent writings of both artists also reflect that the roots of the BAM's collaborative energy can, paradoxically, translate into deeply spiritual, individual quests for enlightenment in the postrace era. In addition, their more recent work suggests that the previous ideals of the BAM perhaps find just as much meaning in black cultural expression, social activism, and liberation struggles today as they once did several decades ago. Still, while Rodgers's readers might expect to encounter the poet's familiar critique of politically inspired art and/or the production of nation-building art forms in her more recent work, given the poet's leading role in the development of Chicago's Black Arts campaign, Rodgers's Black Arts–inspired progressivism takes on deeply and overtly religious and spiritual connotations in her later collections, *Morning Glory* (1989) and *We're Only Human* (1994). Conversely, Jackson's novel *Where I Must Go* (2009) is an aggressive reminder of the relevance of earlier Black Arts principles of collaboration and activism to the contemporary postrace American cultural ideal. However, for each writer, individual imagination and the hopeful dream of tomorrow's promise of social justice realized through principles of collaboration remain at the forefront of their aesthetics.

According to Ed Roberson, who provided the introduction to the 2007 panel discussion on Chicago's Black Arts Movement at Northwestern University, Rodgers's later work reflects a "spiritual intensity" that belied her earlier work as a Black Artist, when she rejected Christianity as an expressive model for the cultural liberation and empowerment of black people. While I agree with this assessment, I want to push the argument further by suggesting that this later aspect of Rodgers's work induces and recalls the earlier nation-building priorities of OBAC and the BAM, despite the narrative emphasis on individual spirituality and/or spiritual awakening. As several of Rodgers's later poems convey, the solitary, individual internal search for answers to universal questions pertaining to human struggle remain profoundly linked to community and nation-building liberation struggles. Yet the democratic, pluralistic, nation-building impulse found in Rodgers's earlier work is expanded into environmental as well as social contexts, and the social liberation of all oppressed people is linked to and balanced between a consciousness for human connectivity to the earth and/or natural resources as much as it is informed by the politics of social realism, identity, and race consciousness.

In "A Love Poem," for instance, the poet writes, "some things we take. / we need / we give," and the ideal of emotional and spiritual balance takes the imagistic form of multicultural harmony as a "city full of people . . . / bloom like marigolds, lilac trees, / and african violets" (75). Inspired by multiple traditions of faith, "A Love Poem" expresses a progressive and fundamentally integrated version of liberation that attempts to transcend the oppressive and socially divisive manifestations of capitalist and consumerist culture that invariably motivate ideology and politics, in favor of a concept of spiritual liberation informed by unifying metaphors of nature. "Contemporary western views of nature are fraught with the dichotomy of duality between man and woman, and person and nature . . . [yet] every form of creation bears the sign of this dialectical unity, of diversity within a unifying principle . . ." (Shiva 40). In addition, in keeping with womanist principles of liberation, as a woman poet invested in spiritual and social ideals of freedom, in this piece and several others in her final collection, *We're Only Human*, Rodgers becomes an ambassador for "sustenance and sustainability" as means of achieving liberation.

> It is the energy of all living things, in all their diversity, and together, the diversity of lives wields tremendous energy. Women's work is similarly invisible in providing sustenance and creating wealth for basic needs . . . The existence of the feminine principle is linked with diversity and sharing . . .

This partnership between women's and nature's work ensures the sustainability of sustenance . . . Sustenance, in the final analysis, is built on the continued capacity of nature to renew its forests, fields, and rivers. These systems are intrinsically linked in life-producing and life-conserving cultures . . . (Shiva 44–45)

Thus, as the narrator of "A Love Poem" expresses "sometimes we take. / we care. / we love," Rodgers preserves the idea of self-preservation and sustainability via metaphors of nature, and ultimately liberation manifests in the form of an integrated spiritual and environmental consciousness that transcends performances or categories of race, religion, ethnicity, sex, or gender.

Whereas many of her earlier Black Arts poems were characterized by the treatment of race consciousness in black communities, in the poem "Visions of Peace," Rodgers's narrator speculates, "suppose . . . / that we / . . . are all divided, . . ." presumably by various religious faiths and cultural traditions in the "afterlife." As globalism inspires the social connectivity of various communities, spirituality and a collective humanistic faith in cultural pluralism become unifying and binding, as "the whole world / . . . no matter the color of skin or eyes, / . . . or the texture of hair" learn to "somehow, peacefully" coexist. As the title for this final collection of poems conveys, the idea that "we're only human" as it relates to the poem "Visions of Peace" reminds Rodgers's readers of their collective vulnerability, and the shared "earthly" fears of being oppressed, endangered, and/or silenced ultimately threaten readers' ability to imagine that in the end, "we [can] all live together." Not only is Rodgers's later work infused with political and social implications of peace, and social justice is continuously perpetuated through woman-centered principles hearkening back to her original Black Arts nation-building aesthetics, but religion and environmentalism also inform the poet's vision of global peace, as "multifarious souls / and quickening spirits" become "fundamentally, / the same." Scholar Roger S. Gottlieb's ideas are useful here. He writes, "If the civil rights struggle shows religion transforming the world of politics and feminist theology demonstrates the political transformation of religion, then the environmental movement reveals the two working together in critically important ways . . . " (153).

Similarly, in Rodgers's Buddhist-inspired piece "Ten Worlds," the narrator expresses that her "buddhist friend" has informed her that there are "ten paths to travel, to search through. / ten ways to laugh or cry and find or be / found in."[4] As individual and collective enlightenment materialize in the narrator's spiritual omnipotence, and she expresses, "i am everywhere spraying a perfume of lotus / and apple blossoms and the perfume is / called Peace," the earth and the natural environment become emotionally assuaging resources toward which the narrator can appeal for sanctity and salvation. Not only does one's emotional and physical liberation manifest in the form of spiritual ascension, but humans and worlds converge in a peaceful, collective ideal, and "bad karma have been eliminated and there / is only good reaping and sowing. /—this is the third eye—." Although Rodgers's poem is idealistic in its proposition for world peace, tolerance, and global justice, the poet reminds readers that balance of the heart and mind, and indeed balance on earth is supreme, as "ten cesspools" and "ten sanctuaries and gateways to heaven" are equally influential images in motivating human behavior in daily life. While racial politics succumb to "green" politics, and the earth becomes the sustaining symbol for nation-building between cultures, "Ten Worlds" encourages readers to look upon themselves and the ubiquitous presence of nature for inspiration, while the narrator's Buddhist friend tells her that there are "ten tall, fat and wide oak trees, / growing next to ten burning bushes. / [and] ten eyes to see one sunset through" for people of all origins. "The religious presence in environmental politics, like a good deal of the entire environmental movement, not only breaks barriers between religion and politics, theology, and social activism, but it also helps develop a world-making political agenda that may avoid being limited to one or another particular social group" (Gottlieb 160).

However, the narrator of Rodgers's poem "For Pilgrims & Strangers" conveys a degree of frustration about the potential for religion and/or religious faith, as "a shared system of beliefs, mythologies, and rituals associated with a god or gods" or as a means of achieving salvation in life or death (qtd. in Mattis and Jagers). As she expresses, "ever since I heard the Word / . . . I dreamed of going / to heaven." While this piece is a clear critique of Christianity, more importantly, Rodgers's characterization of a narrator searching for answers to spiritual questions, only to find that her life experiences are like "broken pieces . . . like a kitchen sink full of / shattered glasses and plates," is at the heart of the poem's message that spiritual and social peace are defined by one's journey toward fulfillment, and that the search for peace and spiritual enlightenment, or an acknowledgment of a "nonmaterial force that permeates all affairs, human and nonhuman," is as important as the realization of both or either (qtd. in Mattis and Jagers 4). The narrator's expressed desire to "stay whole, / through [her] life's wind and / rain storms" is as much a metaphoric translation of her life struggles and her efforts to overcome them as it is an implication of Rodgers's ecofeminist perspective, through which we find a connectivity between her character's physical and environmental worlds. "What is 'deep' about this perspective is the experience—and the conviction—that our surroundings are essential to who we are. And this is not just because they are useful, but because we are tied to them by invisible threads of inspiration, memory, esthetic delight, emotional connection, and simple wonder" (Gottlieb 163). Thus, in this poem, as in earlier Black Arts poems, Rodgers prioritizes the hopeful "questioning," though frustrated journey of the individual toward a comprehension of self as opposed to adopting a scripted ideology or path that will presumably lead to the realization of such comprehension. As the poet integrates and addresses themes of personal and political liberation struggles realized through religious and/or spiritual aspirations, she appeals to her own earlier Black Arts ideals wherein the experiential, unpredictable, and meandering journey toward these goals is as fundamental to community and individual empowerment as the "actual" realization of such goals. The "hopeful" journey that "has to do with a willingness to act in the face of sorrow and loss" for the narrator in the poem "For Pilgrims & Strangers" is a willingness to look clearly at what must be changed . . . without surety of success. "The crucial role of hope is, perhaps, simply to admit that one doesn't know what will happen" (Gottlieb 213).

And yet, in Rodgers's poem "Sheep," not only does the poet dwell within the realm of uncertainty, speculation, and/or imagination, but social, political, religious, and spiritual consciousness inspire group and/or collective activism. As the poem opens, Rodgers's narrator shares her vision of coalition-building that begins with a nightmare wherein she's on a bus "where the passengers sit passively in / the hot and stuffy cars / looking sweaty and faintly ill." While this image conjures narratives of freedom struggles recalling and remembering the civil rights freedom rides of the 1960s, as the narrator and the passengers on the bus sit in tense, agonizing discomfort like "sheep . . . gasping through the heat for every smothering breath," so collectively quiet that one "can hear a pin drop . . . / except for the bleated breathing," the bus becomes a metaphoric context for containment and confinement that informs the urgency of the passengers' desire to break free of their shared imprisonment. Consequently, someone "sees an opening / in the side of the boxcar" and they are able to free themselves, "jump[ing] off the side of the slaveship . . . / to the underground railroad . . . " where they join with others in a multicultural, cross-national freedom, characterized by "bare berlin hands, and east and west," until everyone can "all breathe again. / and [they] can get air." Even as Rodgers invokes images reflective of and narrating the historical imprisonment, liberation, and varied versions of activist struggles of black communities, such images become universally symbolic of the currency of and necessity for collaboration across borders and cultures, and the potential to "ride . . . vigilant into life . . ." rather than "obedient, / into death" is indeed only possible when we imagine ourselves working toward common interests. "In responding to oppression, African Americans have adopted political philosophies that run the gamut from gradualism to radical separatism, and this community has used strategies that range from avoidant to militant . . . Despite their differences, these various philosophies and practices are bound together by a uniform set of survivalist goals" (Mattis 265).

In addition, as discussed within the context of the aforementioned poems, political resistance and social liberation for *all* oppressed groups inform the potential for the realization of collective spiritual enlightenment, and the passengers in the poem "get relief, and . . . ride off into / the sunset or sunrise / (with music playing softly in the background)." Although the ultimate liberation and/or salvation of the passengers occurs through their collective and shared responsibility to break free of their confinement on the bus, the narrator's "nightmare turned dream" sequence also characterizes the power of vision and imagination in the pursuit of emotional and physical freedom. Thus, "dreaming" becomes a stimulus for action, and readers can "imagine" that the narrator is jarred back to reality and/or consciousness with a renewed sense of power fueled by the creative energies of her imagination.

While Rodgers's earlier career and performance as a Black Artist carried with it specific political and artistic implications, as was the case for any self-defined "Black Artist" of the late sixties and early seventies, her activism was most urgently conveyed in her poetry, and her later work continued to carry many of the aesthetic vestiges of this prior movement. As a collective, black women artists, activists, and intellectuals were bound together not only through their chosen expressions of activism, but also through the binding impact and currency of the creative work of artists like Rodgers, who produced material that continues to honor the narratives of struggle and triumph toward which activist communities turn for inspiration and validation. For instance, according to Black Panther activist Assata Shakur, the poetry provided to her by supporters while she was confined in prison in New Jersey, was, in fact, a saving grace.[5]

They gave me the poetry of our people, the tradition of our women, the relationship of human beings to nature and the search of human beings for freedom, for justice, for a world that isn't a brutal world. And those books—even through that experience—kind of just chilled me out, let me be in touch with my tradition, the beauty of my people, even though we've had to suffer such vicious oppression . . . [I]t makes you think that no matter how brutal the police, the courts are, the people fight to keep their humanity. (qtd. in James 147)

Thus, the fruits of the labor of artists like Rodgers—then and now—remain inextricably linked to histories of collaborative freedom struggles as they simultaneously inform the unique, individual activist spirit of those individuals who participate in them.

At the 2007 panel discussion on the legacies of OBAC and the BAM, hosted by Northwestern University, Rodgers reminisced about having been encouraged to attend her first OBAC meeting by her neighbors, dramatists Ann Smith and Duke MacNeal, both of whom were founding members in the theatrical arts branch of the organization. Yet Rodgers made clear her continued investment in Black Arts ideals. Angela Jackson, however, lamented the fact that her work, published during the later years of the BAM, is rarely considered as a product of the movement, despite the fact that she became a member of OBAC as early as 1969, during the height of the BAM era. But, as readers find in Jackson's later published novel, *Where I Must Go* (2009), the influence of the Black Arts ideal of collaboration in the form of activism remains relevant, despite our current postrace-era idealisms, and as race politics continue to contribute to the fallibility of the American Dream in black communities. Furthermore, as a contemporary novel of historical fiction, the plot of *Where I Must Go*, situated within the post–civil rights, Black Arts, and Black Power eras, does anything but romanticize the concept of postraciality. Ultimately, as in Jackson's earlier Black Arts–inspired poetry, the novel implicates the concept of cultural memory as a medium through which contemporary audiences can be reminded of the value of collaboration in the interest of advancing new millennium liberation projects.

According to Manning Marable,

African American leaders currently minimize tactics which a generation ago were at the heart of the black freedom movement—sit-ins, teach-ins, selective buying campaigns or boycotts, civil disobedience, strikes and demonstrations of all types . . . Somehow, black leadership today has forgotten the tactics and lessons of the past . . . (*Beyond Black* 57)

The late Marable's recent project, entitled *Malcolm X: A Life of Reinvention* (2011), is, in itself, a reminder of the value of remembering and/or revisiting the "forgotten," and Marable explores new terrains in focusing on one of the BAM's most influential icons, Malcolm X. Indeed, Malcolm X is referenced on several occasions throughout Jackson's novel, *Where I Must Go*, and Malcolm X's image, along with those of a host of other inspiring figures representing the pantheon of black activist history and culture, provide the visualistic backdrop against which much of the novel's plot takes place. Thus, I read Jackson's *Where I Must Go* as a fictional response to Marable's claim regarding contemporary politics—a jarring, imagistic narrative of innocence lost and lessons learned in the aftermath of a resistance protest facilitated by a group of black college students on the predominantly white campus of Eden University, where "the silent Black population . . . remains at 15 percent of the citizenry" (69). "It required almost forty years of labor, but Angela Jackson's novel . . . seems to have been born at the right time . . . Despite the decade, it is a coming-of-age tale with combustible questions about identity that still loom large," writes one of Jackson's reviewers (Lee). Partly inspired by Jackson's own experiences as an undergraduate at Northwestern University, as well as narratives of the black freedom movements of the 1960s and 1970s, the sequence of events within this novel of historical fiction begins when the main character, Magdalena Grace, leaves home in the fall of 1967, filled with the hope and excitement of being the first person in her family to attend college. Although Maggie is well versed in black history and has read the theories of Frantz Fanon and Marcus Garvey, for instance, her optimism about having earned a scholarship to study art at the prestigious white university and thus her potential to realize the American Dream is clear from the start. Essentially, Maggie believes in the possibility of a future wherein being black won't prove to limit her career goals. However, Maggie's first year is composed of a series of experiences that force her to reckon with the realities of racial discrimination, which culminate in her participation in a student stand-in organized by a group of her friends and other black student leaders on campus. Maggie's perspective about and vision for her future and the fate of her family and community change when she and her friends take control of the campus's financial administration building—a symbol for white capitalist power and its encroachment on black aspirations for educational opportunities, social equality, and political empowerment.

Even as early as the prologue, Jackson's main character, Magdalena Grace, can be perceived as the embodiment of the Black Arts ideals that informed the writer's own earlier poetry, and Maggie feels "inside [her] skin all these women and men" who make up her family's history. Maggie is empowered by the idea of reaching her goal to become an artist and the living breathing proof that the civil rights struggles of her predecessors will be manifested in her own achievements. As Maggie's body is described as "a mosaic made of colors, shapes, designs, textural arrangements, symmetries, studies in contrasts that collide, oils and water that hug like sweat . . . all these forms meshed so fine, so skillfully, that [she] is feeling," readers of Jackson's earlier poetry, included in the collections *VooDoo/Love Magic* (1974) and *The Greenville Club* (1977), are reminded of the writer's ability to weave together and privilege the experiences of diverse yet interconnected black communities, whose narratives are bound by unifying memories and dreams of better futures. In this way, Maggie's perspectives are narrated as vivid images consistent with Jackson's aesthetic sensibilities. Throughout the novel, readers are taken on a visual journey across the campus, including the Black Student Union of Eden University—known as "Blood Island" among the students, who see the doors of the building as a metaphoric portal through which they pass and become "slaves" to their white administrative "masters" at the university. About the inside of the union, Maggie relays, "Fissures run down from the ceiling. The walls the lightest shade of blue, upon which, as if set against a cracked sky, posters preside. The Marcus Garvey. The Malcolm X. A calendar of birthdays of important Blackpeople. Notices of coming events . . ." (43). Through Maggie's detailed descriptions, readers meet the older graduate students on campus, who visit Blood Island:

> They are men in their twenties and thirties who have married and started families with their college sweethearts, who are never seen by anyone at Eden . . . Or they are men who have spent their college summers in the South, riding through brown tobacco rivers of spit while faces stretched into masks of hate leered at them; they have marched and organized with SNCC and CORE, and history taught them new songs that sprout fire in their mouths. They are men who ducked bullets on Asian soil or in the American South. Carefully and nonchalantly they've learned to settle their big feet on possible land mines, exploding ground. (44)

Rather than spin a romantic narrative about Maggie and her peers' dreams of acquiring a college education and fulfilling their working-class aspirations to realize the comforts of the American Dream of a middle-class existence, Jackson lets readers find that Maggie begins to understand rather early in her undergraduate experience that her future may not hold the promise that she hopes, and that her world at Eden isn't all that it seems. Bridging the historical and ideological gap between Maggie and her peers as symbolic representatives of racial progress and those who are less fortunate, who dwell on the outside of Eden's promise and are suspicious of the presumed arrogance of educated blacks like Maggie and her friends, Jackson's narrative of hope and promise begins to take a turn when (black) worlds start to overlap and collide outside of the idyllic, racially harmonious climate and sanctity of Eden's campus. This is most vividly conveyed when Maggie and her college peers take a trip to Great Zimbabwe, a club located in a once prosperous and popular black neighborhood.

> Great Zimbabwe is a mecca for the Black Arts Movement—revolutionary poets who dip and dance like sanctified preachers when they read, saxophonists and flutists who combine the quirky beauty of bebop with the atonal freedom of African ritual music and the lyricism of Ellington, dancers who wide-leg leap to ceilings like spiders on fire under history's inflammatory eye ... Black history from ancient pyramid to urban projects ... to the murdered Malcolm X. From the Queen of Sheba to Gwendolyn Brooks, poet. (102)

It is here where Maggie and her peers meet a group of black locals who are unimpressed with their status as college students on the recently integrated white campus of Eden. "Welcome, my young brothers and sisters, down from the halls of Whiteness," one character mocks (105). This is also one of the first scenes in which Jackson progressively encourages her contemporary, postrace readership to "look back" at and engage a time when a previous generation had to rely upon dangerous ways of challenging social oppression. "Race and institutional racism have not yet declined... To a real extent, the cultural class is intergenerational, symbolized by the radical differences in discourse, political experiences, and social expectations between those African-Americans born before 1964 and those who were born after the great legislative victories of the civil-rights movement" (Marable 206).

However, to "look back" on history, as prompted by the plot of *Where I Must Go*, and through the narrative of Maggie and her Eden University peers is to revisit not only legacies of racism, but also sexism, and the historical objectification of black female sexuality in particular. More specifically, it is the experience endured by Maggie's roommate, Essie, which propels the students' protest and rebellion. When Essie is brutally attacked and becomes the victim of an attempted rape at the hands of white men, and the college administration refuses to pursue the matter on Essie's behalf in the interest of justice, "Essie's story hit campus like a mortar bomb" and Maggie and her friends on the "Central Committee" decide to "take over [the] motherfucker" (270, 271). "If we cannot protect our women, we are not Blackmen," William proclaims (270). Although Maggie knows that "Mama and Madaddy didn't send [her] to Eden to get put out," she is inspired by the titles of books that fill the shelves of the library, and which testify to prior narratives of struggle in the face of fear, such as that she endures now as a revolutionary, books including Margaret Walker's *Jubilee*, W. E. B. Du Bois's *The Souls of Black Folk*, and Lorraine Hansberry's *A Raisin in the Sun*. As she is drawn into the stand-in at the campus financial administration building, Maggie dreams of a vivid sequence of coalescing memories chronicling yet-to-be-fulfilled experiences and terrorizing consequences for her activism.

> First, the dream of Leona, Essie, and me walking in the most lush Technicolor garden . . . Second, the dream of standing on top of the administration building with the glass dome . . . Then the most awful feeling of ineptitude . . . [Third] a full-fledged scenario of chaos, taxing and wondrous to be inside . . . It is like being inside Picasso's *Guernica* or a wonderful collage of printed papers, *Train Whistle Blues: 1* by Romare Bearden . . . So many Black faces and significant shapes. It is that kind of dream. (274–275)

Thus, her dream of cross-cultural and overlapping metaphors that iterate and unify narratives of global liberation struggles becomes a politically inspired proposition for a collaborative transnation-building project compelled by the activist traditions of prior generations. The imagistic manifestation of Maggie's projected kaleidoscope-like perspective is a vivid transcription of Marable's "transformative perspective" ideal, which

> differs from the inclusionist and black-nationalist perspectives, in that its chief objective is the dismantling or destruction of all forms of inequality. Racism is perceived . . . as an unequal relationship between social aggregates, based on power and violence . . . [when] black people have begun to realize that wider power relationships must also be transformed to achieve full human equality. (212)

Marable goes on to suggest that the "new progressive paradigm must grasp the common sense of our people, their recognition of the inequalities in daily life which exist under a racist and capitalist social order, and create the possibilities for new resistance movements" (214). While I read Jackson's novel as a narrative of postrace dystopia, given its dismal yet realistic portrayal and portraiture of racism and the trauma within the lives of young black characters caught in the grip of racial inequality, I also see the presence of "memory" and "nostalgia" in the novel as narrative elements that appear in Jackson's earlier work, and which continue to serve as coalition-inspiring motifs. More specifically, as Maggie becomes aware of her own potential through her activism and alignment with others in the political fight for social justice, she is further convinced of her own power and capabilities to transform and contribute to what will become a perpetual campaign against national oppression and global imperialism. In this way, Jackson's postrace narrative, situated within the historical context of the "past," serves as a potentially arousing plea for those who may be lulled by the rhetoric of postraciality to reconsider the extent to which the initiatives of the past continue to be relevant. At the novel's finale, Maggie lies unsleeping and thinks of a "mural on the raw side of an abandoned building in an area slated for urban renewal that never comes"—quite possibly a reference to the real life Black Arts mural that once adorned the wall of a building on Chicago's South Side, entitled the *Wall of Respect*, which, like the wall of the building Maggie recalls, "[was] bright and big with images of our heroes," and she "thinks of a painting by Jacob Lawrence . . . of how the Blackpeople speak on canvas—eloquent, so powerful, muscular, they defy the two dimensions of canvas. I want to capture us in my own way. I have to educate myself," she thinks to herself (373).[6]

Furthermore, it is important to note the activist participation of young women like Maggie in the plot of *Where I Must Go*, and the fact that the characters' protest was coordinated in response to an act of terrifying violence against a young woman, who herself becomes part of the resistance, for these aspects of the novel reflect Jackson's impetus to prioritize the central role that women played in freedom struggles of this era. Thus, the writer "enlarges the scope of how black radicalism is understood," and counters the "perception that black women activists were summarily excluded from leadership roles . . . " (Gore, Theoharis, Woodard 6, 10). As Essie's experience initiates the activist response of her male and female peers, which then compels a re/action from the Eden University community and administration, the plot calls attention to the interlocking issues of racial and gender injustices, and Essie becomes a symbol for both black *and* feminist power. "The dominant perception that feminist politics and the fight for women's equality occurred largely outside of the black freedom struggle and with little engagement from black women has emerged implicitly and explicitly in numerous studies" (Gore, Theoharis, Woodard 9). In this way, much like the later work of Carolyn Rodgers—Jackson's OBAC and Black Arts kinswoman—with the publication of *Where I Must Go*, Jackson's contemporary readership is challenged to reconstruct the civil rights, Black Arts, and Black Power legacies oriented around the participation of their women in order to grasp the continued relevance of the goals characterized by the activist energies of one of the most contested moments in our nation's history.

Conclusion

You Remind Me... "Post–BAM/Soul" Reflections

Not only can the legacy of the Black Arts Movement be critiqued through an examination of the vast pantheon of material produced by those who were committed to perpetuating its objectives via nationalist and culturally inspired ideals at that time, but it can also be interpreted within existing contemporary mediums of expression invoked by later generations of artists who have seized upon, preserved, and been inspired by the culturally and politically motivated aesthetics promoted by Black Artists of an earlier era. Many scholars have commented on the ways in which some of the BAM's most popular and controversial rhetorical features have appealed to later generations and prompted new dialogues and debates about the resiliency of BAM aesthetics that have been adapted to respond to the cultural, political, and artistic sensibilities of new audiences. Modern and contemporary paradigms of African American expression, including hip-hop and "post-soul" aesthetics that engage narratives of cultural autonomy, race consciousness, and community and/or nation-building ideals through popular media reflect and recall many of the BAM's core elements, as noted by Mark Anthony Neal, for instance:

> Representatives of the black arts movement and a school of black nationalist thought... form some of the intellectual building blocks of the post-soul generation. [Their] work continues to resonate in the work of the post-soul intelligentsia, perhaps because they rightly understood that accessibility to the masses was not necessarily antithetical to high creativity, political activism, and intellectual acumen... It is this nationalist foothold on college campuses that often served to initially politicize the post-soul generation, especially when expressed via hip hop...[1]

Conclusion

In this regard, the "success" and legacy of BAM exists within the constantly morphing and ever-expanding black vernacular tradition, as do its successes, failures, faults, and the unresolved questions raised about its objectives since its inception. Scholars continue to debate BAM's import and new generations of readers continue to both glamorize and vilify its objectives, as well as be compelled by its most provocative aesthetics as means of characterizing identity, culture, community, and belonging.

As products of what Mark Anthony Neal and Nelson George have referred to as the "post-soul" generation, contemporary artists continue to express ideas about identity and community in transnational contexts, and new technology-driven media inform such practices. The work of female Black Artists of the sixties and seventies reflects their interest in moving beyond the ideals of the BAM in a way that appeals to rather than compromises the core principles of the movement's nation-building aesthetic, and it honors what critic Dionne Espinoza refers to as "[e]xpressions of embodiment, oppression, and self-naming ... [that are] central to the politics of interpretation and to the politics of identity."[2] Faced with the challenge of demonstrating a commitment toward the popular aesthetics of this period, for women writers the struggle to introduce universal themes while initiating their own unique poetic and artistic perspectives was especially challenging yet fruitful.

Johari Amini, Carolyn Rodgers, and Angela Jackson played important roles in the advancement of the culturally specific aesthetics for which men of the BAM continue to be credited. And much of their Black Art suggests that not only were they invested in gender empowerment and reorienting the masculinist goals of BAM in order to accommodate their voices, but they encouraged various versions of Black Art and consequently freed it from its commonly perceived "fixed" qualities in favor of a much more amorphous concept that would thrive beyond its most inspired years. Although a "vast amount of cultural criticism, particularly from black feminist and 'womanist' authors has profoundly rethought the nature and limits of black nationalism in the years since the Panthers' heyday," an evaluation of the work of rarely credited writers and/or lesser-known figures such as Amini, Rodgers, and Jackson might compel new ways of thinking about black nationalism of the sixties and seventies (T. V. Reed 69). Even at the height of the BAM, their work offered audiences alternative ways in which to consider nation-building objectives.

As many scholars have noted, Black Arts and Black Power cultures continue to be referenced and emulated by popular artists in contemporary culture in every venue of artistic and political expression. In particular, "Hip-hop culture has continued to draw extensively on African American culture of the 1960's and 1970's and to re-envision the era's cultural politics as its most extensive legacy" (Ongiri 96). Yet much of this "nostalgia" recycles some of the very same fixed masculinist practices for which the BAM has come to be notoriously remembered in spite of the fact that there is so much more to be considered with regard to the movement's legacy. Danny Hoch's contention that "[h]ip-hop's origins are multifaceted, politically conflicting, consistently debated, and highly complicated, because we are still living through many of the same conditions that caused its birth" is noteworthy, since, as he suggests, "aesthetics lie foremost in the social context from which it sprung" (350). He goes on to reference the turmoil of various social and political events in American history as having given rise to hip-hop culture, including the civil rights movement, the turmoil of the militarized political movements, urban blight, the advent of the digital age, an exploding prison population, and the AIDS epidemic, for instance (350). What I find most useful in this critique is the implied reference to the cross-pollinating and ultimately multifarious aspects of hip-hop culture as an extension of earlier cultures and the ideals of prior generations, including that of Black Artists, who were themselves struggling to give birth to a "new" form of expression. Like hip-hop, the goals of the BAM were articulated through a range of voices, yet such goals continue to be perceived in very particular, commercial, and reductive ways.

In spite of the challenges of performing and positioning themselves as politically and artistically conscious writers simultaneously working within specific literary and historical traditions as well as popular frameworks of black expression, Amini, Rodgers, and Jackson reveal in their poetry each writer's ability to experiment with, expand, and explore the parameters of these contexts. Equally significant is their shared status as black women writers working within a woman-centered tradition to shape the social and political boundaries of artistic expression within male-dominated spaces, while they kept visionary eyes toward the future. As we continue to explore the range of voices and facets of the BAM's legacy, it becomes ever clearer that it merits rediscovery as that which was and continues to be far-reaching and indeed productively, paradoxically ambiguous.

Notes

Introduction

1. See the documentary *Cointelpro 101* released by the Freedom Archives regarding the history of government surveillance of activist social justice organizations.

2. See "Power to the People!: The Art of Black Power," introduction in *New Thoughts on the Black Arts Movement*, ed. Lisa Gail Collins and Margo Natalie Crawford (New Brunswick, NJ: Rutgers University Press, 2006), 1–22, for an overview of the collection's focus on some of the more intricate and understudied aspects of the BAM.

3. For instance, see Crawford's essay "Must Revolution Be a Family Affair?: Revisiting The Black Woman" in *Want to Start a Revolution?: Radical Women in the Black Freedom Struggle*, ed. Dayo F. Gore, Jeanne Theoharis, and Komozi Woodard (New York: New York University Press, 2009), 185–205; Pollard's "Sexual Subversions, Political Inversions: Women's Poetry and the Politics of the Black Arts Movement" in *New Thoughts on the Black Arts Movement*, ed. Lisa Gail Collins and Margo Natalie Crawford (New Brunswick, NJ: Rutgers University Press, 2006), 173–186; and Traylor's "Women Writers of the Black Arts Movement" in *The Cambridge Companion to African American Women's Literature*, ed. Angelyn Mitchell and Danille K. Taylor (Cambridge; New York: Cambridge University Press, 2009), 50–70.

4. For more insight about the cross-cultural activism inspired by the Black Arts Movement and Black Power Movement, see, for instance, T. V. Reed's *The Art of Protest: Culture and Activism from the Civil Rights Movement to the Streets of Seattle* (Minneapolis: University of Minnesota Press, 2005) and Fred Ho's *Wicked Theory, Naked Practice: A Fred Ho Reader*, ed. Diane Fujino and Bill V. Mullen (Minneapolis: University of Minnesota Press, 2009).

5. Benston's project, *Performing Blackness: Enactments of African-American Modernism* (London: Routledge, 2000), introduces useful theoretical paradigms for evaluating the performative aspect of BAM culture, wherein the author calls for new ways of considering the subject.

6. For more on this, see T. V. Reed's *The Art of Protest: Culture and Activism from the Civil Rights Movement to the Streets of Seattle* (Minneapolis: University of Minnesota Press, 2005).

7. Baraka, Neal, and Stewart each published short pieces addressing the BAM aesthetic, which appear in *Black Fire: An Anthology of Afro-American Writing*, ed. Baraka and Neal (Baltimore: Black Classics Press, 1968).

8. Ibid.

9. Ibid.

10. See chapter seven of James Smethurst's *The Black Arts Movement: Literary Nationalism in the 1960's and 1970's* (Chapel Hill: University of North Carolina Press, 2005), 179–243.

11. For a critique of this subject, see Angela Davis's "Afro-Images: Politics, Fashion, and Nostalgia" in *The Angela Y. Davis Reader*, ed. Joy James (Malden, MA: Blackwell Publishers Inc., 1999), 289–293.

12. Audre Lorde's poem can be found in *The Collected Poems of Audre Lorde* (New York: W.W. Norton & Co., Inc., 1978).

13. These are but a few names from an impressive list of pioneering black feminist scholars who have developed inspired critiques of black women's traditions, including writing and/or literature of political, social, and cultural resistance. Others include Cheryl Wall, Claudia Tate, and Hazel Carby, for instance.

14. For instance, Ajuan Maria Mance discusses several major works by Carolyn Rodgers in *Inventing Black Women* (Knoxville: University of Tennessee Press, 2007), and Tony Bolden devotes a healthy discussion to Carolyn Rodgers in *Afro-Blue: Improvisations in African American Poetry and Culture* (Urbana and Chicago: University of Illinois Press, 2004), 24. In addition, Rodgers's work is evaluated within the context of feminist culture as well in Kim Whitehead's *The Feminist Poetry Movement* (Jackson, MS: University Press of Mississippi, 1996) and Karen Jackson Ford's *Gender and the Poetics of Excess* (Jackson, MS: University Press of Mississippi, 1997).

15. Rodgers mentions the ways in which poet and writer Margaret Walker influenced her own work at the conference on Black Arts in Chicago, hosted at Northwestern University in Evanston, Illinois, in 2007. The poem "For My People" can be found in *This Is My Century: New and Collected Poems* (Athens: University of Georgia Press, 1989).

16. Bruce Weber wrote an extensive review of Rodgers and her life's work in a *New York Times* online obituary section, published on April 19, 2010. http://www.nytimes.com/2010/04/19/books/19rodgers.html.

17. Madhubuti was quoted as having said such about Rodgers in multiple venues, including the September 2010 edition of *The Writer's Chronicle* and *Chickenbones*, an online journal reporting on literary and artistic stories of interest to black Americans.

18. Rodgers's piece was first published in the *Negro Digest* (Sept. 1969): 18–19.

19. See Bettye L. Parker-Smith's review of Rodgers's *How I Got OVAH* for a complete assessment of the poet's work. Rodgers also made a public appearance at the panel discussion on the Black Arts Movement in Chicago in 2007, hosted by Northwestern University in Evanston, Illinois.

20. The *New York Times* published an article about Jackson and her life's work in October 2009.

21. Thomas is well known for his analysis of the relationship between black American cultural expression and African linguistic culture. For more on Thomas's work, see *Don't Deny My Name*, a collection of his essays, edited by Aldon Lynn Nielsen (Ann Arbor: University of Michigan Press, 2008).

Chapter One

1. Komozi Woodard's preface to *A Nation within A Nation: LeRoi Jones (Amiri Baraka) and Black Power Politics*, ed. Woodard (Chapel Hill: University of North Carolina Press, 1999).

2. See Stephen Henderson's essay "'Survival Motion': A Study of the Black Writer and the Black Revolution in America" in *The Militant Black Writer*, ed. Mercer Cook and Henderson (Madison: University of Wisconsin Press, 1969).

3. See Neal's afterword "And Shine Swam On" in *Black Fire: An Anthology of Afro-American Writing*, ed. Amiri Baraka and Neal (Baltimore: Black Classics Press, 1968), 637–656, for a lengthy discussion of Black Arts goals linked with Black Power nationalism.

4. Martin Delaney was a nineteenth-century black abolitionist, writer, theorist, and physician, who is often considered to be the progenitor of the black nationalist tradition in America. His novel *Black, or the Huts of America* addressed black activism and rebellion during slavery.

5. Ellison's nameless character is introduced to black nationalism when he meets "Ras"—a community activist—after moving to New York City.

6. Brooks reflects on her participation in the BAM and her support of Black Artists in a series of interviews included in the collection *Conversations with Gwendolyn Brooks*, ed. Gloria Wade Gayles (Jackson: University Press of Mississippi, 2003).

7. See "SNCC Position Paper: Women in the Movement," written in 1964 and published in *"Takin' It to the Streets": A Sixties Reader*, ed. Alexander Bloom and Wini Breines (New York: Oxford University Press, 1995), 45–47.

8. This is evident in poems that celebrated the artistic, historical, and political significance of the black female perspective, such as Mari Evans's "I Am a Black Woman" or Sonia Sanchez's "for our lady," both published in 1969.

9. This report, also referred to as "The Negro Family: The Case for National Action," was authored by Senator Daniel Patrick Moynihan in 1965 and, among other things, addressed poverty in the black community.

10. Both poems can be found in *Home Coming: Poems* (Detroit: Broadside Press, 1969).

11. "Concerning One Responsible Nigger with Too Much Power" can be found in *The Collected Poetry of Nikki Giovanni*, ed. Ann Burns (New York: Morrow Publishers, 2003).

12. Evans's poem can be found in the collection *I Am a Black Woman* (New York: Morrow Publishers, 1970).

13. Clifton's poem appears in *Good Woman: Poems and a Memoir* (BOA Editions, Ltd., 1987).

14. Larry Neal, from *Visions of a Liberated Future: Black Arts Movement Writings by Larry Neal* (New York: Thunder's Mouth Press, 1989), 62–78.

15. Cleaver's comments about and attacks on Baldwin's sexuality and literary career were eventually published in *Soul on Ice* (1968).

16. The essay "Here Be Dragons" was first published in *Playboy Magazine* in 1985, under the title "Freaks and the American Ideal of Manhood."

17. For instance, at the Northwestern University panel discussion on the Black Arts Movement in Chicago, hosted in 2007, Sterling Plumpp, Carolyn Rodgers, and Angela Jackson were hesitant to validate or deny Fuller's alleged homosexuality, which may speak to the ways in which black male homosexuality remains a "taboo" subject with regard to BAM legacies.

18. Majors published several poems inspired by his Vietnam War experiences; Madhubuti's "The Long Reality" appears in *THINK BLACK* (Detroit: Broadside Press, 1969); and Rodgers's poem appears in her first collection, *Paper Soul* (Chicago: Third World Press, 1968).

19. *For Malcolm: Poems on the Life and Death of Malcolm X* was published by Randall's Broadside Press in 1967. Also, Baraka's quote appears in the essay "Afro-American Literature and Class Struggle" in *Paradigms in Black Studies*, ed. Abdul Alkalimat (Chicago: Twenty-First Century Books and Publications, 1990), 125.

20. Marable's long-awaited biography and reevaluation of Malcolm X's life and legacy caused quite a stir amongst critics and audiences with its probing questions and theories regarding the murder of the Black Power icon as well as his sexuality.

21. Till was living with his mother in Chicago but visiting relatives in Mississippi when the husband of the white woman to whom Till had made advances, Carolyn Bryant, and his cousin murdered Till several days after the alleged incident. Roy Bryant and his cousin admitted to beating the young Till and throwing him into the Tallahatchie River, where he was found several days later. Till's murder was one of several cases that led to the eventual Civil Rights Act of 1957. Both men were acquitted of Till's kidnapping and murder, and even though they admitted to these crimes in a later interview, due to the protection of the double-jeopardy law, neither man was ever convicted.

22. Sanchez's poem appears in *Morning Haiku* (Boston: Beacon Press, 2010).

Chapter Two

1. James Smethurst provides a context for thinking about the ways in which the ideological and political foundations of BAM were appropriated regionally and institutionally, as well as the ways in which it influenced the relationship between art and politics globally in *The Black Arts Movement: Literary Nationalism in the 1960's and 1970's* (Chapel Hill: University of North Carolina Press, 2005), 179.

2. For instance, see Crawford's "Black Light on the *Wall of Respect*" in *New Thoughts on the Black Arts Movement* (New Brunswick, NJ: Rutgers University Press, 2006), 23–42; and Smith's "Chicago Poets, OBAC, and the Black Arts Movement" in *The Black Columbiad: Defining Moments in African-American Literature and Culture* (Cambridge, MA: Harvard University Press, 1994), 253–264.

3. Margaret Burroughs, personal interview, summer 2000. Also, Black Panther leader Fred Hampton was targeted and killed during a 1969 Chicago police raid, for instance, as part of the government's attempt to "neutralize" the activities of Black Power activists. The instance was a grave reminder of the extent to which social and

political activist groups of this era were perceived as national threats by the U.S. government and the extent to which it attempted to dissolve such groups.

4. Ibid.

5. Johari Amini, personal interview, summer 2000.

6. Ibid.

7. Black Artists such as Larry Neal cited writers like Richard Wright and James Baldwin, for example, for producing work that conformed more to the "literary" standards of white, academic culture rather than the "poetic" form, which was considered to be more accessible to Black Arts audiences, and Carolyn Rodgers and Amiri Baraka, for example, advocated the incorporation of black vernacular in Black Art as a way of engaging urban black audiences.

8. Margo Natalie Crawford suggests, for instance, in her essay "Black Light on the *Wall of Respect*," that "[p]hotography is one of the most neglected genres of the Black Arts Movement," 24.

9. Ann MacNeal, personal interview, summer 2000.

10. Jeff Donaldson, personal interview, summer 2001.

11. See Larry Neal's *Visions of a Liberated Future: Black Arts Movement Writings by Larry Neal* (New York: Thunder's Mouth Press, 1989), 62–78. Although Neal's text was published in *Ebony*, the *Negro Digest* also served as a platform for black writers, including BAM participants, in which writers would provide insights about trends in black writing. For instance, in a 1967 edition of the *Negro Digest* (even before it became the more politically assertive *Black World*), a host of some of the most popular black writers contributed their thoughts to the solvency and potential of "Black Art" and the relationship between black artistic expression and politics. The first issue of this publication under the name the *Black World* ushered in a new political and artistic approach to defining the future of African American culture for its readership.

12. Ibid.

13. This appeared in one of the later editions of *Nommo*, in which writers such as Mari Evans, Gwendolyn Brooks, and a host of others were represented in this collective tribute. In addition, Amini, Rodgers, Jackson, and Plumpp offered favorable remarks in memory of Fuller's contributions at the Northwestern University panel discussion on Chicago Black Arts culture on October 16, 2007.

14. Ibid.

15. From Bill V. Mullen's historical study of leftist politics in Chicago, entitled *Popular Fronts: Chicago and African American Cultural Politics, 1935–46* (Urbana: University of Illinois Press, 1999), 192.

16. Johari Amini, personal interview, summer 2000.

17. Ibid.

18. "To Don at Salaam" appears in Brooks's *Family Pictures* (1970) and "In the Mecca" appears in the collection under the same name (1968).

19. See Joyce Ann Joyce's essay, entitled "The Poetry of Gwendolyn Brooks: An Afrocentric Exploration," in *On Gwendolyn Brooks, a Reliant Contemplation*, ed. Stephen Caldwell Wright (Ann Arbor: University of Michigan, 1996), 246–253.

20. Located in Chicago State University's main campus library, this space serves as both a memorial to Brooks and an educational resource for students and faculty.

21. Ward, Bennett, and Fabio's pieces appear in the collection *To Gwen With Love*, ed. Patricia Brown, Don L. Lee, and Francis Ward (Chicago: Johnson Publications, 1971).

22. Ibid.

Chapter Three

1. Amini expresses this in the foreword to *Images in Black*.

2. From Angela Davis, "Black Nationalism: The Sixties and the Nineties" in *Black Popular Culture*, ed. Gina Dint (Seattle: Bay Press, 1992). Rpt. in *The Angela Y. Davis Reader*, ed. Joy James (Malden, MA: Blackwell Publishers Inc., 1999), 292–293.

3. Johari Amini, telephone interview, summer 2000.

4. Madhubuti's *Dynamite Voices* (1969) outlined the expectations for BAM artists as it related to their responsibilities to black audiences. Amiri Baraka's poem "Black Art" also calls for specific characteristics to which BAM work and/or artists must conform.

5. Johari Amini, telephone interview, summer 2000.

6. OBAC sponsored various mediums of expression in the advancement of nation-building initiatives, including performance art workshops. Also, see *New Thoughts on the Black Arts Movement*, ed. Lisa Gail Collins and Margo Natalie Crawford (New Brunswick and London: Rutgers University Press, 2006), which includes numerous essays that collectively address the multimedia initiatives of the Black Arts Movement.

7. See Paul Laurence Dunbar's poem "We Wear the Mask," published in 1895, which also reflects the treatment of the double-consciousness and/or "masking" motif.

Chapter Four

1. Rodgers's tributary poem to Hoyt Fuller appears in the "Poetry 1967–1975" section of OBAC's *Nommo*, 73.

2. Bettye L. Parker-Smith's review "Running Wild in Her Soul: The Poetry of Carolyn Rodgers" in *Black Women Writers (1950–1980): A Critical Evaluation*, ed. Mari Evans (New York: Anchor Press, 1984), 393–410, is one of the first comprehensive reviews of the poet's work.

3. Randall's and Madhubuti's reviews of Rodgers's work are included in *Black Women Writers (1950–1980): A Critical Evaluation*, ed. Mari Evans.

4. See Jackson's commentary on Rodgers in *Black American Women Poets and Dramatists*, ed. Harold Bloom (New York: Chelsea House Publishers, 1996), 185.

5. For instance, see *The Norton Anthology of African American Literature*, ed. Henry Louis Gates, Jr., and Nellie Y. McKay (New York: W.W. Norton & Company, 1997), 2122–2126.

6. Madhubuti and Amiri Baraka, for instance, placed a high responsibility on black writers to respond to and revise racist social and political practices in their writing and helped to establish the initial standards by which the work of BAM writers would

be judged. Madhubuti's book *Dynamite Voices* is considered to be one of the most influential texts in the construction of BAM ideals as they relate to the responsibility of politically inspired artists.

7. For instance, Larry Neal, Amiri Baraka, and Haki Madhubuti are often credited as being the veritable "forefathers" of the Black Arts Movement, as cited by multiple BAM scholars.

8. Parker-Smith's brief review of Rodgers's work is reprinted in *Black American Women Poets and Dramatists*, ed. Harold Bloom (New York: Chelsea House Publishers, 1996).

9. Nikki Giovanni and Sonia Sanchez, for example, also referred to this in interviews with Claudia Tate with regard to their interpretations of Black Art, published in *Black Women Writers at Work* (1984).

Chapter Five

1. The November 1969 publication of the *Negro Digest* devotes a substantial portion of this issue to various acclaimed writers of this period, such as A.B. Spellman, Maulana Karenga, and Mari Evans, who discuss the political, cultural, and artistic achievements of black Americans at the close of the sixties. Also see Don L. Lee's "Voices of the Seventies: Black Critics," *Black World* (September 1970): 24. Lee reiterates some of the initial concepts and objectives of Black Artists of the Black Arts Movement of the sixties for emerging writers of the seventies. As one of the founding members of the OBAC writers workshop, Lee continues to be an essential and influential figure for black writers of the new decade, and continues to be insistent about the Black Artist's responsibility toward the black community.

2. K. Anthony Appiah and Amy Gutman, *Color Conscious: The Political Morality of Race* (Princeton, NJ: Princeton University Press, 1996), 85–86.

3. This conference, facilitated by Valerie Smith in the summer of 2002, was focused toward the consideration of the Civil Rights Movement within the historical framework of American culture. More specifically, discussions about the way in which this era is memorialized and perpetuated within academic scholarship and the American consciousness and how factors such as gender, race, and audience factor into the representation of this particular historical moment were also engaged.

4. Although the material that I evaluate appears several years after the inception of the OBAC writers workshop, it is important to acknowledge that Jackson writes within an already-established tradition in which the work of women writers was not as popular as that of their male contemporaries. Thus, a critique of her artistic approach may yield the extent to which the pressures and/or expectations of the criteria developed during the original workshop have dissolved or remain consistent.

5. Debra Pollack, "Performing Writing," in *The Ends of Performance*, ed. Peggy Phelan and Jill Lane (New York: New York University Press, 1998), 80. In addition to her explanation of "performative writing" as "evocative," Pollack interprets it as being "subjective," "nervous," "metonymic," "citational," and "consequential."

172 Notes

6. For example, see Tate's *Domestic Allegories of Political Desire*, and Carby's *Reconstructing Womanhood* for analyses of the treatment of the domestic context and black women writing in the nineteenth century.

Chapter Six

1. This discussion brought together former OBAC participants, who talked about the legacy of Chicago's Black Arts Movement within the context of the civil rights struggle. The event took place on October 16, 2007, at Northwestern University, and can be accessed online via YouTube.

2. As discussed in the introduction of this project, Baraka, for instance, speculated that Rodgers had committed herself to a religious lifestyle and had disengaged herself from BAM projects and its legacy. His comments can be found in his essay "Afro-American Literature and Class Struggle" in *Paradigms in Black Studies: Intellectual History, Cultural Meaning, and Political Ideology*, ed. Abdul Alkalimat (Chicago: Twenty-First Century Books and Publications, 1990), 119–142.

3. See http://www.poetryfoundation.org/bio/carolyn-m-rodgers.

4. The number "10" in Buddhism refers to the "10 Hindrances to Enlightenment."

5. Assata Shakur is a former member of the Black Panther Party and the Black Liberation Army who survived in exile after having escaped from prison when she was arrested as a political prisoner after being wrongfully accused of acting as an accomplice to the murder of a New Jersey state trooper in 1977.

6. See Margo Natalie Crawford's "Black Light on the *Wall of Respect*" in *New Thoughts on the Black Arts Movement*, ed. Lisa Gail Collins and Margo Natalie Crawford (New Brunswick, NJ: Rutgers University Press, 2006), 23–42.

Conclusion

1. In *Soul Babies: Black Popular Culture and the Post-Soul Aesthetic* (New York: Routledge, 2002), Mark Anthony Neal discusses the impact of the Black Arts Movement and its political imperatives on the current generation of artists and intellectuals and evaluates its appeal in the marketplace particularly as it relates to emerging ideologies of African American culture. The contemporary artists that I refer to in the conclusion are all products of this generation, and their work reflects similar trends as their predecessors Rodgers, Amini, and Jackson in constructing "alternative" spaces of cultural and individual representation.

2. Dionne Espinoza's quote is taken from the collection *Other Sisterhoods: Literary Theory and U.S. Women of Color*, ed. Sandra Kumamoto Stanley (Urbana: University of Illinois Press,1998), 48.

Works Cited

Alkalimat, Abdul. Personal interview. Summer 2001.
Adeleke, Tunde. *The Case Against Afrocentrism*. Jackson, MS: University Press of Mississippi, 2009.
Amini, Johari. *Black Essence*. Chicago: Third World Press, 1968.
——. *Images in Black*. Chicago: Third World Press, 1967.
——. Personal interviews. Summer 1999–summer 2002.
Baker, Houston. "The Florescence of Nationalism in the 1960s and 1970s." In *On Gwendolyn Brooks, a Reliant Contemplation*. Ed. Stephen Caldwell Wright. Ann Arbor: University of Michigan, 1996. 116–123.
Baldwin, James. "Here Be Dragons." *Traps: African American Men on Gender and Sexuality*. Ed. Rudolph P. Byrd and Beverly Guy-Sheftall. Bloomington, IN: Indiana University Press, 2001. 207–218.
Bambara, Toni Cade, ed. *The Black Woman: An Anthology*. New York: New American Library 1970.
Baraka, Amiri. "A BAM Roll Call." *Chickenbones: A Journal for Literary and Artistic African American Themes*. July 2004. http://www.nathanielturner.com/bamrollcall.htm.
——. "Afro-American Literature and Class Struggle." In *Paradigms in Black Studies: Intellectual History, Cultural Meaning, and Political Ideology*. Ed. Abdul Alkalimat. Chicago: Twenty-First Century Books and Publications, 1990. 119–142.
——, and Larry Neal, eds. *Black Fire: An Anthology of Afro-American Writing*. New York: Morrow Publishers, 1968.
Battle, Juan, and Sandra L. Barnes. Introduction. In *Black Sexualities: Probing Powers, Passions, Practices, and Policies*. Ed. Battle and Barnes. New Brunswick: Rutgers University Press, 2010. 1–12.
Beach, Christopher. *The Cambridge Introduction to Twentieth-Century American Poetry*. Cambridge: Cambridge University Press, 2003.
Benston, Kimberly. *Performing Blackness: Enactments of African-American Modernism*. London: Routledge, 2000.
Bethel, Kathleen E. "Afrocentricity and the Arrangement of Knowledge." In *Afrocentricity and the Academy: Essays on Theory and Practice*. Ed. James L. Conyers, Jr. Jefferson, NC: McFarland & Company, Inc., 2003. 50–66.
Black Creation Annual. "Conversation with Alice Childress and Toni Morrison." In *Conversations with Toni Morrison*. Ed. Danille Taylor-Guthrie. Jackson: University Press of Mississippi, 1994. 3–9.

Boggs, James. "Black Power: A Scientific Concept Whose Time Has Come." In *Black Fire*. Ed. Amiri Baraka and Larry Neal. Baltimore: Black Classics Press, 1968. 105–118.

Bond, Jean Carey, and Patricia Perry. "Is the Black Male Castrated?" In *The Black Woman: An Anthology*. Ed. Toni Cade Bambara. New York: New American Library, 1970. 13–18.

Brock, Lisa, Robin D. G. Kelley, and Karen Sotiropoulos, eds. *Radical History Review's Transnational Black Studies*. Durham, NC: Duke University Press, 2003.

Brown, Fahamisha Patricia. *Performing the Word: African American Poetry as Vernacular Culture*. New Brunswick, NJ: Rutgers University Press, 1999.

Brown, Patricia, Don L. Lee/Haki Madhubuti, and Frances Ward, eds. *To Gwen with Love: An Anthology Dedicated to Gwendolyn Brooks*. Chicago: Johnson Publications, 1971.

Burroughs, Margaret. Personal interview. Summer 2000.

———. "She'll Speak to Generations Yet to Come." In *To Gwen with Love*. Chicago: Johnson Publications, 1971. 129–130.

Carlson, Marvin. *Performance: A Critical Introduction*. London: Routledge, 1996.

Carmichael, Stokely. "A New World to Build." In *Stokely Speaks*. Ed. Mumia Abu-Jamal. Chicago: Lawrence Hill Books, 2007. 145–164.

———. "Toward Black Liberation." In *Black Fire*. Ed. Amiri Baraka and Larry Neal. Baltimore: Black Classics Press, 1968. 119–132.

"Carolyn Marie Rodgers." Obituary. *The Writer's Chronicle* (Sept. 2010): 36.

Christian, Barbara. "The Race for Theory." 1987. In *Feminist Literary Theory and Criticism*. Ed. Sandra M. Gilbert and Susan Gubar. New York: Norton, 2007. 266–277.

Clarke, Cheryl. *"After Mecca": Women Poets and the Black Arts Movement*. New Brunswick: Rutgers University Press, 2005.

Cleaver, Eldridge. "The Black Man's Stake in Vietnam" from *Soul on Ice*. 1965. In *Walkin' the Talk: An Anthology of African American Studies*. Ed. Bill Lyne and Vernon Damani Johnson. Upper Saddle River, NJ: Prentice Hall, 2003. 512–516.

Cole, Johnetta, and Beverly Guy-Sheftall. *Gender Talk: The Struggle for Women's Equality in African American Communities*. New York: Random House Publishing Group, 2003.

Collins, Lisa Gail. "Arts, Artifacts, and African Americans: Context and Criticism." In *Cultural Life*. Ed. Howard Dodson and Colin Palmer. East Lansing: Michigan State University Press, 2007. 221–320.

———, and Margo Natalie Crawford. "Power to the People!: The Art of Black Power." Introduction. In *New Thoughts on the Black Arts Movement*. Ed. Collins and Crawford. New Brunswick, NJ: Rutgers University Press, 2006.

Collins, Patricia Hill. *Fighting Words: Black Women and the Search for Justice*. Minneapolis: University of Minnesota Press, 1998.

Combahee River Collective. "A Black Feminist Statement." In *This Bridge Called My Back*. Ed. Cherrie L. Moraga and Gloria E. Anzaldua. Berkeley: Third Woman Press, 2000.

Conde, Maryse. "Pan-Africanism, Feminism and Culture." In *Imagining Home: Class, Culture, and Nationalism in the Home African Diaspora*. Ed. Disney Lemelle and Robin D. G. Kelley. London: Verso Press, 1994. 55–65.

Crawford, Margo Natalie. "Black Light on the *Wall of Respect*." In *New Thoughts on the Black Arts Movement*. Ed. Lisa Gail Collins and Margo Natalie Crawford. New Brunswick, NJ: Rutgers University Press, 2006. 23–42.

———. "Must Revolution Be a Family Affair?: Revisiting The Black Woman." In *Want to Start a Revolution?: Radical Women in the Black Freedom Struggle*. Ed. Dayo F. Gore, Jeanne Theoharis, and Komozi Woodard. New York: New York University Press, 2009. 185–204.

Croyden, Margaret. "Toni Morrison Tries Her Hand at Playwriting." In *Conversations with Toni Morrison*. Ed. Danille Taylor-Guthrie. Jackson, MS: University Press of Mississippi, 1994. 218–222.

Cruse, Harold. "Revolutionary Nationalism and the Afro-American." In *Black Fire*. Ed. Amiri Baraka and Larry Neal. Baltimore: Black Classics Press, 1968. 39–63.

Davis, Angela. "Black Nationalism: The Sixties and the Nineties." In *Black Popular Culture*. Ed. Gina Dent. Seattle: Bay Press, 1992. 317–324.

Davis, Christina. "An Interview with Toni Morrison." In *Conversations with Toni Morrison*. Ed. Danille Taylor-Guthrie. Jackson: University Press of Mississippi, 1994. 223–233.

Diawara, Manthia. "Afro-Kitsch." In *Black Popular Culture*. Ed. Gina Dent. Seattle: Bay Press, 1992. 285–291.

Donaldson, Jeff. Personal interview. Summer 2001.

Drucker, Joanna. "Visual Performance of the Poetic Text." In *Close Listening: Poetry and the Performed Word*. Ed. Charles Bernstein. New York: Oxford University Press, 1998. 131–161.

Dubey, Madhu. *Black Women Novelists and the Nationalist Aesthetic*. Bloomington, IN: Indiana University Press, 1994.

Evans, Mari. "I Am a Black Woman." 1970. In *Walkin' the Talk: An Anthology of African American Studies*. Ed. Bill Lyne and Vernon D. Johnson. Upper Saddle River, NJ: Prentice Hall, 2003. 518.

Ford, Karen Jackson. *Gender and the Poetics of Excess: Moments of Brocade*. Jackson, MS: University Press of Mississippi, 1997.

Foulkes, Julia L. "Ambassadors with Hips: Katherine Dunham, Pearl Primus, and the Allure of Africa in the Black Arts Movement." In *Impossible to Hold: Women and Culture in the 1960's*. Ed. Avital H. Bloch and Lauri Umansky. New York: New York University Press, 2005. 81–97.

Fuller, Hoyt. From *A Journey to Africa*. *Black Writing in Chicago: In the World Not of It?* Ed. Richard R. Guzman. Carbondale, IL: Southern Illinois University Press, 2006. 138–146.

———. Introduction. Carolyn Rodgers, *Paper Soul*. Chicago: Third World Press, 1968. 1–2.

---. "Towards a Black Aesthetic." In *The Black Aesthetic*. Ed. Addison Gayle. Garden City, NY: Anchor Books, 1971. 3–12.

Fuss, Diana. From *Essentially Speaking: Feminism, Nature and Difference*. 1989. In *Feminist Literary Theory and Criticism*. Ed. Sandra M. Gilbert and Susan Gubar. New York: Norton, 2007. 665–682.

Gates, Henry Louis. "King of Cats." In *Albert Murray and the Aesthetic Imagination of a Nation*. Ed. Barbara A. Baker. Tuscaloosa: University of Alabama Press, 2010. 15–36.

---. Foreword. In *The Greatest Taboo: Homosexuality in Black Communities*. Ed. Delroy Constantine Simms. Los Angeles: Alyson Books, 2001. xi–xvi.

Gilroy, Paul. *Small Acts: Thoughts on the Politics of Black Cultures*. London: Serpent's Tail, 1993.

Gottlieb, Roger S. *Joining Hands: Politics and Religion Together for Social Change*. Cambridge: Westview Press, 2002.

Green, Adam. *Selling the Race: Culture, Community, and Black Chicago, 1940–1955*. Chicago: University of Chicago Press, 2007.

Griffin, Barbara J. "Carolyn Rodgers." *Notable Black Women Writers: Book II*. Ed. Jessie Carney Smith. Detroit: Gale Research, Inc., 1996. 564–568.

Grunwald, Beverly. "Interview with Albert Murray." In *Conversations with Albert Murray*. Ed. Roberta S. Maguire. Jackson: University Press of Mississippi, 1997. 12–14.

Guzman, Richard R., ed. *Black Writing in Chicago: In the World Not of It?* Carbondale, IL: Southern Illinois University Press, 2006.

Harper, Philip Brian. "Eloquence and Epitaph: Black Nationalism and the Homophobic Response to the Death of Max Robinson." In *The Greatest Taboo: Homosexuality in Black Communities*. Ed. Delroy Constantine Simms. Los Angeles: Alyson Books, 2001. 396–414.

Hay, Michelle. "Popular Culture: Pan-African Dimensions." In *Cultural Life*. Ed. Howard Dodson and Colin Palmer. East Lansing: Michigan State University, 2007. 1–64.

Henderson, Stephen, ed. *Understanding the New Black Poetry*. New York: Morrow Publishers, 1973.

---, and Mercer Cook. *The Militant Black Writer in Africa and the United States*. Madison, WI: University of Wisconsin Press, 1969. 65–75.

Hernton, Calvin. *The Sexual Mountain and Black Women Writers: Adventures in Sex, Literature, and Real Life*. New York: Anchor Press, 1987.

Himes, Chester. "Dilemma of the Negro Novelist in the U.S.A." In *New Black Voices*. Ed. Abraham Chapman. New York: New American Library, 1972. 393–400.

Hoch, Danny. "Toward a Hip-Hop Aesthetic: A Manifesto for the Hip-Hop Arts Movement." In *Total Chaos: The Art and Aesthetics of Hip-Hop*. Ed. Jeff Chang. New York: Basic Books, 2006.

hooks, bell. "Postmodern Blackness." In *Feminist Literary Theory and Criticism*. Ed. Sandra M. Gilbert and Susan Gubar. New York: Norton, 2007. 701–708.

Hughes, Sheila Hassell. "My newish voice': rethinking Black power in Gwendolyn Brooks's Whirlwind." In *Gwendolyn Brooks*. Ed. Mildred R. Mickle. Pasadena: Salem Press, 2010.

Hull, Gloria T., and Posey Gallagher. "Update on Part 1: An Interview with Gwendolyn Brooks." In *Conversations with Gwendolyn Brooks*. Ed. Gloria Wade Gayles. Jackson: University Press of Mississippi, 2003. 85–103.

Jabbour, Alan, and Ethelbert Miller. "A Conversation with Gwendolyn Brooks." In *Conversations with Gwendolyn Brooks*. Ed. Gloria Wade Gayles. Jackson: University Press of Mississippi. 2003. 125–132.

Jackson, Angela. Personal interview. Summer 2000.

———. *The Greenville Club*. Chicago: Third World Press, 1977.

———. *VooDoo/Love Magic*. Chicago: Third World Press, 1974.

———. *Where I Must Go*. Evanston, IL: TriQuarterly Books, 2009.

James, Joy. "Framing the Panther: Assata Shakur and Black Female Agency." In *Want to Start a Revolution?: Radical Women in the Black Freedom Struggle*. Ed. Dayo F. Gore, Jeanne Theoharis, and Komozi Woodard. New York: New York University Press, 2009. 138–160.

Jamison, Angelyn. "Imagery in the Women Poems: The Art of Carolyn Rodgers." In *Black Women Writers (1950–1980): A Critical Evaluation*. Ed. Mari Evans. Garden City, NY: Anchor Press/Doubleday, 1983. 377–392.

Jeffries, John. "Toward a Redefinition of the Urban: The Collision of Culture." In *Black Popular Culture*. Ed. Gina Dent. Seattle: Bay Press, 1992. 153–163.

Johnson, Abbey Arthur, and Ronald Maberry Johnson, eds. *Propaganda and Aesthetics: The Literary Politics of African-American Magazines in the Twentieth Century*. Amherst: University of Massachusetts Press, 1991.

Karenga, Ron. "Black Cultural Nationalism." In *The Black Aesthetic*. Ed. Addison Gayle, Jr. Garden City, NY: Doubleday, Inc., 1971. 32–38.

Kent, George E. "The Poetry of Gwendolyn Brooks." In *On Gwendolyn Brooks, a Reliant Contemplation*. Ed. Stephen Caldwell Wright. Ann Arbor: University of Michigan, 1996. 66–80.

Kich, Martin. "The Critical Reception and Influence of Gwendolyn Brooks." In *Critical Insights: Gwendolyn Brooks*. Ed. Mildred R. Mickle. Pasadena, CA: Salem Press, Inc. 2010. 39–55.

Kieta, Michelle Nzadi. "Sonia Sanchez: Fearless about the World." In *Impossible to Hold: Women and Culture in the 1960's*. Ed. Avital H. Bloch and Lauri Umansky. New York: New York University Press, 2005. 279–291.

Killens, John Oliver. "The Black Writer Vis-à-vis His Country." In *The Black Aesthetic*. Ed. Addison Gayle, Jr. Garden City, NY: Doubleday, Inc. 379–398.

Labrie, Peter. "The New Breed." In *Black Fire*. Ed. Amiri Baraka and Larry Neal. Baltimore: Black Classics Press, 1969. 64–77.

Lamar, Jay. "Scooter Comes Home." In *Albert Murray and the Aesthetic Imagination of a Nation*. Ed. Barbara A. Baker. Tuscaloosa: University of Alabama Press, 2010. 191–198.

Lee, Felicia R. "Like Author, Like Heroine: Blazing a Trail in the World of Elite Education." *New York Times on the Web*. 12 October 2009. 13 October 2009. http://www.nytimes.com/2009/10/13/books/13jackson.html.

Lemelle, Sidney J., and Robin D. G. Kelley. Introduction. *Imagining Home: Class, Culture and Nationalism in the African Diaspora*. London: Verso Press, 1994. 1–16.

Lemons, Gary. "When and Where [We] Enter: In Search of a Feminist Forefather—Reclaiming the Womanist Legacy of W. E. B. Du Bois." In *Traps: African American Men on Gender and Sexuality*. Ed. Rudolph P. Byrd and Beverly Guy-Sheftall. Bloomington, IN: Indiana University Press, 2001. 71–92.

Lenz, Gunter H. "The Politics of African American Literary and Cultural Critique: From the Black Arts/Black Aesthetic Movement to a Black Postmodern Multiculturalism." In *Black Liberation in the Americas*. Ed. Fritz Gysin and Christopher Mulvey. Hamburg: LIT, 2001. 203–218.

Lewis, Ida. "My People Are Black People: Interview with Gwendolyn Brooks." In *Conversations with Gwendolyn Brooks*. Ed. Gloria Wade Gayles. Jackson: University Press of Mississippi, 2003. 54–66.

———. "Conversation: Ida Lewis and James Baldwin." *Essence* Magazine. Essence Communications, Inc. 16 (Oct. 1970): 23–27.

Lorde, Audre. "Poetry Is Not a Luxury." 1977. In *The Norton Anthology of African American Literature*. Ed. Henry Louis Gates, Jr., and Nellie Y. McKay. New York: W.W. Norton & Company, 2004. 1924–1925.

———. "Power." 1978. *Walkin' the Talk: An Anthology of African American Studies*. Ed. Bill Lyne and Vernon D. Johnson. Upper Saddle River, NJ: Prentice Hall, 2003. 566–567.

Lubiano, Waheema. "Black Nationalism and Black Common Sense: Policing Ourselves." In *The House That Race Built: Black Americans, U.S. Terrain*. Ed. Lubiano. New York: Pantheon Books, 1997. 232–252.

Lynch, Acklyn. "Black Women Writers in the Past Two Decades: Voices Within the Veil." In *Warpland: A Journal of Black Literature and Ideas*. Ed. Joyce A. Joyce. Vol.1. Chicago: Chicago State University, 1995. 47–60.

Lyne, Bill, and Vernon Damani Johnson, eds. *Walkin' the Talk: An Anthology of African American Studies*. Upper Saddle River, NJ: Prentice Hall, 2003.

MacNeal, Ann. Personal interview. Summer 2000.

Madhubuti, Haki. *Dynamite Voices*. Detroit: Broadside Press, 1971.

———. Introduction. *Warpland: A Journal of Black Literature and Ideas*. Ed. Joyce A. Joyce. Chicago: Chicago State University, 1995. Vol. 1, no. 1.

———. Personal interview. Summer 2000.

Mance, Ajuan Maria. *Inventing Black Women: African American Women Poets and Self-Representation, 1877–2000*. Knoxville, TN: University of Tennessee Press, 2007.

Marable, Manning. *Beyond Black and White: Transforming African-American Politics*. London; New York: Verso Press, 1995.

———. "Groundings with My Sisters: Patriarchy and the Exploitation of Black Women." In *Traps: African American Men on Gender and Sexuality*. Ed. Rudolph P. Byrd and Beverly Guy-Sheftall. Bloomington, IN: Indiana University Press, 2001. 119–152.

Mattis, Jacqueline S., and Robert J. Jagers. "A Relational Framework for the Study of Religiosity and Spirituality in the Lives of African Americans." *Journal of Community Psychology* (Sept. 2001): 519–539.

———. "Religion and African American Political Life." *Political Psychology.* 22.2 (2001): 263–278.
Morrison, Toni. "Unspeakable Things Unspoken: The Afro-American Presence in American Literature." 1998. In *Feminist Literary Theory and Criticism.* Ed. Sandra M. Gilbert and Susan Gubar. New York: Norton, 2007. 266–277.
Mullen, Bill V. *Popular Fronts: Chicago and African-American Cultural Politics, 1935–46.* Urbana: University of Illinois Press, 1999.
Neal, Larry. Afterword, "And Shine Swam On." In *Black Fire.* Ed. Amiri Baraka and Neal. Baltimore: Black Classics Press, 1968. 637–656.
———. "The Black Arts Movement." 1968. *The Norton Anthology of African American Literature.* Ed. Henry Louis Gates, Jr., and Nellie Y. McKay. New York: W. W. Norton & Company, 2004. 2039–2050.
———. "Malcolm X—An Autobiography." In *Black Fire.* Ed. Amiri Baraka and Neal. 312–314. Baltimore: Black Classics Press, 1968.
Neal, Mark Anthony, *Soul Babies: Black Popular Culture and the Post-Soul Aesthetic.* New York: Routledge, 2002.
Newquist, Roy. "Interview with Gwendolyn Brooks." 1967. In *Conversations with Gwendolyn Brooks.* Ed. Gloria Wade Gayles. Jackson, MS: University Press of Mississippi, 2003. 26–36.
Newton, Huey P. "A Letter from Huey to the Revolutionary Brothers and Sisters about the Women's Liberation and Gay Liberation Movements." In *Traps: African American Men on Gender and Sexuality.* Ed. Rudolph P. Byrd and Beverly Guy-Sheftall. Bloomington, IN: Indiana University Press, 2001. 281–283.
Ojo-Ade, Femi. Introduction. In *Of Dreams Deferred, Dead or Alive: African Perspectives of African-American Writers.* Ed. Femi Ojo-Ade. Westport, CT: Greenwood Press, 1996.
Ongiri, Amy Abugo. *Spectacular Blackness: The Cultural Politics of the Black Power Movement and the Search for a Black Aesthetic.* Charlottesville, VA: University of Virginia Press, 2010.
Parker-Smith, Bettye L. "Running Wild in Her Soul: The Poetry of Carolyn Rodgers." In *Black Women Writers (1950–1980): A Critical Evaluation.* Ed. Mari Evans. New York: Anchor Press, 1984. 393–410.
Piazza, Tom. "An Intellectual Godfather to Two Generations of Writers, Thinkers, and Artists." In *Conversations with Albert Murray.* Ed. Roberta S. Maguire. Jackson: University Press of Mississippi. 1997. 110–116.
Pollard, Cherise. "Sexual Subversions, Political Inversions: Women's Poetry and the Politics of the Black Arts Movement." In *New Thoughts on the Black Arts Movement.* Ed. Lisa Gail Collins and Margo Natalie Crawford. New Brunswick, NJ: Rutgers University Press, 1996. 173–186.
Rampersad, Arnold. *Ralph Ellison: A Biography.* New York: Knopf, 2007.
Redmond, Eugene. *Drumvoices / The Mission of Afro-American Poetry: A Critical History.* Garden City, NY: Anchor Press, 1976.

Reed, Ishmael. "19 Necromancers From Now (Introduction)." In *New Black Voices*. Ed. Abraham Chapman. New York: New American Library, 1972. 513–524.

Reed, T. V. *The Art of Protest: Culture and Activism from the Civil Rights Movement to the Streets of Seattle*. Minneapolis: University of Minnesota Press, 2005.

Regester, Charlene. "Black Cinema." In *Cultural Life*. Ed. Howard Dodson and Colin Palmer. East Lansing: Michigan State University Press, 2007. 321–395.

Roberson, Ed. "The Black Arts Movement in the Broader Legacy of the Civil Rights Movement." Northwestern University, Evanston, IL, 16 October 2007. http://www.youtube.com/results?search_query=black+arts+movement+at+northwestern+university.

Rodgers, Carolyn. "A Love Poem." In *A Rock Against the Wind: African American Poems and Letters of Love and Passion*. Ed. Lindsay Patterson. New York: Perigee Publishers, 1996. 75.

———. "Aunt Dolly." In *Working Classics: Poems on Industrial Life*. Ed. Peter Oresick and Nicolas Coles. Urbana-Champaign, IL: University of Illinois Press, 1991. 208.

———. "Black Poetry—Where It's At." *Negro Digest* (Sept. 1969): 7–16.

———. Foreword. In *Black Writing from Chicago: In the World Not of It?* Ed. Richard R. Guzman. Carbondale, IL: Southern Illinois University Press, 2006.

———. *How I Got Ovah: New and Selected Poems*. New York: Doubleday, 1975.

———. "Old Love." *A Rock Against the Wind: African American Poems and Letters of Love and Passion*. Ed. Lindsay Patterson. New York: Perigee Publishers, 1996. 157.

———. *Paper Soul*. Chicago: Third World Press, 1968.

———. *Songs of a Black Bird*. Chicago: Third World Press, 1969.

———. *We're Only Human*. Chicago: Eden Press, 1994.

———. "The Black Arts Movement in the Broader Legacy of the Civil Rights Movement." Northwestern University, Evanston, IL, 16 October 2007. http://www.youtube.com/results?search_query=black+arts+movement+at+northwestern+university.

Rogers, Elice. "Black Power, Chicago Politics, and Social Movements: What Have We Learned?" In *Engines of the Black Power Movement: Essays on the Influence of Civil Rights Actions, Arts, and Islam*. Ed. James L. Conyers, Jr. Jefferson, NC: McFarland & Company, 2007. 43–57.

Rugoff, Kathy. "The Critical Reception and Influence of Gwendolyn Brooks." In *Gwendolyn Brooks*. Ed. Mildred R. Mickle. Pasadena: Salem Press, 2010.

Rustin, Bayard. "Feminism and Equality." In *Traps: African American Men on Gender and Sexuality*. Ed. Rudolph P. Byrd and Beverly Guy-Sheftall. Bloomington, IN: Indiana University Press, 2001. 111–112.

Sell, Mike. *Avante-Garde Performance and the Limits of Criticism: Approaching the Living Theatre, Happenings/Fluxus and the Black Arts Movement*. Ann Arbor: University of Michigan Press, 2005.

———. "The Voice of Blackness: The Black Arts Movement and Logocentrism." *Staging Philosophy: Intersections of Theater, Performance, and Philosophy*. Ed. David Krasner and David Z. Saltz. Ann Arbor: University of Michigan Press, 2006. 278–300.

Shelby, Tommie. *We Who Are Dark: The Philosophical Foundations of Black Solidarity*. Cambridge, MA: Harvard University Press, 2005.

Shiva, Vandana. *Staying Alive: Women, Ecology and Development*. Brooklyn: South End Press, 1988.

Smallwood, Andrew P. "A Critical Assessment of the Educational Mission and Praxis of the Black Arts Movement." In *Engines of the Black Power Movement: Essays on the Influence of Civil Rights Actions, Arts, and Islam*. Ed. James L. Conyers, Jr. Jefferson, NC: McFarland & Company, 2007. 58–71.

Smethurst, James E. *The Black Arts Movement: Literary Nationalism in the 1960's and 1970's*. Chapel Hill: University of North Carolina Press, 2005.

Stavros, George. "An Interview with Gwendolyn Brooks." In *Conversations with Gwendolyn Brooks*. Ed. Gloria Wade Gayles. Jackson: University Press of Mississippi, 2003. 37–53.

Stewart, James T. "The Development of the Black Revolutionary Artist." In *Black Fire*. Ed. Amiri Baraka and Larry Neal. Baltimore: Black Classics Press, 1968. 3–10.

Thomas, Kendall. "Ain't Nothin' Like the Real Thing": Black Masculinity, Gay Sexuality, and the Jargon of Authenticity." In *Traps: African American Men on Gender and Sexuality*. Ed. Rudolph K. Byrd and Beverly Guy-Sheftall. Bloomington, IN: Indiana University Press, 2001. 327–341.

Thomas, Lorenzo. *Don't Deny My Name: Words and Music and the Black Intellectual Tradition*. Ed. Aldon Lynn Nielsen. Ann Arbor: University of Michigan Press, 2008.

———. "Neon Griot: The Functional Role of Poetry Readings in the Black Arts Movement." In *Close Listening: Poetry and the Performed Word*. Ed. Charles Bernstein. New York: Oxford University Press, 1998. 300–323.

Traylor, Eleanor W. "Women Writers of the Black Arts Movement." In *The Cambridge Companion to African American Women's Literature*. Ed. Angelyn Mitchell and Danille K. Taylor. Cambridge; New York: Cambridge University Press, 2009. 50–70.

———. Introduction. In *The Black Woman: An Anthology*. Ed. Toni Cade Bambara. New York: Washington Square Press, 2005.

Van Deburg, William L. *New Day in Babylon: The Black Power Movement and American Culture, 1965–1975*. Chicago: University of Chicago Press, 1992.

Walker, Alice. "In Search of Our Mothers' Gardens." 1974. In *The Norton Anthology of African American Literature*. Ed. Henry Louis Gates, Jr., and Nellie Y. McKay. New York: W.W. Norton & Company, 2004. 2430–2437.

Weber, Bruce. "Carolyn Rodgers, Poet, Is Dead at 69." *New York Times on the Web*, 19 April 2010. http://www.nytimes.com/2010/04/19/books/19rodgers.html.

Webster, Sarah Fabio. "Tripping with Black Writing." In *The Black Aesthetic*. Ed. Addison Gayle, Jr. New York: Doubleday, Inc., 1971. 182–191.

West, Cornel. "Black Sexuality: The Taboo Subject." In *Traps: African American Men on Gender and Sexuality*. Ed. Rudolph K. Byrd and Beverly Guy-Sheftall. Bloomington, IN: Indiana University Press, 2001. 301–307.

———. "Nihilism in Black America." In *Black Popular Culture*. Ed. Gina Dent. Seattle: Bay Press, 1992. 37–47.

West, Tim'm. "Keepin' It Real: Disidentification and Its Discontents." In *Black Cultural Traffic: Crossroads in Global Performance and Popular Culture*. Ed. Harry J. Elam and Kennell Jackson. Ann Arbor: University of Michigan Press, 2005. 162–184.

Whitehead, Kim. *The Feminist Poetry Movement*. Jackson: University Press of Mississippi, 1996.

Wilson, Judith. "A Conversation with Toni Morrison." In *Conversations with Toni Morrison*. Ed. Danille Taylor-Guthrie. Jackson: University Press of Mississippi, 1994. 129–137.

Woodard, Komozi. Preface. In *A Nation within A Nation: LeRoi Jones (Amiri Baraka) and Black Power Politics*. Ed. Woodard. Chapel Hill: University of North Carolina Press, 1999.

X, Malcolm. "Announcement on the Organization of Afro-American Unity." In *New Black Voices*. Ed. Abraham Chapman. New York: New American Library, 1972. 558.

Ya Salaam, Kalamu. "Women's Rights Are Human Rights." In *Traps: African American Men on Gender and Sexuality*. Ed. Rudolph P. Byrd and Beverly Guy-Sheftall. Bloomington, IN: Indiana University Press, 2001. 113–118.

Index

Achebe, Chinua, 70
activism: American, 48; artistic, 16, 56, 74; black, 30, 46, 61, 79, 149, 154, 167; collective, 78–79, 153, 155; cross-cultural, 165; everyday, 111; political, 6, 43, 116, 162; revolutionary, 80; social, 149, 152; suffrage, 45; women's, 45, 65, 74, 154
activist writing, 134
aesthetics: accessible, 122; black, 4–6, 13, 28, 31, 36, 38, 63, 96–97, 114, 147; Black Arts Movement, 11–12, 23, 49, 64, 74, 77, 96, 117, 126, 162; black nationalist, 54; cohesive, 6; community-building, 86; contemporary, 122; conventional, 86; cultural, 96; culturally inclusive, 75; evolving, 12; forced, 86; hip-hop, 162; inclusive, 130; mainstream, 124; musical, 49; national, 73; nationalist, 23, 32, 96, 121; nation-building, 5, 12, 15, 33, 66, 112, 119, 145, 151, 163; natural, 9; Organization of Black American Culture, 12, 121, 140; Pan-African-inspired, 71; politically conscious, 86; politically inspired, 51, 94, 162; politicized, 63; popular, 16, 56, 122, 128, 163; "post-soul," 162; provocative, 163; restricted, 86; socially conscious, 86; socially immediate, 122, 162; visual, 17, 77, 85, 87
African Diaspora, 3, 6, 12, 21, 23–24, 29–30, 49, 55, 116, 118, 133

Afrocentrism, 20–21, 26, 61, 71, 119, 125, 136
After Mecca: Women Poets and the Black Arts Movement, 16
Alkalimat, Abdul, 18, 65, 168
Amini, Johari, 4–6, 11–13, 15–17, 21, 53, 56–57, 61–62, 65, 68–71, 73–94, 98, 114, 116–18, 146, 163–64, 169, 172
  Works: "About Communication," 85–86; *Black Essence*, 17, 87–91, 93; *Black Spirits*, 17; "Coronach," 77–79; "Evolution," 76; "Faux-Semblant," 83–85; *A Folk Fable*, 17; "For Nigareens," 91–92; *A Hip Tale in Earth Style*, 17; "Identity," 81, 83, 85–86; *Images in Black*, 16–17, 76–77, 80, 87, 93, 170; *Let's Go Somewhere*, 17, 70; "Masque," 92–93; "Orbit," 88, 90–91; "Quintessence," 88–90; *Spectrum in Black*, 17; "To a Black Writer," 80; "The Two," 88–90; "When I Thought of Him," 88–89

Baldwin, James, 28, 46–47, 53, 70, 82, 167, 169
Bambara, Toni Cade, 34, 38–40, 52
Baraka, Amiri, 9, 18, 25–28, 33, 36–37, 43, 53, 58, 69, 82, 109, 165, 167–72
bisexuality, 89
Black Art, 4–6, 8, 12, 16–19, 27, 31, 35, 44, 49–50, 57, 61–63, 66–68, 73–74, 76–78, 80–81, 83–88, 91, 95, 97, 99–102, 104, 106–7, 112, 114–17, 129, 146–47, 163, 169–71

183

Black Artist, 3, 5–7, 9–10, 12, 17–19, 23–25, 27, 30–31, 33–37, 39–41, 43, 47, 49, 52, 55–56, 58–67, 69–73, 76–79, 81, 85–86, 90, 92–93, 95, 97, 99–100, 104, 106, 108, 110, 114–16, 118–19, 122, 124, 129, 135–36, 140, 143, 146, 148–50, 154, 162–64, 167, 169, 171

Black Arts Movement (BAM): anti-bourgeoisie stance, 56; cultural base, 124; difference between male and female members, 114; and formation of Organization for Black American Culture, 4, 10; integrationist vs. nationalist debate, 24, 30, 36; legacy, 146; political theory, 73; and role of Amiri Baraka, 69

black bourgeoisie, 26–27, 33, 53

black community, 3, 5–8, 23–27, 29–30, 33, 35, 40, 47–48, 51–53, 55, 68, 72, 77–78, 81, 86–87, 89, 93, 99, 102, 104, 106, 110, 113–14, 116, 121–22, 123, 127, 129, 135, 137, 140–41, 143, 149, 151, 154–55, 157, 167, 171

black family, 21, 40–41, 48, 88, 102, 108, 112, 114, 116, 132, 137–41, 143, 156–57, 165, 167, 169

black nationalism. *See* nationalism

Black Panthers, 38, 45–46, 48, 58, 103, 154, 168, 172

black poetry. *See* poetry

Black Power, 6, 12, 18, 20–21, 25, 27, 29–30, 38, 47–49, 78–79, 89, 92, 98, 103, 108, 119, 134, 147–48, 155, 161, 163, 165, 167–68

Black Power Movement, 3, 6, 13, 25, 30, 37–38, 41, 44–46, 52, 55, 62, 78–79, 81, 89, 98, 165

Black Studies, 61–62, 136

black vernacular. *See* vernacular language

Black Woman, The, 38–42, 165

Black World, 18, 35, 66–67, 95, 98, 117, 169, 171

Blackbird Flies: Remembering Carolyn Rodgers, The, 17

Bontemps, Arna, 147

Brawley, Benjamin, 50

Broadside Press, 53, 58, 61, 98

Bronzeville, 64, 70

Brooks, Gwendolyn, 10, 17, 34–35, 42–43, 52–54, 59, 67, 69–73, 96, 147–48, 158, 167, 169–70

Works: *In the Mecca*, 70, 169; *A Street in Bronzeville*, 70

Burroughs, Charles, 59

Burroughs, Margaret, 35, 53, 59–60, 71, 168

Callaloo, 17

Carby, Hazel, 133, 166

Carmichael, Stokely, 12, 20, 30, 78–79, 82

Christian, Barbara, 14–15

Christianity, 150, 152

civil rights, 6, 25, 38–39, 46–48, 52–53, 58, 62, 70, 72, 79, 89, 120, 141, 151, 153, 157–58, 161, 164–65, 168, 171–72

Clarke, Cheryl, 15–16

Cleaver, Eldridge, 46, 103, 167

Clifton, Lucille, 42, 167

Coalition of Black Revolutionary Artists (COBRA), 65

coalition-building, 4, 6, 57–58, 97, 115, 153

collaboration, 3–6, 10–11, 22–24, 28, 49, 51, 58, 64, 72, 78, 80, 89, 93, 100, 108, 120–21, 129–30, 149, 154–55

Collins, Lisa Gail, 3, 13, 165, 170, 172

Collins, Patricia Hill, 15, 122, 140

Coltrane, John, 64, 106

Combahee River Collective, 48–49

consciousness: Afrocentric, 119, 135; artistic, 72–73; black, 24, 28, 30–31, 33, 35, 37, 50, 55, 82, 87, 107, 118, 122, 127, 129; black racial, 27, 82; collaborative, 81; collective, 53, 79, 101, 122; cultural, 26, 68, 120, 142; Diasporic, 21, 133; double-, 29, 93, 170; enlightened, 126; environmental, 151; fashion, 92; female, 136; feminist, 87; folk, 28;

gender, 139; historical, 140; mind/body, 124; narrator's, 88, 125–26, 134–35, 145, 154; national, 74, 136; nationalist, 121; parallel, 145; political, 73, 125, 148; race, 34, 36, 150–51, 162; revolutionary, 90, 107; self-, 18, 93; sexual, 90; social, 26, 73, 129; spiritual, 153

Cooper, Anna Julie, 45

Crawford, Margo Natalie, 3, 6, 13, 39–40, 58, 65, 80, 165, 168–70, 172

cultural nationalism. *See* nationalism

Davis, Angela, 76, 121, 166, 170

Davis, Ossie, 70

Davis, Ruby, 70

Du Bois, W. E. B., 43, 45, 50, 82, 93, 159

Du Sable Museum, 35, 59–60, 71

Dumas, Henry, 34

Dunham, Katherine, 4

dystopia, 140, 146

Ebony, 66–67, 169

ecofeminism, 153

Eden Press, 148

Ellison, Ralph, 9, 24–28, 32–35, 41, 52, 54, 167

Emanuel, James A., 53

empowerment: black, 28, 44, 106, 122; community, 45, 68, 115; cultural, 21, 23, 27, 29, 49, 62, 65, 114, 116; educational, 62; gender, 15, 163; group, 129; individual, 23, 153; political, 3, 6, 12, 27, 47, 58, 133, 145, 157; self-, 34, 145; sexual, 90

environmentalism, 22, 146, 151

Essence, 18, 47

Evans, Mari, 4, 18, 41–42, 53, 167, 169–71

Evers, Medgar, 52

Fabio, Sarah Webster, 31, 43, 73, 98, 170

family. *See* black family

Fanon, Frantz, 156

femininity, 14, 40, 91, 95–97, 114, 150

feminism, 18, 45, 119

feminist poetry. *See* poetry

feminists, 15–16, 57, 74, 76, 87–88, 117–18, 153, 161, 166; black, 14–16, 39, 45, 48, 118, 163, 166; lesbian, 16, 117; mainstream, 118; white, 117–18

"For My People," 18, 166

Forrest, Leon, 34

Fuller, Hoyt, 28, 35–36, 47–48, 66–68, 95–96, 168–70

Garvey, Marcus, 156–57

Gates, Henry Louis, Jr., 47

gay men, 47–49, 89

Giovanni, Nikki, 4, 41–42, 112, 167, 171

Gray-Ward, Val, 17

Hansberry, Lorraine, 159

Harlem Renaissance, 49–51, 56

Harper, Frances E. W., 48

Hayden, Robert, 32, 34–35, 64

heterosexism, 41, 91

Himes, Chester, 36–37

hip-hop, 162, 164

homophobia, 37, 40–41, 45–48, 89

hooks, bell, 98

Hughes, Langston, 50, 54, 64, 70

Hurst, Catherine, 43

iconography, 13, 76, 79–80, 87, 93

identity: African, 119, 137, 136; American, 33; black, 8, 17, 26, 36, 76, 82–83, 85, 87–88, 92–93, 95, 123, 136–37, 141; collaborative, 127; cultural, 18, 28, 32, 83, 85–87, 118, 132, 134, 136; ethnoracial, 135; feminist, 45; fractured, 135; gender, 91; ideal, 83; national, 17, 25, 141; Pan-African, 136; racial, 25, 32, 61, 82–83, 91, 93, 132, 135; racialized, 83

ideology, 3, 6–9, 14–15, 21, 23, 26–29, 32, 36–38, 41, 43–45, 48, 50–52, 57, 63, 65–66, 71, 77, 81, 92, 97–98, 106–8,

111–12, 116–17, 119, 129, 133–37, 150, 153, 158, 168, 172
integration. *See* racial integration
Invisible Man, 33–34

Jackson, Angela, 4–6, 11–17, 19–21, 56–57, 62, 65, 68, 71, 73–75, 96, 98, 114, 116–22, 124, 126–30, 133–47, 149, 155–61, 163–64, 166, 168–72
  Works: *And All These Roads Be Luminous: Poems Selected and New*, 20; "a beginning for new beginnings," 116, 119–20, 122, 126–27; *Dark Legs and Silk Kisses: The Beatitudes of the Spinners*, 20; "Dreamer," 20; "Early Evenings," 141–43; "Greenville," 138; *The Greenville Club*, 19, 117, 136–38, 142–43, 145, 157; "Home Trainin'," 139–40; "if I tole you," 123–24, 126–27; "In the Echo I Remember," 144; "i/scattered poems," 133–34, 136; "Mak/n My Music," 130, 132; "Other Evenings," 141–43; "Second Meeting," 125–26; *Shango Diaspora: An African-American Myth of Womanhood and Love*, 20; *Solo in the Boxcar*, 20; "a summer story," 130–32; *Treemont Stone*, 20; *Where I Must Go*, 20–21, 149, 155–56, 158, 160–61; "Witch Doctor," 20, 37; *Witness!*, 20; *VooDoo/Love Magic*, 19, 116–18, 120–21, 124, 126, 131–33, 138, 157
Johnson, Helen, 43
Jones, Gayl, 34
Jordan, June, 34

Karenga, Maulana, 43, 171
Karenga, Ron, 31
Kelley, Robin D. G., 20, 119
King, Martin Luther, Jr., 45, 52–53
kinship, 5, 34, 66, 111, 114, 117, 132, 138

kitsch art, 128
Kunjufu, Jawanza, 16
Kuumba Performing Arts Company of Chicago, 17

lesbianism, 16, 46, 89, 117
Lewis, Joe, 106
Lorde, Audrey, 15, 88, 166
Lotus Press, 58
Lumumba, Patrice, 82

MacNeal, Duke, 155
Madhubuti, Haki, 11, 17–19, 43, 52, 61–63, 70, 72–73, 81–82, 98–100, 112, 146, 148, 166, 168, 170–71
Major, Clarence, 52
marginality, 4, 57
masculinity, 5, 11, 13, 38, 44–46, 48, 80, 83, 91, 96, 104, 133, 163–64
McDowell, Deborah, 15
memory, 5, 21, 61, 69, 117–24, 128–30, 132, 135–40, 143–46, 153, 160; childhood, 130, 132, 145; coalescing, 159; collective, 28, 69, 77, 80; cultural, 21, 118, 120–21, 155; subversive, 132; unifying, 157
Morrison, Toni, 13, 34–35, 37–38, 41, 46, 54
multicultural alliances, 6
Murray, Albert, 9, 32–35, 41, 65, 71

nationalism: black, 6–7, 11–12, 20, 25, 28–29, 31–32, 38–39, 43, 45, 48, 54, 69, 71, 107, 110–12, 121–22, 135–36, 141, 159, 162–63, 167, 170; cultural, 10, 14, 122
nation-building: art, 56; concept, 74, 90, 93, 106; goals, 35, 38–39, 74, 76, 81, 91, 106, 110, 116; ideals, 8, 48, 68, 77, 87, 90, 118, 132, 140, 162; initiatives, 3, 34, 170; objectives, 11, 14, 21, 27, 80, 106, 120, 138, 163; paradigm, 107, 130; principle, 17, 63; purposes, 68

nation-building aesthetic. *See* aesthetics
Neal, Larry, 9, 28–29, 36, 43–44, 53, 65, 67, 99, 165, 167, 169, 171–72
New Thoughts on the Black Arts Movement, 3, 13–14, 165, 168, 170, 172
Newton, Huey, 38, 45–46, 48
Nixon, Richard, administration, 9
Nommo, 11, 68, 96, 104, 169–70
nonviolence, 38
nostalgia, 22, 132, 145, 160, 164, 166

Ongiri, Amy Abugo, 13, 164
oppression: class, 15; cultural, 39, 79; economic, 55; gender, 15, 38–39, 45, 163; global, 78; national, 26, 160; political, 89, 163; racial, 15, 29, 36–37, 44, 51, 55, 78, 148, 154–55; sexist, 42; social, 158; triple, 43
Organization of Black American Culture (OBAC), 4, 10–12, 17–21, 47–48, 55–57, 59–61, 64–65, 67–68, 70–73, 76–77, 80, 93, 96–98, 104, 107, 115–17, 120–22, 124, 129–30, 135, 137–40, 146–50, 155, 161, 168, 170–72

Pan-Africanism, 20–21, 71, 116–17, 119, 122, 124, 129
patriarchy, 12, 48, 74, 103
performance art, 86, 170
performance artists, 4, 63–64
performance theory, 73
performative writing, 128–29, 171
performativity, 80
Plumpp, Sterling, 68, 146, 168–69
poetry, 4–5, 11–13, 15–22, 29, 31, 39–40, 43, 53, 62–64, 68–72, 75–77, 81, 86–87, 91, 93, 97–98, 114, 116–19, 136, 147–48, 154–55, 157, 164–65; activist, 87; black, 19, 50, 104, 106, 110, 139; Black Arts, 25, 50, 57, 80, 88, 104; feminist poetry, 57, 74, 117–18, 166, 182; nationalist, 12; oral, 62; women's, 40, 43, 165
popular culture, 5, 77, 79, 111, 119, 127, 170, 172
popular vernacular. *See* vernacular language
post–civil rights era, 12, 30, 36, 50, 55, 59, 98, 155
postmodernism, 73, 98, 120
"Power," 15
Primus, Pearl, 4–5
propaganda, 7, 14, 32, 41, 66, 71, 80, 87, 93

queering, 4–5, 11, 15, 89–90

racial integration, 24–25, 27–33, 36, 54, 124
racial justice, 135–36
Reed, Ishmael, 37, 80
Rodgers, Carolyn, 4–6, 10–13, 15–19, 21, 52, 56–57, 62, 65, 68–69, 71, 73–75, 95–118, 139, 146–55, 161, 163–64, 166, 168–72
Works: "Aunt Dolly," 100–101, 107; "Black Poetry—Where It's At," 19, 104, 110, 139; "Breakthrough," 99–100; *Eden and Other Poems*, 19; "For H. W. Fuller," 96; "For Pilgrims & Strangers," 152–53; *The Heart as Ever Green*, 19; "It Is Deep," 108–10; "Jesus Was Crucified," 107–8, 110; *A Little Lower than Angels*, 19; "A Love Poem," 150–51; *Morning Glory*, 19, 149; "A Non-Poem About Vietnam, or (Try Black)," 52, 102; "Now Ain't That Love," 102; "Once," 113; *Paper Soul*, 16, 19, 95, 97–98, 100–101, 107, 147, 168; *Roots*, 19; "Sheep," 153–55; *Songs of a Black Bird*, 17, 19, 98, 107, 148; "The Sound of Music," 110–11; "Ten Worlds," 151–52; "To White Critics," 101, 112; *Two Love Raps*, 19;

"Visions of Peace," 151; *We're Only Human*, 19, 21, 149–50
Rustin, Bayard, 45, 47

Sanchez, Sonia, 4, 41–43, 53–54, 112, 167–68, 171
separatism, 25, 28–30, 35, 49, 53, 154
sexism, 4, 11, 14, 37–38, 40–42, 44–46, 48–49, 96, 158
Shakur, Assata, 154, 172
signifying, 104, 106
Smethurst, James, 10, 57, 66, 166, 168
Smith, Ann, 155
social justice, 3, 7, 49, 53, 149, 151, 160, 165
spirituality, 18, 61, 146, 150–51
spoken word, 17, 64, 111
Stewart, James T., 9, 35, 165
Student Non-violent Coordinating Committee (SNCC), 38–39, 70–71

Terrell, Mary Church, 48
Terry, Lucy, 50
Third World Press, 17, 19, 58, 61, 72, 95, 148
Thomas, Lorenzo, 21, 63
Till, Emmett, 54–55, 168
To Die for the People, 38
transgender, 89, 91
Truth, Sojourner, 48
Tubman, Harriet, 48

vernacular language: black, 17, 31, 49, 55, 64, 76, 96, 106, 110, 163, 169; popular, 63, 106
Vietnam War, 51–52, 72, 102–3, 110, 168
violence, 36, 40, 47, 52, 54, 72, 77–80, 90–91, 135, 159–60
visual media, 86, 93

Walker, Margaret, 18, 53, 109, 159, 166
Wall of Respect, The, 65, 73, 160, 168–69, 172
Ward, Francis, 17, 72, 170

Washington, Harold, 58
Wells Barnett, Ida B., 48
West, Cornel, 47–48, 121, 133
Wheatley, Phyllis, 50
women writers, 4, 6, 13–14, 16, 22, 39–40, 42, 48, 56, 68, 72, 74, 87, 90, 95–97, 104, 108, 114, 129, 133, 163–64, 171
Wright, Richard, 27, 70, 169

X, Malcolm, 25, 51–54, 82, 121, 156–58, 168

www.ingramcontent.com/pod-product-compliance
Lightning Source LLC
Chambersburg PA
CBHW030625230426
43661CB00053B/2139